TERRITORIES OF THE SOUL

TERRITORIES OF THE SOUL

QUEERED BELONGING
IN THE BLACK DIASPORA

NADIA ELLIS

DUKE UNIVERSITY PRESS *Durham & London* 2015

© 2015 Duke University Press
All rights reserved
Printed in the United States
of America on acid-free paper ∞
Designed by Amy Ruth Buchanan
Typeset in Garamond Premier Pro and Futura
by Graphic Composition, Inc. Bogart, GA

Library of Congress Cataloging-in-Publication Data
Ellis, Nadia, 1977– author.
Territories of the soul : queered belonging
in the Black diaspora / Nadia Ellis.
pages cm
Includes bibliographical references and index.
ISBN 978-0-8223-5915-9 (hardcover : alk. paper)
ISBN 978-0-8223-5928-9 (pbk. : alk. paper)
ISBN 978-0-8223-7510-4 (e-book)
1. American literature—African American
authors—History and criticism. 2. Caribbean
literature—Black authors—History and criticism.
3. Queer theory. 4. African diaspora. 5. Group
identity. I. Title.
PS153.N5E39 2015
810.9'896073—dc23 2015015087

Cover art: Nadia Huggins, *Fighting the currents*,
2014. Digital photograph. Courtesy of the artist.

This book received a publication subsidy from
Duke University's First Book Fund, a fund
established by Press authors who donated their
book royalties to help support innovative work by
junior scholars.

CONTENTS

THE SPACES WE INHABITED ALSO

BECAME TERRITORIES OF THE SOUL.

— Mike Phillips, *London Crossings*

ACKNOWLEDGMENTS

First, of course, my dissertation committee members, who guided this work before it knew what it was. Tim Watson—mentor extraordinaire and a scholar who modeled for me how to create a project of conjunctions—was my first and my steady port of call in Princeton. He read every word of my *essais* with true kindness that was wondrously entangled with keen correction and expansion. And he treated me, always, as if I knew what I was doing. Tim also alerted me very early on to the Wolfenden Report, which both sparked and grounded this project. Daphne Brooks— expansive and elegant enough to enfold me before I even knew what performance would mean to this book; deep and full with learning, style, energy, fire, who asked me, and continues to help me answer, how to bring myself more forcefully into the work. As I revised from dissertation to book, Daphne told me about a reference in Nathaniel Mackey's essays to Burning Spear, which transformed the ending of this project. And Simon Gikandi, of whose work I was an undergraduate fan, and whose formation as a postcolonial student, British postgraduate, and American PhD I echoed in my own trajectory—I felt much less like a geographical-postcolonial weirdo in his wake. He remains, ever, an inspiration for capacity, elegance, and cool under pressure. I thank him as well for drawing my attention to C. L. R. James's letters to Willard Thorpe and Arthur Schlesinger Jr., as well as to the telling discrepancy between the first and second editions of James's *Mariners, Renegades, and Castaways*. The messier, more affect-filled James I was looking for came alive in these discoveries.

I thank the teachers who turned me on to learning and made academia seem the most exciting, challenging, and pleasurable enterprise in the world—and who managed, against my own resistance, to make it seem possible I might do it. At UWI, Maureen Warner-Lewis: pioneer, raconteur, prolific scholar, twinkly eyed and patient teacher. Nadi Edwards, who taught me theory, taught me to seek out difficulty, and who told me, memorably, as he reached for a CD of music I didn't already know, that I should always learn new things. Carolyn Allen, who took an interest in me early and who became my friend and supporter, and who continues to inspire. Carolyn Cooper, whose clarity of vision and extraordinary style also inspires. And Mervyn Morris, about whom there is too much to say, but I'll try: his poem "The Pond" turned something on in my mind as a thirteen-year-old schoolgirl, making me realize it was possible to think through poetry. He taught me to write; and then told me I should apply, just go ahead and apply for that scholarship—and I never would have otherwise. It isn't too much to say that without him I wouldn't be a professor.

I am so grateful for Robert J. C. Young, at Oxford, for taking a chance on a very nervous MPhil student who wanted to write a thesis on Erna Brodber—a choice that probably everyone else at that institution would have found puzzling, and that he encouraged mightily. And at Princeton, Val Smith—whose Civil Rights Memory seminar was life-changing—Diana Fuss, Bill Gleason, and Rachel Gabara, each of whom had particularly profound effects on me and are models to which I still aspire.

At the University of California, Berkeley, Stephen Best took me under his stylish wing and helped me begin my very first academic job. He read rigorously even my most inchoate formulations, made me think hard about what I was trying to do, and offered enormous support in the multitude of considerations of life on the tenure track. I can't thank him enough for his mentorship. I thank as well my fellow (mostly now erstwhile!) junior colleagues—with a special shout-out to Eric Falci, who helped us think of ourselves as a group—who were the most supportive, collegial, and warm bunch of assistant professors one could ever hope for: Kathleen Donegan, Dave Landreth, Steven Lee, Namwali Serpell, Emily Thornbury. To my senior colleagues who read my work and encouraged me, I offer enormous thanks: Elizabeth Abel, Mitch Breitweiser, Abdul JanMohammed, Donna Jones, Colleen Lye, Maura Nolan, Scott Saul, Sue Schweik, Bryan Wagner. Juana Maria Rodriguez mentored me from across campus and showed me what it means to pursue pleasure in thinking and in life. Leigh Raiford continues to provide an inspiring model of engaged academic living while enabling the best consumption of cocktails I've yet experienced in the Bay.

To all my incredible friends, thank you so, *so* much. Special shout-outs to: Elisha Smith Arrillaga, subtlety, intuitive wisdom, and the best social butterfly graces ever; Chaitanya Lakimsetti, wisdom and gentleness embodied; Eng-Beng Lim, fabuloso and *mati,* whom I clearly knew in another life; Swati Rana and Namwali Serpell—we are the NNS!—visions of elegance and California ports-of-harbor; Alai Reyes-Santos, brilliant empath, with whom everything is an adventure; Sara Salih, a decade and a half (and counting!) of friendship and admiration; Pat Saunders, a rock, absolutely unmovable support and extreme mirth to boot; Grace Wang, groundedness and lightness both, without whom the "sun wall," and those stern Berkeley librarians would never have entered my life and, consequently, I may not have finished this book.

Xochipala Maes Valdez taught me so much about who I am, what my work is, and why I should keep doing it. Her good humor, patience, lightning intelligence, and deep wisdom inspired and transformed me. To M.L. it is impossible to offer enough thanks. And thank you J.H. and A.F., sharp, funny, and kind women both, who put my body and soul back together many times.

I have so much appreciation for my extraordinary editor at Duke University Press, Courtney Berger, who believed in the book early and shepherded it through the various stages of review and publication with great care and dedication. I feel truly lucky. To both anonymous reviewers who read the work in manuscript with rigorous care: many thanks for supporting the project, for the call to make its contours clearer, and for the many fine points of suggestion and correction you supplied.

My students are reminders of the ongoing responsibilities and far-reaching implications of being an academic. To the brilliant graduate students with whom I've had the pleasure of working: Sole Anatrone, Lia Bascomb, Amy Lee, Josh Jelly-Schapiro, Gabriel Page, Alexandra Wright—thank you for your curiosity, courage, and for being the future of the discipline. And to my inimitable Berkeley undergrads, whose radicalism and understated charm inspires me every time. I want to thank especially the members of my Urban Postcolonial seminar of fall 2012, which was transformative: in particular Giuliani Alvarenga, Chrystia Cabral, Emily

Chang, Shirin Ghaffary, Jennifer Kim, Nashilu Mouen, Prachi Naik, and Radhika Parashar, who have remained in view and are doing incredible work in the world.

I would also like to thank Nina Simone.

This book is dedicated to my family. You haven't always known what I've been doing, but you've kept the faith. Thank you.

Excerpts of earlier versions of chapter 3 appear in different forms in previous publications: "Black Migrants, White Queers, and the Archive of Inclusion in Postwar London," *Interventions: International Journal of Postcolonial Studies*, January 20, 2013; "Between Windrush and Wolfenden: Class Crossings and Queer Desire in Andrew Salkey's Postwar London," *Beyond Windrush: Rethinking Postwar Anglophone Caribbean Literature*, ed. S. Dillon Brown and Leah Reade Rosenberg (Jackson: University Press of Mississippi, 2015), 60–75. A portion of an early version of the epilogue appears in "Elegies of Diaspora," *Small Axe* 18.1 (2014): 164–172.

THE QUEER ELSEWHERE OF BLACK DIASPORA

Queerness is that thing that lets us feel that this world is not enough.
—Jose Esteban Muñoz, *Cruising Utopia*

When Stuart Hall moved to Oxford from Jamaica in 1951 he arrived embodying a telling mélange of influences, investments, and curiosities. He had come from a family in Kingston that cherished its colonial-identified, bourgeois affectations. He had, accordingly, attended one of the most prominent boys' high schools in the country, Jamaica College, and studied an educational program modeled on that of British public schools among schoolmates that included Michael Manley (political scion and the country's future prime minister). Yet the early 1930s saw the start of labor unrest that would presage the region's self-governance and independence movements. In a lengthy interview with the British historian Bill Schwartz, Hall remembers the feeling of momentousness in those days.[1] He recalls that the colonial engine of the prestige school system was beginning to cede some small ground to an awareness of the particular history, culture, and politics of Jamaica. Some of the more progressive teachers taught from slim pamphlets on Caribbean culture, supplementing the official British and European curriculum. Hall himself sought out works not offered at school in the newly opened Institute of Jamaica.

Hall arrived at Oxford, then, steeped in classic texts of the English literary canon, suffused with a dawning sense of the rightness of West Indian independence movements, and inspired, too, by emblems of modernism—strikingly, by jazz. He had listened to American radio stations and swapped bebop records with close high school friends in Kingston.[2] He had learned about big band music from his brother. Through this music Hall remembers sensing "a special sort of contemporary or avant-garde consciousness that was happening *elsewhere*."[3] The "elsewhere" in that line is marked by italics. It is an emphatic elsewhere, repeated again a few moments later when Hall describes continuing his jazz education while studying for his degree in English literature: "[The music] spoke to our desire to engage wider horizons—a classic colonial form of longing. It didn't represent a firm location or place for me—it wasn't as if I wanted to go, specifically, to America. . . . Rather it was a 'country of the mind.' The main thing was to be able, in one's mind, one's imagination, to have the possibility to be *elsewhere*."[4]

Hall learned about jazz everywhere *but* America: it was a pull from some other place. And I have begun to imagine that in order for the music to remain a potent symbolic force in Hall's imagination it *had* to remain elsewhere. In its ruptured voicings and its relationship to everything Hall imagined about sophisticated black urbanity, jazz became for him a "call to the soul."[5] It was the form that pointed Hall in the 1940s and 1950s to a horizon of possibility. Hall's retrospective account of his intellectual formation provides an entrée into my book's raison d'être while also telescoping its movement. For his narrative of a schoolboy's ambivalent colonial identification giving way to that of a diasporic traveler under the sway of jazz uncannily mimics the movement of this book—from C. L. R. James at Queens Royal College in its first chapter to the unbounded jazz poetics of Nathaniel Mackey in its last. More to the point, Hall suggests that diasporic modernity inhered for him at least as much as, if not more than, anything else, in the call from afar of a black aesthetic form—a call that was answered not by arriving at the place whence it issued but rather and precisely by burrowing into the art itself, from afar, since to have the *possibility* of jazz was as important as the notion that one could travel to the territories of its origins. My book will demonstrate over the course of five case studies—add to the sections on James and Mackey chapters on James Baldwin and George Lamming, Andrew Salkey and queer London, and the young Jamaican artist Ebony Patterson—that diasporic consciousness is at its most potent when it is, so to speak, unconsummated. The urgent sensation of a pull from elsewhere, when not fulfilled, constitutes diaspora culture at its most curious, eccentric, and I would argue, paradigmatic. This is because the examples of diaspora culture I study here, primarily by pairing Caribbean and African American artists in the various world sites where they found themselves in the twentieth century, instance versions of black aesthetic and relational globality in which the most intense, urgent, and productive constitution of the diasporic emerges out of desire (not its fulfillment), agonistic engagement (not easy familiarity), steady evasions of community (not incorporation into community), and imaginative yokings to very distant subjects and aesthetic modes (not accompanied by the possibility of any actual connection in the so-called real world). What I name territories of soul, after the Guyana-born British writer Mike Phillips, are those spaces that embody the classic diasporic dialectic of being at once imagined and material.[6] They are, in this book, like Hall's jazz elsewhere: places and people of black identification that are most lively as horizons of possibility, a call from afar that one keeps trying and trying to answer.

Spying a horizon, Jose Esteban Muñoz might say, provokes two simultaneous and apparently opposing thoughts. One: that the spot in which you are fixed is nowhere near as compelling as the far-off line on which your gaze is trained. And two: that the place marked by that far-off line will never be reached. One knows gazing on a horizon that the sensation of focused urgency it inspires is precisely in relation to its placement always beyond a distance that can be attained. It is Muñoz who explains that this gap between the ground on which one stands and a compelling place beyond can be described by the word *queer.* For *queerness is that thing that lets us feel that the world is not enough.*[7] Wherever there is an outside, a possibility for difference, there is also a perception of the insufficiency of one's present circumstances. In that sense of insufficiency, in the haunting gap between here and there, queerness resides.

This book is about *queered diasporic belonging* because it stakes ground where Muñoz's utopian version of queerness meets black diasporic consciousness. Muñozian queerness highlights insufficiency. Wed to an optimist's ongoing search for better forms is an acute awareness of the uninspiring here and now. In this book I explore diasporic aesthetics and subjectivity where a persistent sense of the insufficiency of existing modes of belonging is matched by an awareness that new forms remain inspiringly elusive. Studying figures across the twentieth century and into the twenty-first who represent an urgent desire for an outside—an outside of the nation, an outside of empire, an outside of traditional forms of genealogy and family relations, an outside of chronological and spatial limitations—the texts I analyze evince striking features of longing, non-fulfillment, and suspension. These features are central to their cultural and aesthetic interest, and to my argument. For idiosyncrasies, tensions, conflicts, and frustrations mark the work of artists who represent alternatives to colonial nationalism, gendered forms of affinity, and the historical alienation attendant to racial scatter. Like the "country of the mind" that etched boundaries in Hall's imagination after his introduction to jazz, the forms of diasporic aesthetics and subjectivity I describe throughout this book become places to belong, alternate modes of political and cultural cathexis.[8] In each case diasporic belonging is forged out of intense affect and eccentric forms of intimacy. I propose, for instance, that C. L. R. James's diasporic political imagination and practice must be understood in the context of his intense affective involvement with performers, an involvement that can be read in his autobiographical writings. These texts of James allow me to track intimacies that are imagined, willed, and often unreciprocated, which lack of reciprocity becomes the basis both of his urgent striving for national and romantic emplacement and, at least in the writing, for the achievement of this emplacement. The harsh closeness of disagreement is another form of intimacy I examine, in the phenomenon of black global artistic colloquia whose quixotic aim was often to articulate common aesthetics. While the communities of such movements as Negritude or the Caribbean Artists Movement in mid-twentieth-century London produced connections around shared artistic endeavors and racial politics, my interest here is in the sustaining entanglements of annoyance and disavowal. When black writers gather to describe an anticolonial poetics, a poetics on which they cannot agree, the affective result is not, as might be expected, inimical to diasporic collectivity. Rather, a mode of collectivity constituted around "negative" affect emerges as a compelling alternative to compulsory sameness. The intersubjective modes and aesthetic forms I study, therefore, are powerful in the *potential* to which they give rise, a potential that suspends rather than resolves at the arrival at some new and satisfying space of exile. In retaining striking traces of the gap between *here* and *there*—between the possibilities spied on the horizon and territory currently occupied—these modes produce urgent feelings of loss, desire, and zeal that mark them, like Muñoz's utopian horizon, as queer.

This book is located, then, in that scholarly place where Hall's diasporic "elsewhere" and Muñoz's queer utopian horizon intersect. This is not a scholarly context that is particularly populous, to say the least. Indeed, my work is to make clearer and more robust the structural relationship between queerness and diaspora. For Muñoz's queerness of the "there and then" is a challenge to nonnormativity that is not limited to gender or sexuality and has implications beyond some of the other recent interventions around queer affinity and time—primarily in its positive affective orientation, a positivity stemming from his marveling in the queer work of raced survival.[9] I follow in the line of queer of color criticism that has brought to light cultural practices of queers of color and the exclusions to which they have been subject, both by normative raced cultures and by queer theories that emerged to critique normativity writ large.[10] And I offer alongside this tradition, to which I am indebted, modes of literary and subjective diasporic cathexis in which I emphasize the structural queerness of black global modes of belonging over particular sexual or erotic practices. The aesthetic structures and modes of relation I describe in successive chapters of this book are queered diasporic forms—and not just in the chapter on London and the Jamaican novelist Andrew Salkey that most directly invokes that phrase. No, each of the foregoing cases is a study in the gap produced, in art and in lives, when there is an earnest desire for alternatives to racial, gendered, and temporal forms of affinity.

African Diaspora studies has been defined by two overarching dialectics and critical orientations. One dialectical formulation describes the cultures of diaspora as a relay between land claims and global movement— for example, a Garveyian claim to "Africa" for all black people is always shadowed by the Black Star Liner's hesitant and thwarted sea voyages. In the other dialectic, diaspora emerges as an interplay between likeness and difference—for example, the uncanny perception of recognition across national boundaries that is cut through, Babel-like, with misalliance. These dialectics have been accompanied by two main critical drifts. On the one hand there is an orientation in the field in which black diaspora culture is marked by unique, locatable practices. Recently, however, scholarship has been inflected by important readings of diasporic culture as constituted through difficulty and loss: see, for instance, Brent Hayes Edwards's study of diasporic (mis)translation and gap (décalage) or Saidiya Hartman's perception that black diaspora is founded on misprision and defined by archival irrecuperability. In this line of thinking, the losses of the Middle Passage and empire emerge as monumental, and they are not to be recuperated so much as confronted.[11] The dynamic tension between sameness and difference and a critical orientation toward locating particular diasporic practices are both clearly exemplified in this much-cited essay. For the most part, however, critical tendencies that emphasize the recovery of diasporic practices and those highlighting archival irrecuperability have emerged as separate endeavors.

In this book I work between these critical orientations. In my account black diaspora is characterized by a distinctive desire to belong "elsewhere," which desire produces a productive tension between attachment and a drive toward intense and idiosyncratic individuation (unencumbered by location, heritage, or even, indeed, by materiality). This productive tension between a quest for affinity and a desire to separate is often marked by frustration. Indeed, it is *failed* affinity that most often drives the tension I observe in my exemplifying texts between a desire to belong and a desire to flee the strictures of ground and community. And so while delineating unique features of diasporic affinities I am also at ease with narrating their failures—if by failure we always understand there to be a utopian reach. Queer theory guides my traversal of critical orientations between pessimism and celebration, orientations that are often held to be worlds apart. For failure in queerness is really just a mark of the insufficiency that makes trying necessary.

I develop my arguments through readings of texts that exemplify different moments in the twentieth- and twenty-first-century black diaspora. I begin with C. L. R. James in chapter 1 because, despite its now being taken for granted that James's roving political life makes him as an exemplary diasporic figure, there is still much to learn about how exactly he managed to embody the hybrid, culturally profligate figure that attracts the attention it does. I focus on what I see as the queer diasporic affinity that emerges in Jamesian surrogation—his preoccupation with bodies that perform communal belonging for him.[12] Rereading James's famous account in *Beyond a Boundary* about his early formation in Trinidad alongside his writings about America—in letters to Constance Webb and the essays that became *American Civilization*—I argue that James managed competing claims to his national, political, and affective inclinations by mediating his attachments through the bodies of performers, particularly West Indian cricketers and American actresses. He metaphorized these bodies for his own filliative ends and surrogated them for his own position in national cultures. The cricket pitch is a site of both colonial *and* imperial emplacement; the movie screen a resting place for James's best hopes for America and his inchoately articulated desire to belong there. And both sites offer only temporary access to the national cultures they present. I thus demonstrate the centrality of James's reliance on performance and affect to craft diasporic belonging, while moving beyond existing scholarship by clarifying the gendered stakes of Jamesian diaspora, especially in the United States. For James's writing about cricketers is suffused with desiring affection. And through a hitherto ignored strand of James's movie watching in America—his repeated screenings of the classic film *Now, Voyager* and his fascination with Bette Davis in particular—I am able to unsettle the sturdy conceit of masculine transatlantic diasporic mobility. I place James alongside Bette Davis's legendary ugly duckling in the Gulf of Mexico, not the famed Atlantic, a re-placement that allows me to argue more forcefully that James's relationship to white American actresses is part of a larger structure of feminine attachment that begins, counterintuitively, in James's early observations of West Indian male cricketers.

The Jamesian archive I peruse here is also queer in that, with the exception of the very well-known cultural study *Beyond a Boundary*, the works I read are often considered eccentric to his oeuvre. Because of their privacy (the letters) and incompletion (the essays) these latter works display a version of James that is at odds with the polished, stentorian figure who emerged in Caribbean and American studies with particular force during the 1990s. The performativity and fragmentation of these works, however, function for me as marks of their queer diasporic import. James's attachments are wild, multiple, and unexpected. Whiteness figures prominently in a set of texts that are a record of Jamesian diaspora, displacing any easy association between black diasporic affiliation and black race, thereby puncturing diasporic essentialism.

In chapter 2 I explore black literary affiliation structured by disavowal and misrecognition by focusing on a generally overlooked moment between George Lamming and James Baldwin at the 1956 Congress of Negro Artists and Writers. Staged at the Sorbonne under the auspices of the influential Negritude publication *Presence Africaine*, the Congress was designed to define something like a black, anticolonial, global aesthetics. And like all such Herculean endeavors, it failed in that respect—but it failed interestingly. I discuss what I have come to consider a missed encounter between Lamming, who actually presented at the conference, and Baldwin, who did not present but who attended and reviewed it. I establish a kind of dialogue between Lamming's and Baldwin's Congress essays and read them as texts that misunderstand, mishear, or otherwise fail to locate affinity in the other, despite their being records putatively about black global affinity. Were a critic looking to Paris '56 for flourishing displays of black diasporic harmony, Baldwin and Lamming would let her down. What is interesting to me, however, is that Lamming's speech, "The Negro Writer and His World," and Baldwin's essay, "Princes and Powers," demonstrate writers seeking fine differentiations from black subjects on the basis of, in both cases, an association with colonial and US cultures—national structures, that is, about which both Lamming and Baldwin had strident critiques. I argue that the fellow feeling that Baldwin and Lamming reveal in their works *despite* their critical errors and misreadings creates the necessity for the disavowal of affinity. In the awkwardness of these essays and the general affective mêlée within the Congress to which they gesture, I am able to describe a form of diasporic affinity that is intense and intimate precisely because it is agonistic.

Chapter 3 moves to London. I read Andrew Salkey's novel *Escape to an Autumn Pavement* (1960) in the context of postwar British immigration and Wolfenden-era discourses surrounding homosexuality. The confluence of national panics about the racial identity and the gender identity of the British nation couches a piece of queer fiction that is marked strikingly by an absence of any positive eros. Certainly Salkey's novel has justly begun to receive attention as one of the earliest fictions by a Jamaican-born writer explicitly to represent a gay protagonist. (At least Johnnie Sobert *thinks* he is gay—he happily moves in to live with a gay man, and he is overly intrigued with his rough male neighbor.) And it might have been enough to read this troublesome novel for the purposes of continuing to recuperate a black queer diasporic tradition—where queer would register solely as same-sex desire. But that is not my sole project here. Instead I read *Escape to an Autumn Pavement* alongside British postwar documents in the new field of Race Relations, in RAF and War Office files, in the papers of London East End social worker Edith Ramsay, and in the unedited sound recordings of the Hall Carpenter Gay and Lesbian Oral History Project archive housed at the British Library. Collectively these archival documents destabilize the task of finding the "gay black subject" in a way remarkably similar to Salkey's thwarted and thwarting novelistic hero.

This elusiveness of the queer diasporic subject in both novel and archive can be experienced, in the wake of Jose Muñoz's elusive horizon, as a pleasurable discovery. If the queer diasporic subject enacts an attitude toward nation *and* diasporic community that is evasive, recalcitrant, skeptical, and rebellious then we have a subject who upends forms of sociality in which gender and sexual norms persist from nation to migration and from straight to gay. As I discuss in chapter 3, queer diasporic elusiveness resonates with the "anti-social turn" in recent queer theory, but it is distinguished from this line of theory by a Muñozian-style embrace of the utopian. At the end of the novel, Johnnie "escapes" to the sidewalks of London but doesn't know where he is going. Under the aegis of utopianism, this seemingly problematic novelistic dénouement becomes instead an example of a form of diasporic belonging I propose throughout this book: suspended and eschatological.

Finally, in chapter 4, I read interlocking essays and fiction by the African American poet, critic, and novelist Nathaniel Mackey alongside the signal work of the reggae musician Burning Spear, the album *Marcus Garvey*. In a sense, this final chapter is quite distinct from the first three, in that it draws from work produced half a generation removed, and later, from the publication of Salkey's novel and the cultural milieu of mid-twentieth-century United States and postwar Britain. In addition, I read Mackey and Burning Spear somewhat as outliers, distinct artists each of whose work is in strange apposition to the other, rather than situating them in a familiar context of black diasporic ferment. However, these two contemporary artists are a fitting culmination to my queered diasporic canon. For I begin this book with James "at the window" of his colonial home in Tunapuna, Trinidad, leave off from Salkey's attenuated protagonist elusively adrift on London's streets, and arrive at these artists' astonishing formal and musical effects, and their aesthetic and subjective propositions, in which the materiality of the body is even more intensely called into question.[13] Mackey's and Burning Spear's contributions to my formulation of queer diasporic affinity is in the trope of spirit possession, an aesthetic that presents the most radical elsewhere of all. For here is a subjective state with an extremely untethered relationship to normative time and an expansive reach beyond the strictures of geographical reason. Over the course of a long and prolific career Nathaniel Mackey has returned to Dogon rituals and the Yoruba deity Legba time and again to develop an ongoing poetics of black literature in which it is permissible to imagine the intimacy of four continents (to invoke Lisa Lowe's powerful articulation in a different context).[14] The music of Burning Spear, nondiscursive, *performs* an aesthetics of possession that is similarly exemplary of the potential to belong in the black diaspora—though in contradistinction to Mackey's incantatory, almost infinite sentences is Burning Spear's fragmentary enunciations, endlessly on repeat. Spirit possession concludes this book as a structure of diasporic belonging because it both encompasses the earlier forms of affinity I have been interested in throughout the book—performance and surrogation; likeness across difference; suspension and failure—and offers possibilities for belonging that exceed the ground and materiality of any one location. In the long history of black Atlantic dispossession, spirit possession, whether as embodied practice or aesthetic appropriation, provides a space for reclamation in multiple ways.

My textual selections reflect early queer theory's move to displace essence with performance since, in a sense, I disentangle literary tradition from aesthetic effect in black literature. The figures grounding each chapter are significant enough in their own ways to warrant study in the context of global black literature, and there is new resonance for African Diaspora studies to be found in juxtaposing them. This is particularly true when the chapters are seen as staging a set of conversations between Caribbean and African American figures, as these chapters do. However, my work here is not to insist on a traditional literary genealogy. Indeed, if anything, my work is exactly the opposite of that enterprise. Each chapter enables the consideration of eccentric, troubling, or failed attempts to construct diasporic community that, by virtue of being attempts, amplify the call for something even better. As the question of where to belong in the wake of racial scatter undergirds all my texts, my textual archive reflects diasporic profligacy. Together these texts instance a queered diasporic canon in which an eschatological attunement to a better that must be coming encompasses a critique of the insufficiency surrounding identity in the modern world. A queer eschatology—the feeling that Johnnie Sobert has in *Escape from an Autumn Pavement*, for instance, that one "must wait and wait and wait"; or the ongoing propositions of Nathaniel Mackey, which build on each other over decades and suggest an infinite stretching beyond into the future—habituates itself to <u>modes of suspension or tension</u> that inform theoretical accounts of diaspora, classic ones, and now my own.

Belonging in a Territory of Soul: Erna Brodber's b l a c k s p a c e

Before yielding to the main body of the book, I want to provide one example of a space, and a set of cultural and political practices, that exemplifies a structure of belonging and a metaphorical space of multiplicity and suspension that I have named "territories of the soul." In the late summer of 2011 the Jamaican writer Erna Brodber sent me a fragment from a government paper she wrote in 1989. "The excerpt comes from a document called 'Programme Audit, Jamaica Cultural Development Commission,'" she told me. "The rest of the paper is the boring stuff about management, with the usual flowcharts."[15] By happenstance of pagination, one of those flowcharts came along with the four pages Brodber sent me. Its effect is rather stirring, actually. The schematic forms alongside the memo's language only make more vivid the work of the administrative alongside the more rarefied labor of the imaginative in the making and maintenance of nations. As Ian Baucom has noted in a different though not entirely unrelated context, even the most startling procedures of nationalism are undergirded by bureaucratic sangfroid.[16]

The memo Brodber sent me proposes, in part, the restitution of Emancipation Day as a national holiday in Jamaica.[17] The celebration of slavery emancipation had begun on that grand day, August 1, 1838, when British West Indian slaves were given "full free." The rituals of emancipation had been multiple, complex, and ongoing for over a hundred years, with the government providing its imprimatur on certain events, such as the grand celebration at Spanish Town in 1838, and at other times discouraging or outright denouncing enthusiastic jubilees.[18] Sometimes, with the backing of local governments, churches took the occasion of emancipation celebrations as an opportunity to instill dubious messages of moral rectitude into the formerly enslaved. These rather more staid church teas had banners encouraging newly freed men and women to work (a rather ironic message for those whose lives had been defined by unrelenting labor). At other times, though, freedom's revelry proved to be so vociferous it threatened to put a damper on the Crown Colony's belief in its orderly and liberal administration, causing one parish magistrate in 1847, for instance, to condemn the "illegal revelry" that had been going on for ten days.[19] Whether encouraged, co-opted, or censured, Emancipation Day was a potent practice of national memory.

Yet when another kind of freedom was being plotted—the separation of the colonial island from its imperial motherland—slavery's remembrance became a political stumbling block. Though founded on the labor union movement, the Jamaican political party system was led primarily by what Deborah Thomas describes as "creole nationalists": largely "brown" (i.e., light-skinned), educated, and bourgeois figures who chose to emphasize a vague notion of mixed ethnic nationalism, stirred together with ersatz folk cultural forms, over and against the largely African and enslaved heritage of the island's majority.[20] This vision of an independent Jamaica could not sustain a robust engagement with a slave past, not least because shame about this aspect of the country's history and a paradoxical dependence on the British parliamentary forms that sustained it were key features of nascent West Indian nationalism. On August 6, 1962, then, Independence Day officially supplanted Emancipation Day as the island's celebration of freedom. A new conception of nation, forged through cultural policy and governmental decree, would apparently override practices and experiences of black collectivity that had always existed alongside, and separate from, the state.

It is to this transfer of ceremonial ritual that Brodber's paper speaks. In its guise of dry consultancy memorandum, the "Programme Audit" is about nothing less significant than the role, possibilities, and stakes of slavery's memorialization in Jamaica. Moreover, the suggestions of the "Programme Audit" are based on extensive interviews Brodber conducted with Jamaicans for her research on the generation of black subjects with living memories of those who were emancipated—the so-called second generation of "freemen," whose parents or grandparents had celebrated the granting of "full free."[21] For these people, Brodber discovered, a fierce attachment to the working and ownership of land was profoundly connected to memories of those passed on who themselves had worked with very little possibility of ownership. A strong relationship to the topos of Jamaica, then, would always be accompanied by, indeed *underwritten* by, a complex relationship to the spiritual presence of ancestors who were understood both to inhere in this land and to have passed on from it. These folk belonged to the nation, yes; but the nation as they understood it was free in the sense that their ancestors had understood freedom, not in the sense that the current Jamaican government did. They belonged to land made of soil and memory.

Brodber's memo gestured to a form of national belonging *not* operative in the state but organized and sustained by black subjects whose rituals of slavery's remembrance had created powerful structures of affinity among them. By the lights of Brodber's research, when the government had shifted its emphasis to Independence and away from Emancipation, it had mis-read the meaning of land ownership, and its concomitant metaphor of national independence, in the lives of the working black majority. Land was crucially important to the primarily rural folk Brodber surveyed, but land had meaning because of the memory of those who had died working it, those who had been brought to it from elsewhere. By suggesting changes to the structure and programming of the Jamaica Cultural Development Commission, Brodber was making radical propositions about how, in the celebrations of nationhood, the government might balance its ideology of multiethnic inclusion with the memory of African enslavement.

The memo reads:

> We submit that the first week of August is asked to note two import-ant national points [Independence and Emancipation], each of which deserves to be clearly heard. We therefore suggest that the Arts Festival [associated with Independence] be divorced from the Independence celebrations and be scheduled perhaps in the spring, close to the end of the official tourist season, where it can be its own significant event making a statement to Jamaicans and the world about the high quality of and particularity of Jamaican art.
>
> We suggest that the first week of August be devoted to marking the political advance of Jamaicans. We further suggest that the programmes for this week deal with Jamaica's definition of herself as a multi-racial so-ciety in accordance with the claims of her national motto ["Out of Many, One People"]. To this end we suggest that the Afro-Jamaican celebration of the 1st of August as emancipation day be put back in place, that other days in the week be assigned to other ethnic groups as research to be mounted will dictate, and that the week peak with the independence celebrations, a statement of ethnic solidarity and of political maturity.[22]

Brodber's proposed relegation of Festival to the tourist season (her use of the term "spring," a season that exists only in the touristic register of the tropical nation, only emphasizes the point) is not a sign of her disparagement of culture. In fact it is the opposite. Apart from being a historian, sociologist, community activist, and some time governmental consultant, Brodber is also an acclaimed novelist, known in particular for her formal innovations. No, in seeking to distinguish between the government's arts policies and its memorials, Brodber was attempting to retrieve for the arts some of their autonomy and power. It was an effort to give back to "the folk" the music, dance, and theater that the government had bastardized for its own ends. (This aspect of the memo therefore demonstrates an astute reading of the instrumentalizing function of art in Jamaica's statecraft and economy.) Brodber goes on to suggest that Emancipation Day celebrations happen at the local, not national, level "with the assistance of the parish cultural programme officer who would draw on the research of the parish arts development officer and the regional office to add historical and cultural depth to the programmes designed to celebrate the day in the villages."[23] Here it is the parish, the locality, that is emphasized, not the national. It is as if Brodber was seeking to wrest control of emancipation away from the national government; as if placing its administration at the more diffuse and granular local level would return it closer to the celebrants themselves. If the government had passed over the opportunity to memorialize emancipation before, Brodber here suggests that the processes of remembering be taken out of state hands.

Meanwhile, Brodber was doing exactly that herself. The Cultural Development Commission's programs had thus far highlighted Jamaica's 1962 Independence from Britain—its legal instantiation (and no less marvelous for it when you think about it). But in her work as a historical sociologist, Brodber had been conducting extensive interviews with Jamaicans in far-flung villages who remembered celebrating Emancipation Day and who experienced a far deeper resonance with that festival, and with the collectivity that practice conjured up. They felt less enthused by the belated, and one suspects increasingly anticlimactic, Independence celebrations for which the government offered its hefty sponsorship.[24] As Brodber points out, celebrating the nation could be burdensome.[25] And so why shouldn't people be offered the opportunity to spend valuable energy and resources celebrating the nation as they understood it? Modern-day celebrations of Emancipation Day imply a national imaginary comprising the cultures of successive generations of the descendants of black slaves. Brodber gestures to other ethnic histories that belong within the nation too (and no, the government has not as yet undertaken her suggestion to research and celebrate Chinese, Indian, Jewish, or any of the other ethnicities represented in the island in any substantive way). But she suggests that her contribution to the government's parsing of these issues, and the work of August 1, should be reserved for remembering the day in 1838 when slaves of British colonies in the West Indies were finally granted full legal freedom.

Brodber's memo points to the discrepancy between the legal and the imagined entity that is simultaneously referred to as *Jamaica*. The commemoration of freedom mapped on to local spaces, which spaces in turn contained specific histories and cultures that were separable from the state. So while Emancipation Day has since been reinstated as a national holiday, and the government has begun supporting various celebratory events, these continue to be mixed in with the Arts Festival that Brodber suggested be kept separate. And local Emancipation Day celebrations are still distinct from the government-sponsored ones, which continue to be enmeshed with the national project.

Brodber signed her memo thus:

> Erna Brodber
> b l a c k s p a c e (Ja.) Ltd.
> December 1989

b l a c k s p a c e refers to Brodber's organization, under the auspices of which she carries out a variety of activities: her consultancy work; a summer school; a "reasoning" workshop in African Diaspora history and culture; and the annual Emancipation Day celebrations she revived in her village in the 1990s, long before the government decided to take her advice. Brodber's Woodside celebrations have become legendary and they draw visitors from Kingston and abroad, with an impact beyond their relatively modest numbers. It is inconceivable that the success of the Woodside celebrations did not influence the national government's decision to reinstate Emancipation Day, and Brodber has mentioned the notice her memo received in Parliament, though she has never been given official word about the implementation of her advice.[26]

b l a c k s p a c e also refers to her home in the small village of Woodside, St. Mary Parish, the home in which she was born in 1940 and to which she returned in the 1980s after years of study in Kingston, the United States, and England. She christened the homestead b l a c k s p a c e in a gesture of reclamation: Woodside had previously been a coffee plantation owned by white colonialists and worked by black slaves. Her family's wood and concrete home, the land on which the house was built, and, by symbolic extension, Woodside itself, was now imaginatively and nominatively a space of blackness. In the memo's signature, Jamaica is parenthetical, circumscribed, and limited. b l a c k s p a c e is elongated, stretching across as much of the page as it can. And yet Brodber's home is not an internal colony: it is as much a part of Jamaica as is King's House, the nation's symbolic seat of state power in Kingston. And so, not unlike "Jamaica," b l a c k s p a c e refers simultaneously to a locatable place, to a variety of activities and performances occurring within it, and to a *concept* of autonomy wed to the legacy of slaves whose history is enmeshed with the land. Both terms, *b l a c k s p a c e* and *Jamaica*, are gestures of freedom that require land. Yet the land itself eventually cedes importance to the practices that develop on it, the imaginative work enabled by rituals of remembrance that invoke ancestors and yoke present-day celebrants to the slaves who worked and died there. These rituals in turn imbue the land with meaning, offering multiple subjects—including those who have traveled from outside Woodside to attend—a way to claim a form of belonging that is mediated through ritualized attachment to land.

This dialectic between ritual and land, the way the literal ground of b l a c k s p a c e becomes the deeply felt experience of being in black space, is the dynamic of belonging to a territory of soul that I will trace throughout this book. Brodber is a writer who conceives of her social remit as much wider than her particular island and who lives her imaginative, political, and literary life in reference always to a time that is past yet somehow accessible. b l a c k s p a c e is circumscribed geographically and racially (Brodber sometimes prefers only those of African or Asian descent to attend certain gatherings there). And yet this circumscription opens up a sense of encounter with black subjects far removed in time and space, and so it is uniquely inclusive and capacious. To be immersed in Brodber's work, whether her evocative and elusive novels, her programs at b l a c k s p a c e, her groundbreaking historiography, or even, yes, her government memos, is to be confronted with a feeling of being in multiple places and multiple times at once. Beginning with *Jane and Louisa Will Soon Come Home* (1981), her startling first novel, Brodber evinces a version of national belonging—indeed, national return, a nation chosen and claimed—that exists alongside a sense of belonging somewhere else, too. Even deep "inna the kumbla," as the refrain in *Jane and Louisa* goes, perhaps from deepest inside the *kumbla*, is the feeling that a wider universe opens that is always at once just beyond reach and decidedly in view.

Territories of the Soul concludes with an epilogue that brings us to another kind of Jamaican blackspace, this time in Kingston. For a period in May 2010 the Tivoli Gardens community became a space of death, a *territory of souls* in the most haunting way. Through an astonishing set of artworks by Ebony Patterson I read the week, now best known as the Tivoli Incursion, when Jamaican police and military forces entered the community in search of a drug lord, killing an estimated seventy-six civilians in the process.[27] Patterson's detailed, filigreed, and ecstatic mixed media pieces render seventy-two of those deaths using the aesthetics of reggae's young spawn, Jamaican dancehall. Dancehall culture was prominent in Tivoli before the incursion, and its aesthetics have always accommodated the experiences of circumscription and violence that May 2010 brought into vivid focus.

When you arrive at the close of the book, then, I hope you will see, as I do, how Patterson's visual elegies articulate a future for diasporic belonging in which local performance practices, however unwittingly and usually in situations of dire extremity, call out to the diaspora, carving black space out of materials that, at first glance, should never allow it. Even in regions and experiences of the most violent circumscription, the call of the diasporic elsewhere can be heard. This book ventures to suggest that territories of the soul have long been taking up residence in black subjects, through art, culture, and music. Our contemporary moment provides ample evidence that more than ever these queered forms of identification exert a compelling and necessary force.

ONE

THE ATTACHMENTS OF C. L. R. JAMES

In the countryside of Trinidad, around the 1920s, a young girl named Anita Perez worked in the cocoa plantations from morning til night and dreamt about a boy. Each night, laconic Sebastian came down from the hillside, where his several acres and settled home meant he did not have to work, and he sat on a bench by the door of Anita's house. Chiefly, he smoked; for Sebastian was self-conscious and Anita shy. They admired each other and ritually enjoyed their quiet company for two years. Anita, meanwhile, hoped he loved her and was never sure. Finally, prompted by the image of herself in the mirror veering toward the haggard—and by the nosy and self-satisfied inquiries of a married aunt—Anita became desperate. Would she ever be married? Would Sebastian take her and her mother away from their dull life in the cocoa? Anita's aunt sprung into action: to the town of Siparia Anita would go to visit the statue of La Divina Pastora, the patron saint of the town, who granted the wishes of those who importuned her. Anita went to Siparia, arrived at the church, stood before La Divina, and offered the only thing of value she had: a small gold necklace. This necklace she usually wore on Sundays, and it was a delicate gesture of a thing that distinguished her from the girl who worked ten hours a day in the fields, a gesture to the self who aspired to charm, leisure, and romance—everything she hoped Sebastian would offer her. Anita draped the chain around La Divina and prayed for the love of a man. A week later, returned from Siparia, Anita was met by a taxicab that had been ordered to bring her to Sebastian immediately. So quick had been the results of Anita's pilgrimage that she was startled. For when Sebastian had made his nightly constitutional to the Perez family house only to find Anita gone, he had known instantly that he could not stand to lose her. He declared himself the moment she returned to their little countryside town, not even waiting for the cab to arrive at his house but running down the hill to meet it. The lovers were to go out to a dance together in the next night or two, and so it would be complete. Everyone would know that Sebastian loved Anita, and marriage and all the rest were sure to follow. As Anita prepared for her entrée into the publicity of feminine romance, she dressed carefully. Arranging her blue Sunday muslin dress while admiring in the mirror the beauty her new-found excitement lent her, Anita suddenly thought everything perfect, except for one missing thing: her little gold necklace. With regret in her voice she found herself wishing she had it. It was the second time Anita youthfully forgot herself, vis-à-vis the speedy good fortune La Divina had sent her. Earlier, when met by the cab on arriving back home, she had been so overwhelmed by the speed of the occurrences with Sebastian that she had almost forgotten it was the saint who was responsible. And so it was that at the dance a little cloud formed between Anita and Sebastian, who tired quickly and was miffed at Anita's wanting to stay out. And in the car home, the two were silent, each a little worried and annoyed. Anita set aside her brief notion that she might kiss Sebastian that night, perhaps even make love with him. We shall make it up tomorrow night, she thought. Back home and undressing, Anita hung her dress and replaced some hairpins in the cigarette tin in which she kept her thises-and-thats. Stunned, she looked at the tin and saw that her necklace had been replaced there too.

Maybe you can't have everything at once. Perhaps multiplicity requires a relay. You can have the delicacy of the gold necklace confirming your femininity once a week. Or you can have the love of a man to take you away from the drudgery of the field. But once you wish for both at the same time, once you dare to imagine "having it all," the one falls away, the other returns.

C. L. R. James's story "La Divina Pastora" (1927), my version of which I have offered as an overture to this chapter, is one of two short narratives he wrote that feature young working-class girls striving for more than they have.[1] ("Triumph" [1929] is the other.) And I start here—in 1920s Trinidad—even though my chapter is going to take me further afield and later into James's career, because it was in reencountering these stories in the wake of my study of James's writing on America that I got a hold of what James offers to a rethinking of diaspora.

It is not, as I originally thought, that James provides a *model* of what it looks like to belong in multiple places. It is that he occasions the possibility of describing what this multiplicity feels like.

Certainly, James clarifies an account of diasporic belonging that emphasizes multiplicity because his life in different countries exemplifies the possibility, sometimes the necessity, of claiming multiple spaces as sites of attachment and affiliation. But it is not *only* this that James offers. Like his numerous forebears—Claude McKay, say, or Una Marson—James is a figure of Caribbean exile par excellence. And yes, James's multiple excursions and stretches of residence in England, the United States, Mexico, and the Caribbean offer an example of cultural and political cosmopolitanism that makes him a compelling figure for this study. But the effect of scattering that *diaspora* describes, when applied to a single person, conjures up an image of subjective splitting that, while figuratively compelling, requires some explaining, some effort to describe just how multiple national cathexes are possible.[2] In this chapter, I will be interested to demonstrate not just the fact of James's attachments to multiple places but also how these attachments were forged. For apart from multiplicity, James models a structure of diasporic belonging that is enabled by the mediation of other bodies. The gendered dimension of these mediations is very compelling, and to my mind the most striking contribution to a rereading of James for contemporary understandings of the experience of black diaspora. Far from overlooking James's early stories of women's dilemmas, as the voluminous scholarship on him generally does, I want to begin by offering these narratives as paradigmatic of James's formative curiosities, however subterranean or transmuted they became in his later work.

For early on, James was fascinated by "women's troubles," a term I use as a call out to Lauren Berlant, whose account of feminine emotional prostheses informs my reading of James's American career. James's barrack-yard fiction, so-called, which includes the aforementioned stories as well as his only novel, *Minty Alley* (1936), evince a keen interest in the feminine management of economic, affective, and sartorial affairs. For instance, a persuasive rendering of the allegorical meaning of "La Divina Pastora," it seems to me, is not the more obvious bromide *be careful what you wish for*. Rather, were I to allegorize "La Divina" for Jamesian diasporic belonging, I would say that the story means Anita must choose between the labor of the land—onerous, though potentially meaningful in the Brodberian b l a c k s p a c e sense—and the work of feminine beauty—easier but extremely tenuous in its effects. That these choices are in direct opposition to one other is only half of the lesson (*you can't have it all*). The other half of the lesson, buried at the heart of Anita's story, is that if she wants to find somewhere to rest, she must work. For Anita *does* want somewhere to set herself down, some permanent veranda she can lean back on. And in order to attain this space of her own, labor she must, whether in the cocoa or in front of the vanity mirror.

James's attention to the poignancy of Anita's plight, a peculiarly feminine poignancy because one of her two choices rests on the uniquely feminine gossamer of beauty, establishes his interest in the gendered features of spatial dominion. Setting oneself down, resting for the evening—this kind of easeful leisure presupposes a confident sense of belonging. Anita never achieves it, nor, in a sense, did James, who though confident in his political engagements in many places, lived a peripatetic and restless life, one increasingly marked—if his letters are any indication—by a desire to stay some place he ultimately would not be allowed to. But the labor attending the desire to belong is interesting labor, especially when it is informed by the work of others, as it is for James. His attachments to the Caribbean, to England, and to the United States each required different laboring bodies, at least one of which—that of the white American actress—James's critics have paid almost no attention. If we are to get anything out of C. L. R. James's journeys over his long, radical life, apart from an adoring interest in the spectacle of his brilliance and his ability to work in multiple settings, then we have to pay attention to the people, the performers, who embodied what he thought of as national character. James's relationship to specific kinds of performed embodiment helped him to understand, to attach, and to imagine himself into various social formations. This was a cathexis of a rather feminine kind—at least if we consider the stark duality of Anita's choice in "La Divina Pastora" as particularly feminine in its precarity and emphasis on embodiment. For in James, even in his investment in "male" forms, such as cricket, I detect a desire to rest in the body of another, and I sense that this desire is in tension with a roving tendency of his to labor on his own.

Even before James found himself embroiled in an emotional drama with an American woman who figured for him America itself, even before he wanted to help transform America as well as to be "universal," somehow above its nationalist confines, we can observe him desiring two things at once—the magnificence of West Indian triumph on the sporting field and a cultural solubility with Englishness. James managed that twin demand by forging an attachment to England through absorption in the body of the West Indian cricketer. In the case of James's American cathexis, the role that femininity, precarity, and indeed eros, played in his fifteen-year stint in the United States is made vividly clear through his relationships to female actresses. I do not believe the perspective of James as a lovesick man taking in Bette Davis movies of an afternoon has been sufficiently re-marked, much less folded into an account of his political meaning. In this chapter, I will do just that, with a specific focus on how a counterintuitive reading of James in America provides a model for diasporic belonging. James's national attachments as a black Caribbean radical relied in pro-found ways on his reading of, and experience with, feminine desire and disappointment.

Loving James and Giving Him Up; or, James in Ellis Island and Other Confined Spaces

C. L. R. James seems to belong in many places. And judging by the sheer number of scholarly works in multiple disciplines produced in his name, he belongs to many people. Born in Port of Spain, Trinidad, in 1901, James traveled and wrote to such an extent and with such prodigious profligacy that he very quickly became a "man of the world" in every sense of that term. Moving to England in 1932 (leaving his first wife, Juanita—the at-tachment to her apparently less compelling than that to the imperial cen-ter), James made his way in radical circles, introduced by Learie Constan-tine, the West Indies cricketer playing in the north of England, and became a Marxist. From there, he traveled to the United States, commissioned by Trotskyites to work on "the Negro Problem." That James had no previous experience with the particularities of US race politics proved no barrier to his belief that America was exactly where he belonged, even that America needed him, and he set about his work with alacrity. When he was finally deported in late 1953, he appeared to be genuinely shocked. The letters he wrote from Ellis Island while he awaited deportation orders show him to be incredulous that America could not feel his love as demonstrated by his mastery of what he argued was its key text, *Moby-Dick*. He felt pro-foundly misunderstood. For a black radical, this is a curious sentiment to have about America at a moment when leftist trust in the government's capacity to understand, let alone sympathize with, radical politics was approximately nil. Yet in February 1953, James wrote a letter about his book of Melville criticism, *Mariners, Renegades, and Castaways* (1953), to Arthur Schlesinger Jr., then professor of history at Harvard, making a case for his literary criticism as a form of investment in the American national project. Displaying a customary ease with institutional prestige and a typically sanguine estimation of his own work, James writes:

> I send you a copy of my book on Herman Melville. I believe my book will interest you because I think it demonstrates among other things, that no other writer grasped the totalitarian personality, the nature of the modern intellectual neurosis, and at the same time had so profound and comprehensive a conception of the great uneducated masses of the world in contemporary civilization. It is to me very illuminating that all this should receive such remarkable expression in the work of an American.
>
> The special circumstances of the publication are fully explained in Chapter VII, but I am confident that this will at least prove no obstacle to your serious consideration of [the] book.[3]

The passage is extraordinary in several ways: in the broad sweep of James's claims; in the slippage between Melville and James himself, demonstrated by that ambiguous phrase "no other writer"; in his note of surprise that "an American" should have had the wherewithal to gather up all the important issues of modern society. It is extraordinary as well in its intriguing combination of hubris and innocence, and in its intense, if covert, intertwining of the intellectual and the personal. For "the special circumstances" James notes in his letter to Schlesinger are, of course, that he is writing from his holding cell. He had been detained in Ellis Island ostensibly for visa violations, though his alliance with the American far left certainly didn't help, and he was housed with the communists. Within a few months, he would be sent back to England.

The letter to Schlesinger established James's sense that he belonged in the community of American Melville scholars even as it was an implicit plea for help in the exigencies of his political trials. James only delicately mentions his troubles to Schlesinger, but he included in the package to him a letter he wrote to Willard Thorp, English professor at Princeton, which contained slightly more information about his political woes as well as the emphatic insistence that "I am asking no one, absolutely no one, to use any influence or say a few words to any influential person or anything of the sort."[4] The 1953 chapter 7 of *Mariners, Renegades, and Castaways* expands on the difficulties of his detention in great detail—the bad food and how it exacerbates his stomach problems; the callousness of the staff; the loneliness—belying this assertion that he wants no help.[5] James is abject in that chapter, and he folds his abjection into his critique of America's failures to live up to the revolutionary potential of the *Pequod*. Nevertheless, help from these high literary quarters was not forthcoming.

It was his revolutionary friends who found a way to publish *Mariners*, and it was this first edition he circulated to Melville scholars, as well as members of Congress, in a plea to remain in the United States. The 1978 edition excised chapter 7.[6] (The 2001 version introduced by Donald Pease restores it.)[7] James was apparently unconcerned about his readers seeing him explore personal pain. Indeed, he writes letters to members of the highest echelons of cultural prestige because he thinks the quality of his mind gains him access there, and because he expects his personal pain to be transmuted by the rigor of his argument. Furthermore, James's most profound point in *Mariners* is that what Paul Gilroy might refer to as the "conviviality" of the men of different races on the ship is what produces the revolutionary potential of American democracy.[8] Far from exhibiting reticence about the personal in his *Marines* project—a reticence presupposed and imposed by the editors of the 1978 edition who excised the book's most personal chapter—James's political interest in Melville's novel is generated by the affiliative and homosocial bonds of shipmates that the novel depicts. And it is within that key of the affective that James diagnoses America's failure, allegorized by the fact of his being locked away in inhospitable circumstances.

James's letters about his Melville book written in the middle of the century and in America deposit us at the very center of a complex of issues surrounding the relationship between his affections and his ideas, the differences in his ties to England and America, and his sense of the performative aspects of the autobiographical form. The letters are typically Jamesian in their conflation of the intellectual, the personal, and the political. And they demonstrate James's relationship to precarity. At a moment of extreme personal exigency, faced with the loss of home, community, wife, and child, James turned to literary criticism.

The Melville letters also remind us of the tension in James's affection for America and England. The ironic and withheld quality of his missive to Schlesinger suggests James's affectation of what he named, in *Beyond a Boundary* (1963), English "restraint." But the letters are about his new-found enthusiasm for Melville, which is unrestrained. In *Beyond a Boundary* James expounds on his sense of the innate hold Englishness has on his affections. In his draft essays on American culture, posthumously published as *American Civilization* (1993), and in his letters to the American woman who would become his wife, Constance Webb, there is a loosening of that restraint that makes the texts sometimes overwhelming. This loosening, I think, is related not just to the romantic love that spurs the texts, but also to James's sense of what emotional cast is fit for America. These documents are a trove of insights about how James forged his attachment to the United States. And yet one of the things I discovered as I traced the origins of his American cultural enthusiasms is that James's attachment to England, the national feeling that came first and that he theorizes in *Beyond a Boundary* (arguably his most famous book), does not disappear during the decade and a half that he spent in the United States. Far from abandoning England and Englishness during his radical adventure in America, James felt that the colonial mastery of English forms made the mastery of, at least by his lights, relatively nascent American popular culture easily comprehensible. That sense of ease is everywhere in his pronouncements on American culture—pronouncements that were often undertheorized when compared with his work on revolutionary Haiti (*The Black Jacobins* [1938], his other heavily cited book) or on Caribbean and British cricket.

Before further exploring the differences between James's American and English attachments, let me reiterate: the underlying structural form that attachment required was the performance of others. In the realm of two separate performance spheres James experienced and described his attachment to nations he nevertheless considered quite different. Cricket, the sport England exported to select colonies as a civilizing mechanism, fully did its work on James. He is explicit in *Beyond a Boundary* that cricket, alongside Victorian literature and the schoolroom, created his investment in certain modes of behavior categorizable under the term he prefers, *restraint*. Restraint was responsible for—here is the irony—the development of Caribbean nationalism and was its grounds for independence. For decades after James wrote *Beyond a Boundary*, the cricket pitch was the premiere theater for the enactment of West Indian self-governance, a fact James was first to explain precisely in the writing of that book. But there was a complication in James's investment in restraint. For something like its opposite—the watchword in James's American texts is *vitality*—conditions his relationship to America. And the theater for the working out of that affective link to the United States, the space for exploring the excessive emotional transparency he denied himself in Englishness, was quite literally the theater—cinema, to be precise. To locate the embodied surrogate for Jamesian belonging we must toggle between the cricketer in Englishness and the female American screen star, whose iconographic circulation in photographs and whose apparently radical availability on-screen made James feel he could *have* America; made him feel he could be just as present; and made him experiment with both of those notions in the person of Constance Webb, to whom he wrote the most about America. The epistolary collection *Special Delivery: The Letters of C. L. R. James to Constance Webb, 1939–1948* (1996) is a companion piece to *Beyond a Boundary*, though to my knowledge the works have not been considered by these lights. In both books James demonstrates that belonging requires the labor of performance. But the stark choice James faced at some critical moments in America such as his Ellis Island incarceration—his version of Anita's necklace, as it were—is that even as he was increasingly seduced by American vitality, he expressed his admiration for it with a sometimes muddled rhetoric of restraint, naïvely imagining that this English presentation would translate to a perception of his cultural superiority vis-à-vis America, a place where blackness was abjected. James even then believed his mastery of Englishness, even though it came via colonial oppression, could be of utilitarian political value—witness his belief in those letters from Ellis Island that his learning could broker his release. This, of course, could never be the case—and certainly not while McCarthy-era immigration attitudes prevailed.

James, then, occupied a unique position between the two Anglophone imperial powers of the twentieth century. In the time of James, which is to say the entire twentieth century, the West Indies was a mediating region between the empire of Great Britain and the emerging empire of the United States. As colonial islands slowly plotting their separation from the motherland, most West Indian nations remained attached to the forms and politics of Britain. But as the balance of power shifted to the United States after World War II, and indeed as the United States ventured deeper into the region during this period, West Indians made their way to America. They had to accommodate themselves to a different world power, the first one having failed them in multiple and predictable ways. James models what that shift between the United Kingdom and the United States was like for many of his generation in the Caribbean. And his significant blind spots in the field of US race relations make sense in the wake of his explanation that he was inculcated by Englishness into an understanding of himself as a universal subject. All of which is to say that it should not be surprising that the Caribbean was all at once: the heart of James's other national belongings, the ground of his theorizing, and the place he could not bear to stay. James is only one of the men of a generation of West Indians for whom exile was the only way to belong, though *his* way of belonging is particularly illuminating. To understand why we must go back to young James in Trinidad, to the retrospective vision he gives us in the autobiographical book he wrote when he was in his early sixties—and I will turn to *Beyond a Boundary* in a moment.

Before that, one final detour: a dip into one of the wide pools of James studies. In order to illuminate the backdrop—indeed to prepare the reader— for what will be a very different approach to the stentorian figure that is the C. L. R. James many people think of when his name is invoked, I want to briefly recall the fact that for a moment, James became metonymic for all Caribbean intellectual production. His putatively implacable logic, his masterful accomplishment of several varieties of Western discourse, his self-presentation as supremely rational, his apparent lucidity—all these became triumphs not just of this particular individual but of the West Indian mind. But putting James at the service of a Caribbean ideal often meant creating false dichotomies that were not supported by his work. Selwyn Cudjoe's 1992 *Transition* review, "C. L. R. James Misbound," is particularly good at capturing this tendency. Cudjoe argues that Anna Grimshaw, the editor of several collections of James's work (I discuss these more later) made ill-advised choices in compiling one of the first major editions in over a decade of James's early work: "To this reviewer, it seems that any perspicacious reading of *The C. L. R. James Reader* leaves James looking more like a cultural critic than . . . political thinker, philosopher, and revolutionary organizer . . . which, in my opinion, is what gives James his claim on our scholarly attention."[9] Embedded in the culture–politics dichotomy are other unsaid oppositions: art–praxis; feeling–thinking;

feminine–masculine (Grimshaw–Cudjoe). James is supposed to be the kind of prominent figure who works at the crucial job of nation-building while still having time on the side to encourage the arts. Yet he wrote constantly against these dichotomies. He stressed the importance of art to any successful revolutionary society; he studied poetry and film alongside Hegel all his life.

But Cudjoe is not alone in his desire for a James who left culture to the ladies. In a sense Cudjoe is merely indicating a larger desire not just for James but for the kind of Caribbean male leader he represents. James has become symbolic of the most patriarchal form of Caribbean cultural nationalism. Some prominent narratives of West Indian nationhood rely on the silent fecundity of the female and the firm leadership of the learned male or the rebellious, charismatic leader.[10] James reflects both these masculine images. He is a towering figure of Caribbean achievement, and a celebrant-symbol of masculine physical capacity and intellectual mastery. Furthermore, he secured his knowledge through a solid colonial high school education and the discipline of a brilliant autodidact and thus could be seen as institutional as well as rebellious—an irresistible Caribbean combination. James never attained elected office and lived most of his life outside the West Indies—facts that confirm him as a metaphor of some of the Caribbean's most important political traditions: transnationalism, Pan-Africanism, and the centrality of politics beyond the strictly electoral realm.

This Jamesian figure was created in earnest in the late 1980s and early 1990s, in the decade after his death. It is no surprise that in the period of disappointments after West Indian independence movements, Caribbean thinkers and activists would create an indigenous intellectual hero. By 1990, when a collection of essays was published by University of the West Indies graduate students titled *Celebrating C. L. R. James: Tribute to a Scholar*, the Caribbean was already in the aftermath of several post-independence traumas. Trinidad had been through an Eric Williams–imposed state of emergency in 1970 after the Black Power Movement began to gain influence, and there was talk of a general strike. In Jamaica, where *Celebrating C. L. R. James* was produced, the violent 1980 elections had profoundly wounded people's hope in the country's postcolonial promise. The 1979–1983 period in Grenada was marked by upheavals and traumas, beginning with the rise to power of communist-leaning Maurice Bishop, his eventual assassination, and the nation's invasion by the United States and other Caribbean nations in order to overthrow the military government that had taken power. After the excesses of Caribbean leaders—Bishop's curtailment of civil rights; Jamaican prime minister Michael Manley's socially progressive but economically deterring policies and his successor Edward Seaga's adherence to Reaganism—the image of James as a different kind of leader, politically active yet somehow politically pure, an intellectual, would have been a salve. And so:

> C. L. R. James was, arguably, one of the most outstanding personalities of the 20th Century. In a life which spanned nine of the Century's decades, he embraced most of its great social movements with passion, eloquence, and brilliant insights. To some, he is best known for his tireless struggles against colonialism, imperialism, racism, and Stalinism; inspired by an overarching and infectious vision of the possibilities of establishing a just, humane and participatory society. Others will remember him for the scope of his knowledge and appreciation of literature and philosophy, and his ability to illuminate their relationship to politics and the workday world. For [others still], he is quite simply the best writer on cricket and society that the game has ever known. No one exposed to him or his work is ever quite the same again.[11]

Bringing due attention to an overlooked Caribbean intellectual meant that superlatives were necessary. Norman Girvan here sums up the renaissance quality James doubtless possessed but that it became increasingly important that he be *seen* to possess in the wake of the disappointments of West Indian independence. Paul Buhle's edited collection of essays on James's work, *C. L. R. James: His Life and Work* (1986) demonstrates a similar impulse. In his introduction, Buhle begins by emphasizing the multifariousness of James's accomplishments and also goes on to note: "One special dimension of James's activity must properly be treated at the outset. As several of the essays note in passing, James has worked in groups all his days. Most often, he was the outstanding intellectual, with guiding influence over whatever documents the groups produced and the political directions its members took. But he never imagined his collaborators to be ciphers or extensions of himself. And even when no formal group existed, he has gathered assistants and associates for a similar mode of expression."[12] Buhle's slight defensiveness about James's collaborations gently contradicts his assertion that James was often "the outstanding intellectual, with guiding influence" over his groups' direction and output. (And we know that many of James's collaborations were troubled: the Johnson-Forest Tendency collapsed in part because the women who made up the other two-thirds of the trio, Grace Lee Boggs and Raya Dunayevskaya, would not act as mere functionaries for James's aims.) In Buhle's introduction to James's political style, we have an example of critical conflict around the Jamesian legacy. Impossibly, he was meant to be the shining light, the singular intelligence, at the same time that he was the cooperative collaborator.[13] The slight sense of refutation we detect Buhle's assertions about James's cooperation, coupled with many later critical examples, suggests that the emphasis on James's legacy at this stage was in fact the singularity of his genius, an emphasis in problematic tension with the thorny collaborations that marked his output.

The image of the singular thinker came about at this stage for important reasons. Buhle's use of the term _intellectual_ in this context has all the force of a history that denied that category to black subjects. It is an emphasis echoed in Walter Rodney's essay in Buhle's collection, which notes that "James qualifies to be called an 'academic' or 'intellectual'; and as a participant in the struggle for African advance, he becomes a 'revolutionary intellectual.'"[14] It is there when Richard Small remarks James's "exceptionally trained mind."[15] And indeed, Buhle's biography, _C. L. R. James: The Artist as Revolutionary_ (1988) summarizes some of the popular hopes for James's intellect and how these hopes reflected a history of Western humanism that excluded black people: "[James] has often been called a Renaissance Man. That label seems imprecise, if only because his many-sidedness represents not a break from medieval constants but rather an expansion upon the particularly human possibilities of our time. He has also been called a "Black Plato," a characterization in some ways wildly inaccurate but not lacking a glimmer of truth."[16] As early as 1960 George Lamming was describing James as "the sharpest and most interesting mind that the British Caribbean has produced in three centuries of learning."[17] Derek Walcott's tribute to James at a watershed conference on James at Wellesley College included this note: "The scale of James as an intellect again can be easily praised on an academic level. . . . But the width I refer to is not the width that has to do with experience. It has to do with a sensibility that was ready to absorb everything."[18]

Added to the complicated burden of James as singular intellectual is a curious and subtle, apparently contradictory demand. James was also by now becoming metonymic for all of West Indian intellectual production—what Buhle calls "West Indian genius." Edward Said best sums up this dual purpose of the Jamesian legacy: "[James is] the father of modern Caribbean writing . . . [and] a centrally important 20th-century figure, a Trinidadian black whose life as a scholar of history, political activist, cricket player and critic, cultural maverick, restless pilgrim between the West and its former colonial possessions in Africa and America, is emblematic of modern existence itself."[19] James was somehow both a maverick and the founding figure of an established tradition; scholar and restless wanderer.

In the wake of the establishment of James as an intellectual worthy of serious critical attention, his work began circulating as never before, available for scholars and critics in fields from politics to literature. The London firm Allison and Busby had already brought out one edition of selected works, *The Future in the Present*, in 1977. During the eighties it added two more, *Spheres of Existence* (1980) and *At the Rendezvous of History* (1984). In 1994, Humanities Press edited a collection of James's writing titled *C. L. R. James and Revolutionary Marxism*.[20] It was a sign that James's stature was secure when, by the midnineties, reassessments of his work became more the norm. In his collection *Rethinking C. L. R. James* (1996), Grant Farred struck a cautionary note when he wondered: "What does [James's] new intellectual, ideological and political capital mean for James studies? How will James's work be utilized now? What are the possibilities and the pitfalls endemic to his new status?"[21] Well, the pitfalls, as I see them, must now be clear in the critical history I have been summarizing. The James recovered by this period in Caribbean and American studies was a successful, masculine, affect-free intellectual who shored up prevailing concepts about Caribbean governance and nationalism. He was also, to my mind, lacking in sustaining interest. For only a very particular and partial reading of the phrases "Renaissance Man" and "Black Plato" would fail to be interested that James was also the man who wrote letters about how handsome the cowboys in Nevada were—being in Nevada, by the way, because he had to redo his quickie Mexican divorce from his first wife in order to marry a second wife who was half his age.[22]

There is a photograph on the cover of the first reissue of *Minty Alley*—a bronze bust of James in which all the lines are smooth, clear, and untroubled.[23] It is centered on the novel's front like a stamp. But if you stare at the image long enough, and at James's oeuvre long enough, the clear lines of this statuesque figure begin to blur, puzzlingly at first, then pleasurably. Stuart Hall was one of the first major critics to draw attention to the deficiencies of too gratifying an image of C. L. R. James noting that "Major intellectual and political figures are not honored by simply celebration. Honor is accorded by taking his or her ideas seriously and debating them, extending them, quarreling with them, and making them live again."[24] If there is one thing that happens when we look closely at James's autobiographical work, it is that he begins to live again. And it is a life of a most interesting, desiring, painful, and conflictual sort.

Excessive Restraint; or, Little Nello at the Window

The most famous section of *Beyond a Boundary* is subtitled "The Window," and it inaugurates the book. James locates us in Tunapuna, a town, he says "of about 3,000 inhabitants, situated eight miles along the road from Port of Spain," Trinidad and Tobago's capital city. Those three thousand inhabitants included James's family, whose house, he notes, was superbly situated behind the village cricket ground, with a window of that afforded clear views of the cricketers: "By standing on a chair a small boy of six could watch practice every afternoon and matches on Saturdays. . . . From the chair also he could mount on to the window-sill and so stretch a groping hand for the books on the top of the wardrobe. Thus early the pattern of my life was set."[25]

There is something slightly scandalous about imagining C. L. R. James, Caribbean Great Man, as little Cyril, "a small boy of six"—which is probably why James introduces him in this objectifying way, before returning to a reconstituted first person. James also enjoys potentially confounding and dazzling his readers by being simultaneously scrappy and bookish, in love with sport and in love with literature at once. The section that follows is justifiably famous: a breathless description of how his love for cricket concretized in the person of one Matthew Bondman:

> I was an adventurous little boy and so my grandmother and my two aunts, with whom I lived for half the year, the rainy season, preferred me in the backyard or in the house where they could keep an eye on me.

When I tired of playing in the yard I perched myself on the chair by the window. I doubt if for some years I knew what I was looking at in detail. But this watch from the window shaped one of my strongest early impressions of personality in society. His name was Matthew Bondman and he lived next door to us.[26]

Bondman was a disreputable character. He was, James notes, "generally dirty. He would not work. His eyes were fierce, his language was violent, and his voice was loud. His lips curled back naturally and he intensified it by an almost perpetual snarl."[27] James's aunts and grandmothers hated Bondman. He walked around barefooted and his sister was bad. The whole Bondman family—the name itself surely too close to the slavery days James's family was actively working to forget—took on a scandalous aspect that young James clearly relished, given that (and especially because) his own family embodied the colonial Victorian uprightness exemplified by the books he scampered to reach on the high shelves of his home. But James is emotionally activated by the lawlessness of the Bondmans, by the physical intemperance of Matthew and his sister. And this interest is only heightened by what is Matthew's sole saving grace according to the James family: the fact that he is an excellent cricketer. It is of sustaining intellectual interest to James that even the female arbiters of his family allow that Matthew Bondman's physical grace performs a kind of moral alchemy on his character. This is how James discovers the fundamentally political role of cricket in the colonial setting and how he is able to describe its relationship to race, class, and processes of nationalism and decolonization. Achieving mastery of one British form, however ill-suited a colonial subject was to several others, demonstrated the potential for reforming the historically enslaved and undisciplined colonial into an enlightened citizen. Self-governance on the pitch could mean self-governance in the body politic. And winning—beating the Brits at their own game—well, what could be a clearer sign that it was time to allow the colonies to transform the lessons of political economy and reasoned enterprise for their own ends?

But I am interested in something else as well. James's description of Matthew Bondman is of an intense, even romantic cast. It suggests a kind of intemperance in James's appreciations, and it is curious that such unabashed delight has generally gone unremarked in the analysis of James, cricket, and national attachment. James does not write about Bondman in a detached and disembodied way. "He had one particular stroke that he played by going down low on one knee," James writes. "It may have been a slash through the covers or a sweep to the leg. But, whatever it was, whenever Matthew sank down and made it, a long, low 'Ah!' came from many a spectator, and my own little soul thrilled with recognition and delight."[28] And it wasn't just Bondman. In 1921 James wrote a sonnet to a cricketer. In this fact—one apt to be passed over not in spite of James's love for cricket but because that love is now so acknowledged and legitimated—resides much of what makes cricket interesting not just as a metaphor for decolonization but as theater, ironically, for colonial cathexis. James wrote the poem at the request of a cricket fan who had seen in the papers the week before some of James's poems written in a comic vein. This fan wished James to write a serious poem in honor of the Trinidadian cricketer Wilton St. Hill, who was then demonstrating his prowess in matches against England and other nations during an intercolonial tournament on the island. James agreed to this challenge, and the poem reads in part:

> O Wilton St. Hill, Trinidadians' pride,
> A century and four came from your bat,
> And helped to win the victory for your side
> But more than that you did, yea, more than that.[29]

Though he is partially self-ironizing about his efforts when he excerpts the sonnet in *Beyond a Boundary*, James also admits that he was "in a sense" serious about the poem he had produced.[30] James's love for English literary form and the attachment of those forms to the body of the West Indian cricketer are both indicated. As is the curious fit of those attachments— there is something mannered in that "O" and that "yea" that contradicts the physical vigor required of cricketing. Though in a way, this is precisely the paradox of cricket and why it functioned as it did in the colonies: it both disciplined the body through its long hours under the hot sun in a pristine white uniform and simultaneously required displays of immense dexterity and physical strength. In contrast, a sport such as rugby required brawn but not elegance. It was notably not introduced into slave societies and tended to thrive only in some settler colonies. What message would all that violent, messy contact between the races send to the colonial subjects Britain was trying to rule? As Orlando Patterson and Jason Kaufman argue in an article on cricket's cultural diffusion in the colonies, the sport functioned as "the umbilical cord of Empire."[31] "English elites encouraged their colonial subjects to play cricket because of the game's professed ability to discipline and civilize men, English and native alike."[32]

In the final line of James's sonnet is the way performance has a specific kind of power in his account of colonial affections. "But more than that you did, yea, more than that," James writes about St. Hill's performance on the cricket pitch. In that excess, the "more" of St. Hill's sportsmanship, is the surplus that is produced by any performance. James's work in *Beyond a Boundary* is partly to demonstrate that the spectacle of sports performances, as much as or more than the politics of sports performances, creates bonds of affection that generate national and transnational allegiances. What is particularly interesting in James's case is that the allegiances created by these performances shift. The superior performance of the black cricketing body stirs up profound and reactive feelings in James that produce for him the idea of the Caribbean nation. But these feelings just as much confirm James's sense that the performances of West Indians at home bind them inextricably to what he sees, even after his Marxist transformation, as the grandeur of British forms.

Which brings us to a sentiment James expresses not long after quoting his poem. Speaking of himself as a schoolboy in Port of Spain, he writes: "I was an actor on a stage in which the parts were set in advance. I not only took it to an extreme, I seemed to have been made by nature for nothing else. There were others around me who did not go as far and as completely as I did."[33] Using the language of performance to describe his early subjectivity, James describes himself as somehow both enacting external directives and simultaneously innately suited to the code. There is no longer a distance between an interior self submitting to the rigors of performance direction; rather, that interior self is now made "by nature" to incarnate British forms. This is one moment of several throughout the memoir in which James actively maintains a paradox between performance and nature, reflecting on the ritualized quality of the habits he learned but then soon enough writing of them as instinctive. Remembering, for instance, his "fierce, self-imposed discipline," an aspect of the code James says he picked up from English boys' magazines and subscription books, he claims: "These [forms of discipline] we understood, these we lived by, the principles they taught we absorbed through the pores and practiced instinctively."[34] They were instinctive practices become instinctive only through repetition.

Alongside that performative paradox is another: restraint, that category of withholding of which James, ironically, gave too much. Restraint is almost talismanic in *Beyond a Boundary*. The term becomes a catchall for a variety of habits, manners, performances, and assumptions that James names "the code." The code is the code of cricket, but it is also the rule of Victorian novels, of his Oxbridge schoolmasters, of his parents. The code establishes James's sense of the generative power of performance, for the code *creates* the interiority of the colonial subject through the theater of a culturally elaborated sport (and through novels, schoolmasters, and parents). For James, the performance of Victorian restraint reflects this affection for Britain, and the way this was formed and fostered through the spaces and objects of its imperial display. In the autobiographical realm of *Beyond a Boundary*, performance enacts affective connection.

The argument I am making here about the relationship between James's loves and his subjective formation is in some relationship to Bhabhian mimicry and, less obviously at first, with Anne Cheng's account of subjectivity and melancholia. Bhabha bears mentioning because what perhaps first comes to mind when considering the achievement of excellence in colonial performances is his signal account of the ambivalences of native mimicry—*almost the same but not white*.[35] And while Bhabha's subtle and sturdy theorization of the acquisition of Englishness in India (and, let us not forget, the ambivalences of *English* colonial discourse as well) is resonant here, I am struck by the way James's account of his colonial formation roughens its texture, if it does not at some points actually contradict it. Bhabha rightly notes that the formation of a raced colonial Other in the mold of the English subject is a threat to the imperial order, giving lie to the myth of English singularity. "Mimicry," he writes, "is at once resemblance and menace."[36] But Bhabha's emphasis on colonial desire from the perspective of the colonizers rather than the colonized is what gives his account a curious lack of fit with James's, with which it would otherwise seem to have much in common. For Bhabha, (English) colonial desire produces what he calls "metonymy of presence"—those stereotypes and those agitated, racist accounts in colonial discourse that represent the colonizers' desire for, simultaneously, a differentiated racial other and something like a mirror image.[37] In James's reading of his attainment of English forms, the emphasis and the perspective are reversed: the beautiful West Indian cricketer is a metonym for a wholeness of English identity to which James has access. There is no interdiction here; there is, rather, a colonial enabling of Englishness.

Which suggests Anne Cheng's account of the psychoanalysis of raced subjectivity.[38] All subjects, she argues, are formed through a process in which the idealized, hegemonic subject casts a shadow on the raced ego. Rather than mourning this process or seeking a compensatory narrative for it, she argues, one might as well see it as providing an instrumentalizing melancholia, the *active* formation of subjectivity by the raced subject using the cultural tools available. James's account of his colonial subjectivity is, of course, not remotely affectively downbeat. Indeed, it is the opposite—full of joie de vivre. But it is precisely in this way that it exemplifies Cheng's version of the agentive function of affect in raced subjectivities. Something like colonial affection suggests the structure of love and desire on the part of the Caribbean subject toward various objects of Englishness: language, monuments, books, ideas, manners. But the "colonial" part of the formulation modifies "affection" in a way that illuminates the complex and contradictory force at work. One might think of that force, with a few tweaks and modifications, as melancholia. If affection marks love and desire for Englishness, then melancholia is the reminder of the problematic ways that desire came to be there in the first place.

Let me be clear: I am not arguing that James's attachment to British forms is melancholic, or at least not in any sense other than Anne Cheng's. But melancholia offers a suggestive template for considering the relationship between England and the colonial subject in that it suggests not just the racialized subject's responses to loss and rejection but the racializing culture's strange incorporation of the Other. Cheng writes: "With phenomena such as segregation and colonialism, the racial question is an issue of *place* (the literalization of Freudian melancholic suspension) rather than of full relinquishment. Segregation and colonialism are internally fraught institutions not because they have eliminated the other but because they need the very thing they hate or fear."[39] Furthermore, the idea of racial melancholia that Cheng offers points out that the Freudian description of melancholia involves the subject nourishing himself or herself on the lost, rejecting, and desired object, introjecting or assimilating the object into the ego itself. Melancholia in her account is not pathological in any simple sense because it involves the subject in a drama of ego-formation and almost willful response. In Cheng's reading, the melancholic subject is working to maintain his or her relationship with the desired in complicated ways, and thus Cheng's account is amenable to notions of subjective agency, and agency is central to my account of James's attachments. Cheng sets the stage for my reading of James in *Beyond a Boundary* when she asks: "Is not the conversion of the grief of being black into the enjoyment of whiteness a very *cultural* lesson of mastering personal displeasure as social pleasure?"[40] A positively affective response to the valued and desired object is a fascinating way of tracking the colonized subject's agency in relation to the processes of colonialism.

In *Beyond a Boundary* we are able to see just how influential the colonial upbringing was, how primary its interventions were, and how sustaining it was. For even though James records the ways he rebelled against some of the expectations of the code, what is striking is the ways he did not; how his behaviors and attitudes were governed by a deep appreciation for it and an implicit sense that it was right. What is striking as well is how contemporary James's feelings for the code are. He wrote *Beyond a Boundary* after decades of radical activism and after years of living in America. Yet famously he was able to say: "Thackeray, not Marx, bears the heaviest responsibility for me."[41] He means not just that *Vanity Fair* made alive for him the brutality of the English caste system. He means that Thackeray got there first; that the Victorian writer was primary in the formation of his subjective ideas and in how he would go on to perform those ideas. One of the most powerful aspects of James's affective account of colonialism is how clear he makes it that these primary loves endure. Writing about his school principal, "Mr. W. Burslem, M.A., formerly, if I remember rightly, of Clare College, Cambridge," James is affectionate. He writes of Burslem's kindness to him, describes him as devoted, conscientious, and self-sacrificing. And James is aware that this sense of a colonial educator is at odds with contemporary understanding of the effects of English education in the colonies. Yet what he is trying to make clear is that his own experience of the "Eden" of school has fundamentally cast his affections in one direction. His conclusion about Mr. Burslem, despite his "autocratic disposition," despite all he represents, is stunning in its fundamental accession to the affective: "In the nationalist temper of today Mr. Burslem would be an anachronism, his bristling Englishness a perpetual reminder not of what he was doing but of what he represented. I write of him as he was, and today, forty years after, despite all that I have learnt between, what I think of him now is not very different from what I thought then."[42]

James describes an interlocking pattern of colonial influences in his memoirs. At one point, he pauses to note that though he has been describing the influence of his school and schoolmasters and reading on his inner life, he should also make clear the way his entire family helped to create the context of his colonial formations: "What was it that so linked my Aunt Judith with cricket as I, a colonial, experienced it? The answer is in one word: Puritanism; more specifically restraint, and restraint in a personal sense. But that restraint, did we learn it only on the cricket field, in *The Captain* and the *Boy's Own Paper*, the pervading influence of the university men who taught me, as I once believed? I don't think so. I absorbed it from Judith and from my mother—and it was in essence the same code—and I was learning it very early from my *Vanity Fair*."[43] A few moments later, quoting from *Pendennis* to make a point about the language of restraint in Victorian literature, James writes:

> This is not the aristocracy of the early eighteenth century. It is the solid British middle class, Puritanism incarnate, of the middle of the nineteenth. If Judith had been a literary person this is the way she would have spoken. The West Indian masses did not care a damn for this. . . . But they knew the code as it applied to sport, they expected us, the college boys, to maintain it; and if any English touring team or any member of it fell short they were merciless in their condemnation and shook their heads over it for years afterwards. Not only the English masters, but Englishmen in their relation to games in the colonies held tightly to the code as example and as mark of differentiation.[44]

The strictures of the code, then, were enforced by a wide-ranging crew of colonial society, including those working-class members to whom it did not directly apply, and the English expatriates who took it on as a mark of differentiation, becoming more "English" than they would have been at home.

The influences were overlapping and they were also ritualized, crystallized on the cricket pitch, which is why the memoir eventually gives way to sports analysis and not, say, literary criticism. Cricket best symbolizes the process of the code for James because, unlike reading, cricket blends the ritualistic with the corporeal, instinct and habit, the body and the mind. Sports require performance in a way that reading does not, and therefore the habits they inspire are arguably more enduring. Sounding like James sixty years before the fact, the British writer Cecil Headlam noted of cricket in India that it "provides moral training, an education in pluck, and nerve, and self-restraint, far more valuable to the character of the ordinary native than the mere learning by heart of a play of Shakespeare."[45] And performing on the sports field generates a relationship between bodily performance and language that connects the colonial schoolboy to the Victorian bourgeoisie. James writes of playing cricket at his school: "We were a motley crew. . . . Yet we rapidly learned to obey the umpire's decision without question, however irrational it was. We learned to play with the team, which meant subordinating your personal inclinations, and even interests, to the good of the whole. We kept a stiff upper lip in that we did not complain about ill-fortune. We did not denounce failures, but 'Well tried' or 'Hard luck' came easily to our lips. We were generous to opponents and congratulated them on victories, even when we knew they did not deserve it."

If he is able to clarify the performative elements of "the code" then James can also elucidate the affections to which the code gave rise. It is not often remarked just how lavish the emotional language is in his *Beyond a Boundary*. Throughout the book, he describes his attitudes toward Caribbean colonial artifacts in wildly emotive terms. There is also a strangeness in Jamesian language that comes from the tension between his excessive affect and what we might think of, in his own terms, as his excessive restraint. James inherits from the Victorians strategies of emotional distance that leave reservoirs of emotional excess sometimes to lap at the boundaries of civility. Occasionally, these reservoirs flood and spill over. Yet even when they do not, the affect in James's writing consists of what Denise Riley calls "unexamined rhetoricity"; that "tension, unease, or . . . feeling of dispossession [that] can result from the gulf between the ostensible content of what's said, and the affect which seeps from the very form of the words."[46]

Some of the early passages in *Beyond a Boundary* are replete with moments of this form of unease, particularly when citationality introduces a literal form of affective interpolation, producing queasy, unmarked tonal disjunctions. At one point, James remembers how he made sense of the multiple significance of his second childhood cricketing god, Arthur Jones. It was only years after observing him, James writes, when he was in his teens and at school, that he came across a passage in a book that reminded him of Jones's batting. James indents and quotes from the text, as I will here:

> It was a study for Phidias to see Beldham rise to strike; the grandeur of attitude, the settled composure of the look, the piercing lightning of the eye, the rapid glances of the bat, were electrical. Men's hearts throbbed within them, their cheeks turned pale and red. Michael Angelo [*sic*] should have painted him.[47]

"This was thrilling enough," James comments. "I began to tingle." Then he continues the citation: "Beldham was great in every hit, but his peculiar glory was the cut. Here he stood, with no man beside him, the laurel was all his own; it seemed like the cut of a racket. His wrist seemed to turn on springs of the finest steel. He took the ball, as Burke did the House of Commons, between wind and water—not a moment too soon or too late."[48] The more obvious resonances of this passage are rung on throughout the book. Young James thrills at the integration of art, politics, and sports in this passage. The Burke reference attaches to cricket the English parliamentary tradition of rhetorical style. The classical reference gives James's passion a history and a philosophy as well as sanctioning the equally obvious but less remarked homoerotic element of sports writing in this tradition. (The classical tradition comes with its own culturally sanctioned admiration of the male body beautiful, a tradition that is frankly homoerotic, which homoeroticism is only amplified with the reference to Michelangelo.) James's careful attention as a boy to Bondman and Jones, later expressed in the text when he is in his sixties, is if not homoerotic, certainly heightened—as are the physical descriptions of cricketers later in the book. To skip over this fact is to go along with a critical tradition that has not known what to make of the fact that James's political understanding of cricket is suffused with affection, not just for the sport but for the players. There is a network of aesthetic appreciation in James's writing—including the letters to Webb, to which I will turn shortly—in which beauty as a good in itself coalesces categories—men, women, clothes, poetry, speeches, music—and allows them to gain meaning in relation to each other.

Beyond a Boundary initiates the field of Caribbean cultural studies in idolatry, a term that recurs throughout the text and helpfully bridges the affective landscape of James's colonial affections with that of his American ones. Idolatry applies in *Beyond a Boundary*, especially in the first three chapters, to everyone from Thackeray to W. G. Grace. The religious language that permeates the text highlights the primacy and ritualistic quality of James's love. *Idolatry* also suggests that his affections are misplaced. Recall the secularization of the Holy Trinity that occurs at the end of the first chapter: "I had completed a circle. I discovered that I had not arbitrarily or by accident worshipped at the shrine of John Bunyan and Aunt Judith, of W. G. Grace and Matthew Bondman, of *The Throne of the House of David* and *Vanity Fair*. They were a trinity, three in one and one in three, the Gospel according to St. Matthew, Matthew being the son of Thomas, otherwise called Arnold of Rugby."[49] In another moment, James writes that only after many years did Matthew Bondman and Arthur Jones "[fall] into place as starting points of a connected pattern . . . the end, the last stone put into place, of a pyramid whose base constantly widened, until it embraced those aspects of social relations, politics, and art laid bare when the veil of the temple has been rent in twain as ours has been."[50] Egyptian history, with its traditions of Israelite slavery, combines with biblical imagery to make a provocative whole. The idea of the Caribbean as a holy temple violated by the forces of history and colonialism is particularly striking.

And yet as we know, this imagery does not yield in James's writing to prophetic injunctions against colonialism. Rather, he uses religious language to heighten and legitimize his idolatrous loves. In other words, though James uses a language of transference for many of his affections, idolatry has no rigid structure of reference. James is promiscuous in his sense of what deserves devotion. Of Matthew Bondman and British literature: "I was in my teens at school, playing cricket, reading cricket, idolizing Thackeray, Burke, Shelley."[51] *Vanity Fair* "became my Homer and my bible"; he finds in the novel "the same rhythms and the same moralism" he had found in Bible stories and the Old Testament.[52] Of art: "I had already begun a life-long worship of Michelangelo."[53] Of his school: the "race question" never disturbed their "little Eden."[54]

There is a moment in *Beyond a Boundary* when James writes about himself and his generation of men who grew up in the colonial Caribbean in a way that is so pointed as to be almost fatalistic. James describes social habits and attitudes that inform an entire generation and class of men who played cricket and inherited the British code, men whose interiority was forged by the performance of that code, and whom James does not imagine could emerge from that formation: "Read the books of Worrell and Walcott, middle-class boys of secondary education, and see how native to them is this code. . . . There is a whole generation of us, and perhaps two generations, who have been formed by it not only in social attitudes but in our most intimate personal lives, in fact there more than anywhere else. The social attitudes we could to some degree alter if we wished. For the inner self the die was cast."[55] James's central paradox in relation to Englishness as produced through cricket—extreme restraint—encapsulates the importance of James to the definition of West Indian belonging as paradoxical. It is here that we begin to understand the peculiarities of Caribbean subjectivity among the decolonizing generation. James elucidates the discordant image of migrant Caribbean people as, at once, intelligent and troublesome, quiescent and rebellious. James both acceded to the expectations of the West Indian colonial ideal and resisted them. Sylvia Wynter's lake of contradictions is still the best description of the Jamesian intrigue: "a Negro yet British, a colonial native yet culturally a part of the public school code, attached to the cause of the proletariat yet a member of the middle class, a Marxian yet a Puritan, an intellectual who plays cricket, of African descent yet Western, a Trotskyist and Pan-Africanist, a Marxist yet a supporter of black studies, a West Indian majority yet an American minority black."[56] Wynter's essay on "the pluri-consciousness of the Jamesian identity" and the way it disturbs the binaries on which colonial society is based seeks the unifying principle beneath all this internal conflict—what she calls either the Jamesian poiesis or the Jamesian theoretics.[57] To my mind, any West Indian singularity that James embodies inheres in his explicit need to belong both to the imperial center and to the idealized, utopian space of America. Such a singularity inheres in the difficulty he found in actually living in the West Indian island that enabled these multiple national imaginaries. And it belongs to the way he specifically positioned the Caribbean as a node for the elaboration of Western modernity precisely because it enabled what we might follow Wynter in referring to as a pluri-consciousness.

James's language of performance is a way of understanding how these multiple national attachments occur. Sports performances or film performances evoke emotional responses for James that exceed his own subjectivity and create social, political, and national allegiances. There is no Jamesian theoretics without affect; none of the freedom, complication, and range of James's life and writing without his ability to cathect to English and American forms. Ultimately, I agree with Wynter that it was James's primary sense of inclusion in the English fold, fostered by his high school, Queen's Royal College, gave him the ability to move into the American space with such confidence and ease. In this sense, the very different modes of performance that enabled his attachment to England and to America do not emerge as contradictions but as mutually constitutive oppositions. The English code might have stayed with him as he traveled to America, but arguably it was his habituation to restraint that primed him for the very different performances and affective principles to which he was drawn once he arrived there. The counterpoint of restraint in American feminine vitality emerges most powerfully for me when I consider James in love and at the movies.

Bette Davis's Eyes and Other American Prostheses

James found Bette Davis while living in New York City and going to the cinema after a day of work. It is a bit of a winding road from Nello at the window to James in love in America, though Matthew Bondman's capacity to perform embodied citizenship for James is not, as I have been indicating, entirely dissimilar from Davis's embodiment of the American democratic ideal. From one point to the other, however, one body to the other body, there is much in between. The body of the cricketer produces the unique quality of British colonial subjectivity that James names *excessive restraint*. This form of subjectivity is transmuted, ironically, into incipient self-governing West Indian nationalism—the same body metaphorized for different national ends. (Which national ends, by dint of that body's singularity, it is clear, are not so separate.) Meanwhile, the mechanism by which Matthew Bondman becomes James's access point to embodied colonial and West Indian citizenship is the linguistic transfer of embodied performance to the page. James watches the men, finds an analogue in Victorian literature, and produces as best he can linguistic forms of exuberant withholding, written displays of mastery that are Bhabhian in their excessive likeness to Englishness.

In America, substitute Nello at the window for James at the movies. That portal to the theater of colonial performance can be likened to this other portal, the cinema screen, though its aptness as a point for affective transfer is even more potent, sharing as it does the name for the conduit of psychoanalytic transfer we call projection. The movie screen onto which Hollywood stars are projected facilitates screen idols onto which James can project. In New York cinemas, James finds screen idols—Greer Garson, Ava Gardner, Ingrid Bergman, Bette Davis—and discovers their fitness as symbols for American disorder, revolutionary potential, and individual presenting—that capacity for individuals to be most vitally themselves. The 1940s stars and their genres—noir, melodrama—are symptomatic for James of American workers' post-Depression depression. And the stars also embody the potential for the masses to overcome their rage against capitalist oppression and inhabit America's energetic potential for revolution. Some stars do this better than others: in James's writing on America, I have become intrigued by how Bette Davis figures as one of those exemplary figures.

One other layer: Bette Davis is an un-American heroine, to be sure. But her implications are magnified by James's telling muddling of the screen icon and the "real" American woman he fell in love with, the young Californian model-actress-activist-writer Constance Webb. As a magnificently famous screen icon, Bette Davis possessed that quality of quasi-religious import wherein the circulation of her image, extractable from her actual physical person, made it possible for her to stand in effigy—as both an image for larger cultural desire and, as Joseph Roach has argued, for the cultural absences fueling that desire.[58] The film star thus endowed must seem "at once touchable and transcendent," apparently contradictory features enabled by the existence of mental images of her boosted by, but not entirely dependent on, actual physical representations. Consumers of—believers in—celebrity partake of a fantasy in which they imagine themselves "in communication with the special, spectral other." Roach writes: "An image thus synthesized as an idea . . . will very likely have only a coincidental relationship to the identity of the actual human person whose peculiar attraction triggered the hunger for the experience in the first place."[59] "Bette" was that force that, as James put it to Webb, "sweeps on like a battleship."[60] And "Constance," whom James met only once before he began writing to her, and saw only once more in the intervening years before they met again and married, was his "Cleopatra in a suburban drawing-room," that striking conjunction of imperious beauty and emotional accessibility often required of female film stars.[61] A telling obsession around 1943 was for Webb to send James her headshots: "Now, Constance, I have a standing grievance against you. You never sent those [pictures] you promised. I am waiting anxiously for these."[62] "Now. PICTURES PLEASE," came the plaintive demand a few pages later.[63] "I am not possessive, but very demanding. Face, and all of you; from head to shoes."[64] For years Webb would be an icon, like the screen idols James watched of an evening. This iconicity made her wonderfully suitable for national surrogation—though not particularly ideal for actual marriage—and made their correspondence—or at least the side of it that survives, James's letters—an archive of gendered attachment.

In a screen icon such as Bette Davis and in Webb, James found women through whom to experience and theorize American exuberance. He used them as testing grounds for his own emotionality. Where the cricketer impelled a literate form of affective appreciation modulated by formal distance or even irony, much of James's writing in America comports with very little sense of remove. The essays in *American Civilization*, still haughty, are more scattered, draftier; the letters to Webb are direct and often strikingly emotionally transparent. This bifurcation—colonial Englishness on one side, American exuberance on the other—should be seen to enhance rather than to mask a coherent idea of diasporic belonging, for it highlights that sense of the extremity of choice which is attendant to a life made in circulation. The quite remarkable gender difference of James's attachment to America introduces a polyphony that gives the structure of his diasporic belonging its Anita-like sense of sometimes-precarious toggle.

Several James critics have pointed out that his work on America presents a radical scholar taking popular culture seriously in a way that previews the cultural studies model that took root in academia a generation later. Much of James's American work had been lost or overlooked before a period of editing and republication by the anthropologist Anna Grimshaw, who was James's final editorial assistant, renewed interest in it. Grimshaw's edition of *The C. L. R. James Reader* (1992) included little-known essays by James about American film, literature, and politics. And her publication in 1993 of *American Civilization*, the book James had written but not revised or published in 1949–1950 and had meant to be his major statement on American democracy and culture, established in ways previously unacknowledged that James had taken a keen interest in the culture—not just the radical politics—of the United States. In addition, Scott McLemee's 1996 collection of James's essays on the "Negro Question" brought together work that had been archived away and mostly unread since it had first been written during the American years.[65] James had spent the fifteen years he resided in the United States—New York City mostly, with some travels through the south and west—observing and postulating on the nation's cultural forms.

His time in the United States overlapped exactly with the voluminous correspondence he maintained with Webb, and the letters' themes overlap with those of the essays in *American Civilization* that he wrote six years after he began writing to Webb. His relationship with Webb became one context in which he worked out his ideas about America—even if he awkwardly positioned himself in the letters as Webb's teacher. Grimshaw's edition of the letters is therefore a companion piece to *American Civilization*—Grimshaw says as much in her introduction to the latter. In both texts, James's ideas are inchoate—the essays are unrevised, the letters are personal and exploratory. In both texts, James takes seriously the potential of American freedom bolstered by its revolutionary origins, its youth relative to Europe, and the promise of happiness embedded in its founding documents. And he struggles throughout his American adventure to reconcile the dialectical model of historical development to which he adhered with the idea of human individualism and creativity that he valued just as highly. The essays composing *American Civilization* were, after all, at one time titled "The Struggle for Happiness," after the heading of one of its chapters.[66] While the essays and the letters are both cramped by James's fealty to a particular historical method, there are striking moments in both texts when his political heterodoxy (he eventually broke from Trotskyism, and his Johnson-Forest Tendency was a splinter group created out of disagreements with the Socialist Workers Party) and his artistic inclinations allow him to gesture outside what could sometimes be rigid cultural analyses. He once wrote to Webb about her decision to become an actress: "Now you are a creative person and express yourself to society in a certain way. Sweetheart, no revolutionary of any sanity or experience would dream of your doing anything else—*as long as you did something about it.*"[67] James's work on America is by and large an attempt to *do something about* his consumption of the nation's popular culture. And what is fascinating about the letters and the essays is the role that actresses play in framing the debate about American joy. These women are open vessels for feeling—conveyers and enablers. Their whiteness—for, with one exception to which I'll refer at the end of this chapter, it is white actresses James writes about—is a screen for James's American projections. Their femininity is a symbol of American feeling; and their feeling is a prosthesis enabling James's American attachment.

In the wake of Lauren Berlant's study of American femininity, "women's culture," and the intimate public, this should not be surprising. Berlant argues that the advancement of an idea of women's exceptional talent for feeling was robust in certain areas of popular and consumer culture from the mid-nineteenth century on. Novels and films presenting women in emotional predicaments called into being a collectivity of women who were conditioned to imagine themselves *as* collective, because they shared intimate knowledge of the struggle to be a woman (manifest racial, class-based, and geographical differences notwithstanding). And this collectivity was sustained and re-presented in media that everywhere deployed women embroiled in love plots, solving varieties of intimate predicaments, giving bravura performances of affective management and display. Since the normative basis of the intimate public of American femininity was whiteness, and since white femininity has a fraught relationship with the public sphere, difference was managed through racial prosthesis, Berlant argues. Her analysis of the multiple texts of *Imitation of Life* (the original novel and the two film versions) for example, argues that the white heroine (Bea in the novel) requires both the body and the "trademark" of the black woman (Delilah) as a way to manage the labor of bourgeois self-sufficiency and its concomitant demand for public display. Bea performs what Berlant names *code-crossing*, "borrowing the corporeal logic of an other [Delilah], or a fantasy of that logic, and adopting it as a prosthesis."[68] In *Imitation of Life*, Delilah's work generates Bea's income, and her minstrelized visage becomes the image of Bea's company. In this way, Bea can "have it all" while surrogating certain key tasks to another. She can ally with another woman (with whom she has in common, say, single motherhood and the need to make her own living), but she can instrumentalize Delilah's specific dilemma as African American, overburdened with a problematic public corporeality, for her own profit-making ends.

James's relationship to white femininity reverses this paradigm. He needs a feminine prosthetic in order to grasp America. Black femininity won't do because James understands that the public quality of black female corporeality in the United States is abject, not enlivening. The history of the Aunt Jemima trademark (introduced in 1893 and on which, Berlant points out, *Imitation of Life* bases Delilah's storyline) demonstrates the positive utilitarian function of the icon of southern black womanhood for suturing the north-south rupture of the nation. But this is accomplished by presenting a figure that all sides of the schismatic nation can agree to find inhuman—a haunt of slavery both nostalgic and cautionary.[69] No, what James needs is a public intimate feminine. This appears to be a contradiction, not because of the tension between "intimate" and "public," which is resolved in Berlant's description of the term as "juxtapolitical," but in the tension between *feminine* and public. For proper white femininity is supposed to be marked by its privacy. The performing woman, the *actress*, mediates between two demands: the one for respectable womanhood to be private, and indeed oppressively excluded from the public sphere, and the necessity to reinforce this privacy through representations (filmic and otherwise) of this gendered requirement to stay inside. Actresses took one for the team. They agreed to manage the fraught air of the disreputable attendant to their profession and, in the name of "women's culture," to purvey normative images of femininity that assured the viewing public that they were, as public figures, aberrations.

Berlant notes that whether portraying queer versions of nonnormative attachment or highly conventional romantic and familial scenarios in which women's cathexis to others is supreme—whether in screwball comedy, melodrama, or tragedy—the modern love story emplots women as "teachers of compassion and surrogates for others' refusals or incapacities to feel appropriately and intelligently."[70] When writing to Webb in a 1942 letter about his multiple screenings of *Now, Voyager*, James positions her as a potential instructor in emotion: "I am learning plenty, I can assure you. [But] if you were near I'd talk to you about it, day after day and being a woman and quick you'd teach me much that I am missing."[71] And women are not just instructors in affect. The emotionality accompanying a screen idol's iconic feminine milestones can be powerful enough to impact James's own rhetoric. For instance, in *American Civilization*, he buttresses his point about the symbolic importance of the film star with a lengthy quote about Rita Hayworth in which her excessive physical beauty makes her image into a religious object, a talisman to assure military success. The quote, an excerpt from an article on Hayworth by Winthrop Sergeant, is rather florid: "She was born in 1918. By 1941 the dark-haired baby had blossomed into a red-haired girl whose undulant figure and speculative smile were already becoming as familiar to Americans as those of the Madonna were to the Italians of the Renaissance."[72] Eventually the citation gets away from James, as if in reproducing the press response to the icon, he himself has become transfixed. A half a page later of finely printed quotation regarding the popular hubbub around the birth of Hayworth's first child, James simply concurs, analysis temporarily failing him: "Sergeant's attitude is absolutely correct. This is indeed a phenomenon. And such a mass of feeling, good will and international emotion was aroused by her marriage and the birth of her baby as probably was never seen in the world before." Unlike the West Indian cricketers, whose emotional restraint on the field draws a veil around their feelings, whose restraint is indeed a mark of their fitness as symbols, Rita Hayworth's appropriateness as surrogate lies in the accessibility of her most intimate emotional moments. "To point out the great limitations as an actress of this from all accounts simple unassuming young woman in the typical fashion of intellectuals is to cut oneself off from recognizing the tremendous social significance of what she represents."[73]

Displacing the cricketer in the structure of national attachment to America, then, is this other body, this magnificent prosthesis, the female movie star. Her liveliness makes her appear radically accessible. Her kinetic animation, even though it has been photographed and is necessarily mediated and deferred, presents for James an overwhelming model of America's youthfulness and its powerful democratic potential. He argues in *American Civilization* that "the great stars are all *characteristic* people, selected by the masses who pay their dimes, because they represent something that the people want," and he goes on to give a detailed analysis of how some famous actors and actresses represent certain kinds of mass desire.[74] He is also writing about a structure of surrogation similar to that which exists in the Caribbean with cricketers. The body politic requires figures whose performances elevate their own crises and bind them together as a nation. But by James's account, the affective principle of the male cricketer and the female star are very different. For James, American film divas convey live presence, a presentness that is routed through performed and embodied affectivity. Bette Davis is not just a master of her craft, an impressive manipulator of her charisma. She is an "*American* woman," displaying something that stars of European provenance such as Greta Garbo, Ingrid Bergman, and Marlene Dietrich ("representatives of the older civilization") do not have.[75] Bette, James decides, has "a tremendous vitality."[76] The adjectival *vital* denotes that which is constituted by an "immaterial force or principle which is present in living beings or organisms and by which they are animated and their functions maintained"; that which "maintains or supports a life"; that which is "paramount, supreme, or very great" (*OED*). Its noun form, *vitality*, also involves the resonant denotation of "endurance" (*OED*). The linguistic lacuna that makes it possible for James to provide *American* as an ineffable quality in Bette Davis registers that sense of *vitality* as an immaterial force, some unnameable energy lighting up the actress from within and separating her from other, merely European extraordinaires. (Thus we notice that even as James retains an ideal of European learning, in the register of film performance, it is American women who prevail.) Meanwhile, the genius of the West Indian batsman, while subtle, can be delineated in great detail and is marked by the precision of physical movement — talent and accomplishment rather than life force.

The implications of the move from the body of the cricketer to the body of the American film star are significant. *Beyond a Boundary* emphasized the cooperative enterprise of the team, whereby the exceptional cricketer shined within the elegant construction of the game's boundaries — indeed shined *precisely* because those boundaries were so carefully constructed that superlative elegance stood out. The subsumption of each individual player to the structuring power of the team was both political and aesthetic. The finely ordered lines of play created the conditions for one batsman's flair, which was articulated by James as a highly organized arrangement of the body that then mirrored, in a sense, the organization of the pitch, of the team, of empire. Matthew Bondman, after all, is a body *out of order* until he bats, at which point the beauty of the stroke restores him, redeems everything. The reason the cricketer's body enables attachment to England is because its formal expression repeats other English forms: the public school system, the sonnet, the essay. Matthew Bondman's mastery over his body in the theater of English sport authorized James's mastery over other forms of Englishness — forms apparently less embodied, but meaningful to James to the extent that they could be brought back to the body: the boy gazing out the window at the men in physical expression.

Order is not remotely the point of James's screen sirens. James is compelled by the violence of the context in which Hollywood stars appear. Of film noir, he writes: "The whole popular so-called entertainment world began its turn to violence, sadism, cruelty, the release of aggression immediately after the consciousness of the Depression had seized hold of the country."[77] And he is compelled as well by the torrent of emotion, the potentially disordering chaos, of women's emotional fixes in noir and in drama. He reads actresses' performances as skillful, yes, but not in the way Bondman is skillful. His paean to gorgeous performative excess in the context of cricket is always counterbalanced by an interest in the cricketers' bodily control. Hollywood actresses, in particular those who figure an American type, are powerful vessels of their own affective torrents, and they are ports of harbor for everyone else's. They might be sturdy, yes, but they are compelling to him because of some sensation that their emotion could at some level capsize everything.

These seafaring metaphors are intentional. James wrote to Webb that he had watched *Now, Voyager* "6 times and will see it if necessary 6 times more."[78] And the oceanic circulation that connects diasporic James to sea-voyaging Bette is everywhere, once one begins to notice it. James, like Bette's most famous ugly duckling, *Now, Voyager*'s Charlotte Vale, comes alive on a ship. He begins writing to Constance Webb from a ship he boards to cross the Gulf of Mexico back to the United States, after a trip to visit Trotsky in Mexico. In one of these early letters he pursues a brief imaginative journey to Brazil with one of his shipmates—having not yet seen *Now, Voyager*, he couldn't have known that Charlotte *literally* takes that journey to Brazil, and that her prevailing sexual and affective attachment to a man of uncertain accent named JD is ignited there. And yet here, and in several other ways I will detail below, James accompanies Charlotte/Bette on her oceanic journey of amorous discovery. By writing to Webb from ships, and carrying on his love for her through those letters from afar, he forges a connection between the screen idol and the neophyte actress/model that consolidates his love for America in his love for American women.

Merely for the sake of academic propriety, I wish it were possible to separate out the pleasure I take in recasting James as a feminine heroine from the intellectual aptness of this gesture—but it is not. A large part of what is to be gained from reading James's American writings in light of the romance he pursued with Webb, and with America, is a recasting of James himself, from stentorian West Indian man of letters to a nervy, melodramatic, and often lovesick romantic hero—a man with a nervous stomach and hands that shook so violently from anxiety that he sometimes found it impossible to write. This recasting does not just open up to us a new, more interesting James—burnished from the fusty, even ossified, figure that emerged in the wake of his revival in the 1980s and 1990s—a James who comes through differently in light of his American investments. Bette's ship journey and James's also give us a new way into the prevailing metaphor of black diaspora: the circulation of bodies and ideas through sea travel. To provide just the briefest rehearsal of contemporary influential scholarship providing these compelling seafaring metaphors: Gilroy's counter-modern Black Atlantic; Michelle Stephens's ship of state, Peter Linebaugh and Marcus Rediker's "motley crew" of multiracial laborers—their "many-headed hydra" of counter-nationalist diasporic affiliation (the early research of which inspired Gilroy).[79] The circulations of black culture come to us anew when seen through the sexual awakening of a young American white girl in the cargo hold of a ship—not least because such a view into diasporic circulation highlights, by contrast, the oppressions of the circulation of *black* bodies, at the same time that it provides an arresting and deeply strange inverse image. Let me propose, by way of the analogy between C. L. R. James and Charlotte Vale, a vision of black diaspora's polymorphous perversity. One never knows the means of cathexis that will enable the diasporic traveler to imagine himself out of one space and into the other. Perhaps in certain circumstances, a shy and traumatized white girl, embodied by a powerful white actress, can serve just as well as a Du Boisian dark princess.

Yogita Goyal's recent treatment of diaspora through the lens of romance—by which she means both narrative genre and the formal and affective features that attend all sorts of discourses—"the spectacle, the theater, the extravagance"; "the spectacle, the myth, the drama"—is a useful salve to the dryer pontifications around diaspora that often mirror the pieties of nationalism that diaspora is supposed to thwart.[80] But in a way, my own interest in James and the movies, and James and Webb, is unseemlier even than the romantic genre. It tries to take seriously romance in the interpersonal realm too: love letters, disappointments, fantasies, separations, misunderstandings. With *Now, Voyager* as intertext, some of these apparently pettier concerns start to make wider political and cultural sense for James's role in diasporic formations—however counterintuitive that may seem. Joseph Roach's formulation for filmic charisma, a countenance that offers "the effortless look of public intimacy," is a signal part of the operation of Bette Davis by which James is held, seduced, and prompted into theory.[81] He would not be the first viewer to be transfixed by a screen actress mightily in command of her gifts. He might, however, be the first West Indian radical through which it is possible to offer this effect as a general theory for belonging in America. Continuing his definition of "It," that ineffable quality attending figures who demand attention, Roach writes that this particular genius is characterized by "characteristic manifestations of public intimacy (the illusion of availability), synthetic experience (vicariousness), and the It-Effect (personality-driven mass attraction)."[82] All three of these elements are touched on by James in his writing on American film stars, with one other feature germane to this project: all three elements also constitute the conditions of belonging in a place of uncertain belonging.

When Charlotte Vale is first introduced to the doctor, Jaquith, who will become her psychiatrist and mentor, she is a shrinking, painfully anxious woman swathed in yards of unshapely fabric that passes for a respectable dress. She can barely speak. Silent though she may be, she is nevertheless enraged that her family has arranged for her to see a therapist. She resists him in the only way she can then manage, which is to run out of the drawing room where they have been introduced. When Jaquith pursues her to her bedroom she finally explodes in language, screaming at him and unleashing in a torrent exactly why her confinement in the family home is inevitable, given the iron-fisted rule of her mother. As far as Charlotte is concerned, she will never be allowed to leave the house, never be allowed to express her robust sexual instincts, and she will forever remain a child imprisoned by her mother with no possibility of healing.

Jaquith disagrees. And in trying to mollify her temper and describe in the least arcane and intimidating way what his psychiatric method entails, he says simply this: "I just put up a signpost: not that way, this way."[83] Charlotte startles at this invocation of choice. But by the end of the film, a fully realized and independent Charlotte has, indeed, made some serious choices. Having reignited her passionate sexuality with a man she meets on a cruise after her stay in Jaquith's sanitarium (Jerry, aka JD), she finds herself deeply and persistently in love with him, despite the significant impediment of his already having a wife and family. JD is willing to risk the scandal of adultery to be with Charlotte, his love for her similarly overwhelming. But after years of separation and a triangulated reunion via JD's daughter Tina, who is herself now in Jaquith's sanitarium in treatment for a nervous breakdown, the two lovers compromise. They will mediate their love through JD's daughter. Charlotte will house Tina and practice the various good sense methods of mental hygiene she has learned from Jaquith, along with other techniques she is innovating in her own large mansion. (Her mother has finally died.) And JD will visit often, allowing the lovers ample context for their chaste but intense attachment. When JD doubts that this will be enough, it is Charlotte who holds their ground. "Don't let's ask for the moon," she tells Jerry in the film's iconic last lines, "we have the stars." In a line previous, one that may very well be iconic for *my* project, Charlotte notes, "We can both try hard to protect that little strip of territory that is ours."

No Anita-like loss for Charlotte, then. Respecting the limits of her multiple choices, she chooses the path of sublimation and mediation. For she can have a scandalous and finite affair with JD; or she can have the pleasure of ongoing, uncensored contact with him, as well as familial surrogation, since his daughter is now considered also Charlotte's daughter and they come as a package deal. This is a rather mature configuration for the genre of romantic melodrama, yet it all makes very good sense. And Charlotte too has used prostheses of a sort. Her glasses, the physical indication of her "ugliness," are finally broken in half by Jaquith when he decides she is sufficiently healed and has no need of them any more. And those cigarettes, ubiquitous in code-era film as phalluses, proliferate in *Now, Voyager*. Certainly they fulfill that glamorous sign of sexual attraction that both titillates and charms a modern audience inured to seeing sexual appendages of all sorts in contemporary cinema. But if we think of Charlotte's cigarettes not just as phalluses but as extensions out into the world, ways for her to focus the atmosphere around her so that it might be tactile and manageable, then these too are prostheses. (Charlotte used to hide her cigarettes; by the end of the film they are a sign of her glamour.) This is important to consider because if we believe Berlant's argument that women's film in the mid-twentieth century had the function to represent women teaching men to feel, to offer their bodies, their brimming eyes, as emotional prostheses for men, then it is interesting to note that women had their own props too. And the cigarette functions not as phallus, I would say, but as wand. The focusing and directing arrow pointing "this way, not that," which is the thing you need especially when your doctor decides to break your glasses.

There is a great deal of pleasure in unpacking the unexpected similarities between *Now, Voyager* and the narrative of C. L. R. James's letters to Constance Webb, and I will aim to exercise some restraint in simply listing them—though, by way of emphasizing the gender reconfiguration I hope this chapter is accomplishing on James, there is a lot to be said for doing just that. For instance, like Charlotte Vale, James first stokes his passion for Constance Webb on a ship—love seems to "sweep on like a battleship," so to speak—and he begins to write her love letters immediately. This despite their having met only once, a Charlotte and JD–type "love at first sight" situation that is rare to find outside the confines of film. Sea voyages recur in important and different ways in both texts. In *Now, Voyager*, for instance, we are told in a flashback that Charlotte first discovered sexual passion as a teenager on a tourist cruise to Africa (she canoodled with the ship's dashing wireless operator on deck before sneaking off to make love to him in a car in the cargo hold). No rereading of diaspora that seeks to pair it with this unlikely film will be impervious to the resonances of a ship's cargo hold and its transatlantic destination, as I have already indicated above. (At one point the sailor informs Charlotte: "There's nothing to be found like you in all of Africa," having presumably tested his theory during other ports of call.) And so my rather whimsical set of comparisons does come bracketed with the knowledge that for black diaspora subjects, oceanic cargo holds will never *not* revive the slave ship. And the erotic adventures of a constrained white girl, caught out in the end and punished by her mother, is not an analogy for the extreme confinement of chattel slaves; it is its obverse image. But as Anna Grimshaw notes about her editorial decisions in preparing *Special Delivery*, a notable feature of the letters James wrote while sailing from Mexico to New Orleans after meeting Webb at a speech in California, as well as the letters he wrote to her while in Nevada awaiting the US divorce that would allow them to marry, is that something in the separation gives James's letters in these moments a palpable urgency. And it is striking that distance and time spent apart are key features in both the Charlotte-JD and the James-Webb dyads. James's long odyssey toward

Webb is full of moments when her absence or her recalcitrance, even her rejection, is transformed by the sheer force of James's imaginative will into a moment of connection. James sets many a movie scene with Webb in it. The entire first half of his correspondence with her can be seen as an extended film act in which she features as his lover. In the letters, James feels he has control. He can set the scene, make what does not exist come to life. He is enamored with the language of theater because it gives him the scope to deal with his feelings in ways that seem *active*. Beginning on April 15, 1939, James writes a long letter to Webb about his time in Mexico with Trotsky and the long boat journey from there to New Orleans. Importantly, he does not post the letter immediately upon completing it—holding onto it until he is confident enough in his feelings to let her know them. On the third writing day, James says: "Here we are, sweetheart, 7:45, and I am writing to you already."[84]

> All unknown to yourself you have been my dear companion on this journey. I saw you that afternoon in the church, then that impudent Carlo said at your house "Isn't she lovely?" and I had to rebuke him. You remember? When we came back you were in a red dressing gown and all sleepy and exciting. I was sorry I didn't see you on the last Saturday. . . . You must not write such eager letters and at the same time appear suddenly before lonely men, wearing red dressing gowns, rubbing your eyes like a big baby who needs to be put to bed.[85]

This is his "Cleopatra in a suburban drawing room," and he returns to her twice more.[86] It is the sense-memory that seems most personal and profoundly connected to his love for Webb. It was this woman to whom he wrote. When he was actually with Webb, when she wrote him letters, she seemed always to disappoint him. And how could she not, if his image of her was so specifically tied to an emotional memory he had created and preserved?

The second half of the correspondence is marked by this sense of disappointment. James comes up against the limits of his literary and performative power, and he is sometimes enraged. Webb had always been essentially unavailable—either married or partnered; living in California or New York while he traveled and worked; focusing on her own career. The astonishing letters of 1945, and again in 1947, when James rants at Webb for her perceived inconsideration reveals all that feeling he had been mustering and harnessing. It also reveals the ways James's affection for Webb was misplaced, fueled by his own image of her, mediated. In one letter written in the summer of 1945 James is despondent that Webb's letters are more tepid than he would prefer. He has a reckoning: "For four years I have carried the image of this woman deep inside of me. It is time I tore it out. Hostility? Bitterness? Not as far as I know. . . . Only it's time I stopped philandering around and dreaming dreams of you and seriously begin to think of someone else."[87] It is not that James should not have loved Webb but rather that his love was always affixed to a version of Webb that did not strictly exist. It was an effigy to which he prayed, and his letters transform when the real woman exceeded the limits of the likeness he had fashioned. "I was loyal to what was only a memory and a vision," is what he writes glumly as their relationship disintegrates.[88]

And yet it was a long disintegration. James and Webb patched things up in 1945, which is why he pursued a divorce and spent time in Nevada. From Nevada, things were rocky again, and James wrote an illuminating and desperate letter in which he makes clear how much he learned about feeling from Webb, this other actress teaching him to love. Scribbled, Anna Grimshaw notes, on the back of his essay "Dialectical Materialism and the Fate of Humanity," a letter was sent from the ranch in Nevada on October 7, 1947: "This is the man who loves you. I took up dialectic five years ago. I knew a lot of things before and I was able to master it. I know a lot of things about loving you. I am only just beginning to apply them. I can master that with the greatest rapidity—just give me a hand. I feel all sorts of new powers, *freedoms*, etc., surging in me. You released so many of my constrictions. What are you going to *do*? I am bursting all over with love for you."[89] The idea that James might somehow *master* love is in tension with his surge of freedom. No longer restrained, he credits Webb with releasing him. And yet where could this gush of feeling land? It was so unrestrained, so disconnected—with all those American freedoms, those female-induced freedoms, James still did not wind up living in the United States with his love.

And so the narrative, by some lights, looks like this: by the time James had overwhelmed the unavailable young Webb with letter after letter, finally won her heart, married her, and had a child, the relationship was over. Of the three hundred–odd pages of his correspondence to her, more than two-thirds were written before the two were a couple in any conventional sense. The last third, once the relationship had dissolved, are an astonishing set of texts in which James appears indeed to have been taught how to feel. The James we have in the letters at the end of *Special Delivery* are, as he himself might say, *vital*. They are emotionally accessible. They break apart and stutter, they lack all the composure we associate with James's prose. And they endure, going on and on and on.

James's writing about film stars in the essay on popular culture in *American Civilization* ("The Popular Arts and Society" [1949–1950]) is, ultimately, rather barren and austere. His main idea about popular film, fiction, and comic books can be fairly easily summarized: the "masses" require an outlet for their bitterness and rage against the oppressive vagaries of capitalism, and thus the popularity of artifacts of sexuality and violence—film noir, the great detectives, the femme fatales—are sustained, if not at some level brought into being, by the workers themselves requiring the balm of glamour and the catharsis of violence. "The masses have fostered a system whereby a certain selected few individuals symbolize in their film existence *and their private and public existence* the revolt against general conditions. If the great body of the public did not need stars, there would be no stars."[90] This is how the idea is put across in *American Civilization*. In the letters, however, something else and something deeper and more interesting emerges. For one thing, as I have been arguing, the emergence of white femininity *as such* as a fit symbol conduit for national attachment re-introduces that sense of precarity marking James's earlier considerations of belonging (through the black women in his barrack-yard fiction), that sense of potential psychic danger and of emotional frailty that he skips over in *Beyond a Boundary*. Further, with Webb, James allows himself fixate. No longer a series of names roughly equivalent to each other—Rita Hayworth, Bette Davis, and Barbara Stanwyck are mentioned in one category as if these actresses might be indistinguishable from each other. No, it is Bette who dominates; and, of course, Webb herself. "You are, my dear, a very beautiful person. I can point out, I daresay, faults here or there. But the ensemble is lovely, very striking, very human, very vital, with emotional depth, and I always thought, intellectual power above the average."[91] In both these women, James responds to what he thinks of as American feminine attributes, and in that repeated word "vital" we note the slippage for him between the mass "type" and the embodied woman, Webb herself, of whom he demands greater and greater openness and with whom he is increasingly open.

A counterpoint to this series of letters about vital American femininity and the movies is a smaller and also fascinating thread about the theater, and it is here that I will end. In three extended letters to Webb, James writes about his plan to create a play for Ethel Waters, another American actress whom James says he admires, "beyond idolatry."[92] James had seen Waters in *Cabin in the Sky* and thought that she gave "one of the most satisfying performances I have ever seen in my life. The musical comedy business is, as far as I can see, very difficult. She triumphed."[93] James decided that Waters deserved to act in serious theatrical drama ("The good lady should play Medea in Euripides or Lady Macbeth") and began writing a play about Harriet Tubman in which she would star.[94]

James sent to Webb two detailed treatments of the play, which would involve a love triangle between a southern white woman who gets involved in the abolitionist movement, a former slave with whom she falls in love, and an aristocratic racist landowner determined to keep them apart. As with his play about Toussaint L'Ouverture, which starred Paul Robeson in London in 1936, James's primary theatrical concern was to represent the movement of history. He was clearly concerned about how to profess a political message "through *living people with all their passions, loves, hates, jealousies, etc.*"[95] Confusingly, and ultimately tellingly, James's script summaries never include his treatment of Ethel Water's character Harriet Tubman. The love triangle is worked through in both of James's script treatments, and he continues to profess his admiration for Waters and his keen desire to meet her, as well as his even keener hope that she would agree to do the play. He says that he will abandon his plans for the play if Waters decides not to do it. But James never describes his interest in Tubman's character nor his sense of what Ethel Waters would bring to the role. His admiration for Waters and Tubman do not become transformed, at least not in his letters to Webb or in the Tubman play (which in the event was not produced), into symbols of affective significance.

The reasons for this I have already indicated. Despite James's black radical politics, his utterly foundational scholarship on the first successful black revolution in history, and his pioneering work to establish political independence in the West Indies, despite even the insight into working-class Trinidadian women's dilemmas demonstrated in his early fiction, James did not cultivate a robust political imaginary for black women. He acceded—and I do not ascribe intent here, only effect—to the racist, sexist logic by which black women's bodies could not count for affirmative national imaginaries. And, too, his impulse to master totalities—*all* of the American nation; the *whole* of American character—meant that, by and large, he studied the mainstream heroines of his day, and these, inevitably, were portrayed by white actresses. Ethel Waters was a remarkable exception. By dint of her masterful presence she got through to James—though he was never able to make good on the potential she hinted at for him to chart a different, black feminist, trajectory for American vitality.[96] She is the exception that proves the rule. For James, performing bodies labored to help him figure out where he could belong. There were black men; there were white women. But if we read James's attachments as affectively charged, it is not as depressingly familiar as all this. Remember Anita's necklace: James began his career imagining the travails of working black women wanting nothing more than spaces of their own. In charting his own strangely inspiring course, he all but became one of those women.

TWO

THE FRATERNAL AGONIES
OF BALDWIN AND LAMMING

On September 19–22, 1956, at the Sorbonne, luminaries from around the globe attended the first Congress of Black Writers and Artists in Paris. Conceived by Alioune Diop and attended by black intellectuals of the first order—Leopold Senghor and Aime Cesaire; Jean Price-Mars; Richard Wright—the event was in the spirit of the great Pan-African conferences that had occurred at the beginning of the twentieth century.[1] Given the setting in Paris, the provenance of its most prominent voices, and its association with the radical Francophone journal *Presence Africaine*, the Congress also became a staging ground for debates about the stakes of black global unity against colonialism. And while arguably the heyday of Negritude had been more than a decade earlier—if the movement's most intense fervor might be marked by, for example, Cesaire's *Cahiers du au retour aux pays natal* (1939) or the life of the journal *L'Etudiant Noir* (1930–1935)—the published proceedings in *Presence Africaine* of the discussions taking place at the Congress suggest that attempts to define global black kinship were as urgent, and as fraught, as ever.[2]

Also in attendance over those three days in September were George Lamming and James Baldwin. Baldwin was then in this eighth year of exile, on and off, in Paris; Lamming had been living in London for six, having moved from his native Barbados. Both men had something to say about the occasion. Lamming actually gave a speech, published in the *Presence Africaine* special issue as "The Negro Writer and His World."[3] Baldwin's "Princes and Powers," first published in *Encounter* (January 1957) and later republished in his second essay collection *Nobody Knows My Name* (1961), was a lengthy account of the Congress, including comments on Lamming's presentation.[4] If my previous chapter provided an occasion to rethink familiar metaphors of diasporic circulation through the lens of C. L. R. James's gendered enthusiasms, then this chapter occasions the reformulation of a different (and differently gendered) metaphor of diasporic affiliation: brotherhood. The global black brotherhood represented by the Pan-Africanist enterprise of the Congress was going to be put under pressure by the stark disagreements and striking misalliances that would be on display at the gathering. Preferring to see these misalliances as proper to the structure of diasporic siblinghood, rather than as a threat to it, I will read Baldwin's and Lamming's essays as together producing a structure of diasporic filiation constituted by what I call *fraternal agony*. In their writings during this period about diaspora and about each other, Baldwin and Lamming present as siblings engaged in everything of which agony admits: contest, pain, rumination. There is also affinity, rivalry, unwarranted critique, studious nonchalance. And each of these elements is underwritten by a structure of mutual disavowal by which the thing that is (the affinity between Lamming and Baldwin) is presented as the thing that it is not (i.e., a fundamental difference between them).

Why do Lamming and Baldwin help me to re-metaphorize diaspora as brotherhood? And how am I using the metaphor of fraternity—so richly (and so problematically) a part of black global politics for at least two centuries—in a way that complicates rather than adds weight to any facile notion of black affinity as family reunion, and with a priority on masculinity, at that? I will take these questions in turn.

Why Lamming and Baldwin? For one thing, they were interested in each other. There was "Princes and Powers," to which I have already alluded and will turn momentarily. But Lamming, too, wrote about Baldwin. In his famous book of essays, *The Pleasures of Exile* (1960), Lamming devoted a chapter to Baldwin's first essay collection, *Notes of a Native Son* (1955).[5] Lamming's chapter evinces, to my mind, a set of misunderstandings of Baldwin's work that parallels—if not in literal error of fact then in performance of agonistic differentiation—Baldwin's misreadings of Lamming at the 1956 Congress. Very few critics have been interested in observing these moments of Baldwin and Lamming's mutual gazing. Then, too, I am struck by the temporal coincidence of Lamming's and Baldwin's early works. In 1953, both produced masterful first novels that were autobiographical family sagas. Baldwin's *Go Tell It on the Mountain*, the story of John Grimes and his stepfather, was the first in a career of reflection on cultural "stephood"—on what it meant to have partial acceptance by a surrogate father; what it meant to experience an a priori sense of loss, a constant missing presence whose place cannot be filled by the figure who purports to fill it.[6] Lamming's family novel, *In the Castle of My Skin*, is an allegory of motherhood and colonial indifference. This novel, too, represents primal parental loss as fundamental to black subjectivity. The differences between the novels, particularly the primacy of the father in the one and of the mother in the other, is one telling difference between African American and West Indian relationships to white hegemony and the West.

Furthermore, Lamming and Baldwin are writers for whom exile was fundamentally important in their early imaginations of themselves as artists. In this sense, they are paradigmatic of certain movements within African American and Caribbean midcentury responses to white and colonial hegemony. Baldwin moved to France, like many of his compatriots, to free his writerly imagination from the grip of US racism. Lamming moved to England from Barbados believing, like so many other Caribbean writers, that he had to leave the island in order to make his way as a writer in the metropole. The difference between the US and the West Indian versions of exile is brought into focus by the coincidence of the publications of these writers' powerful first novels. For Lamming, England was a motherland of whose maternity he would soon be disabused. For Baldwin, Paris was a surrogate parent—the real father, America, having disowned him. Both writers would eventually return home, and both these returns were framed as acts of reclamation. For Baldwin, the lost parent would now be forced to attend to him. For Lamming, losing the mother was a step in creating a sense of rebirth. By joining the civil rights movement, Baldwin was insisting on being brought into the fold. By adding his voice to the movement for Caribbean self-governance, Lamming was insisting on the necessity of making a new family. These separate national gestures nevertheless involve diasporic engagement. Lamming's determining the content of West Indian nationalism involved reflections on his relationship to global black culture—thus, the moments in *The Pleasures of Exile* of considering, somewhat troublingly, Harlem and Ghana; and thus, his turn later in the book to working out the possibilities of Haitian ritual as a structuring metaphor for Caribbean (post)colonial aesthetic subterfuge. For Baldwin, an increasing investment in the politics of the United

States would not preclude contentious exchanges with blacks elsewhere, exchanges with—as we will see later in the chapter, West Indian students in London, say—which clarify the particularity of the nation into which he was born and which he would later re-claim.

A structure of diasporic brotherhood emerges between Baldwin and Lamming because they have a lateral connection to each other on the basis of a mutual relationship to an entity above them (or behind them, depending on perspective): a relationship, that is, to "the West." Baldwin and Lamming both develop a genealogical paradigm for black racial belonging in the West, separately theorizing the diasporic subject's relationship to the United States and to Britain as one of unclaimed sonhood. In separate essays, Lamming and Baldwin figure themselves as lost sons reflecting on parents who disavow them. Moreover, Baldwin and Lamming write essays about each other marked by black artistic misrecognition. This ramification of disavowal—the parents, the sons—is precisely what holds the entire structure together. Heather Love's work on contentious queer friendship, though it describes by some lights a very different phenomenon, elucidates this beautifully and underwrites much of how I read Baldwin and Lamming's exchange, despite their not being in "queer" relation in a strict sense. To recall: Love's *Feeling Backward* describes the desire of readers to find "positive" retrospective emotion binding together abjected subjects whom we feel should be aligned. And yet often, and certainly in the twentieth-century queer novels Love reads, it is not uniformly warm images that accompany narratives that, nevertheless, depict queer dyads: "As we consider the history of queer representation," Love writes, "it is crucial that we recognize how central the failure of community is in such representations. Such a recognition in turn asks that we expand our sense of what counts as relationship . . . and suggests that we might need to rethink what counts as legitimate or significant political emotions."[7] Like Jonathan Flatley in *Affective Mapping*, a text whose powerful argument for melancholia as politically agentive also underwrites my understanding of this moment and these agonistic affects, Love wishes to recuperate failure. And more than that, which is what I will show here, Love shows how negative images can be ones that evince close intimacy. Of Willa Cather's fierce and finite friendship with Sarah Orne Jewett, for instance, Love observes that Cather eventually imagined their once expansive "world of romantic friendship as a 'shrinking kingdom,' a back garden that she surveys with a mixture of desire, longing, and regret." Baldwin and Lamming were never friends. But their telling moments of missed connection at the '56 Congress place them in a small kingdom of black contention, and their crossing texts, misreading each other, describe a profound "absence, loss, and proleptic mourning."[8]

Negro, with a Difference

Lamming's presentation at the 1956 Congress began by evoking three black writers from different points in the transatlantic nexus—Richard Wright, Roger Mais, and Amos Tutuola. Ultimately, however, the piece occasions Lamming's perception of a crucial separation among global blacks, a separation whose axis turns on a hazy notion of ineffable African difference. The Nigerian Tutuola comes to exemplify this difference at the point in the speech where irreducible difference is most pointedly described. Because the text is elusive, and because it is crucial to get down the facts so that I can turn to what Baldwin makes of them, I will quote from this portion of "Negro Writer and His World" at some length:

> The case of the British West Indian writer is, I think, somewhat different. He occasions surprise . . . I'm sure, but he also creates a certain confusion. He confuses because, for a variety of reasons, he seems so perilously near to the Other whose judgment begins with the unconscious premiss [sic] that he is, in fact, *different*. The novels which have come from these territories in the last few years seem to betray themes[,] anxieties, desires, and illusions that appear identical with those of his English equivalent. His conception of what a novel is seems to be the same. His preoccupation with the use of the language would not seem to differ in any noticeable way. He does really *speak English*. . . . It confuses because he looks like M. Tutuola, but seems to belong to a wholly different pattern of calculations and ambitions. He seems so much nearer to us than his equivalent in Nigeria, and yet we know, in a way we cannot explain, that he is much nearer to his Nigerian equivalent than he is to us. He is Negro, yes, but he is a Negro with a *difference*.[9]

Lamming begins to ventriloquize an Englishman summing up the situation of the Nigerian versus the West Indian writer, and so Lamming's own relationship to this "Negro with a difference" is complicated to parse.

The "us" to which the West Indian writer is near in that penultimate sentence is the white British writer. The passage begins with Lamming coolly describing in the third person the "West Indian writer" and ends with Lamming holding the place of the white writer, explaining why his implied "I" here is different from the subject he actually is, that same West Indian writer the passage objectifies. It seems safe to say that Lamming is wry and ironic about his problematically favored status: he later goes on to imagine his symbolic Englishman noting that the West Indian is "a colonial who has been in closer touch. . . . He is a product."[10] And notice also that the "Other" here is not black but white—an important inversion, albeit by universalizing the existentialists. Nevertheless, this passage reflects the curious tenor of Lamming's presence at the Black Writers and Artists Congress—one of detachment, not solidarity; of imaginative sympathy, at least linguistically, rhetorically, not with his fellows in the African diaspora but with the English. In this essay about black writers, the accent is on what *differentiates* their experiences in the metropole, not what unites them.

In "The Negro Writer and His World," Lamming was writing to and from a tradition that was capacious and transnational, but in this moment his emphasis was on the singularity of the West Indian writer in England. Indeed, what is it that he finally argues *does* unite the three writers he began with—Tutuola, Wright, and Mais? He writes: "Politics is the only ground for a universal Negro sympathy. This is a situation that embarrasses many a writer who is Negro."[11] The implied distinction between politics and art here is one shared by Baldwin in his review of the Congress. (Might it have been suggested by Lamming?) It is a surprising bifurcation for Lamming, whose essays are often considered to be a fruitful melding of the two categories, and whose aesthetic project of Caribbean nationalist art is precisely about the indissoluble connection between art and politics, culture and history. But the distinction is important for understanding Lamming's gesture here, at the Congress of Negro Writers and Artists. Lamming feels united with these artists on the basis of a black relationship to the white Other; he feels distinct on the basis of his relationship to England.

Migration was not a word I would have used to describe what I was doing when I sailed with other West Indians to England in 1950. We simply thought we were going to an England which had been planted in our childhood consciousness as a heritage and a place of welcome. It is a measure of our innocence that neither the claim of heritage nor the expectation of welcome would have been seriously doubted.... Today I shudder to think how a country, so foreign to our own instincts, could have achieved the miracle of being called Mother.[12]

With the retrospective distance of thirty-three years, George Lamming shudders at the intimacy he and his fellow migrants presumed with England. He shudders also at the primacy of the relationship between England and colony that conjured the image of maternity for its reckoning. Lamming's shudder is a gesture marking an interior landscape of strong, surprising feeling: fear and horror. The shudder reminds us that Lamming's most profound interest is to represent the experience of the colonial subject in as direct a way as possible. His aesthetic experiments, his themes, his most famous set-pieces are all aimed at illustrating the subject formed by English colonialism in the places of its formation: the body and the interior landscape of thought and emotion.

But if West Indian "instincts" contrast so profoundly with English ones, then why should Lamming have felt such affinity? Lamming's answer throughout his oeuvre, and certainly in *The Pleasures of Exile*, is that English institutions, language, and culture had inculcated themselves so deeply into the subjectivity of Caribbean people that there was no way they could feel otherwise. But this answer—which recalls the starting point of C. L. R. James's analysis—only produces a paradox: if Caribbean instincts could be encroached on by imperial habits, then this suggests not so much their difference as their similarity; not so much the distance between the two as the nearness.

Revisiting *The Pleasures of Exile* reveals the not very often remarked fact that Lamming, through his affinity for Englishness and the English language, confessed to a feeling of *separateness* from his fellow black artists in America and France throughout the middle of the twentieth century. The West Indian subject of *The Pleasures of Exile* is uncannily close to the English subject, which ironically highlights that the most prominent complaints against the vast numbers of new Caribbean migrants arriving in postwar England was that they were foreign, "dark strangers" threatening to change the pristine and undifferentiated landscape of England. (I will turn to this problem in the next chapter.) Lamming's essays suggest it is just as well to imagine that the hostility against West Indians was not that they were so foreign but that they were so familiar—the surrogated double, in Joseph Roach's designation, that "often appears as alien to the culture that reproduces it and that it reproduces."[13] Kingsley Amis's claim that new voices from "the tropics" were using the English language better than contemporary British-born writers might be one example of the sense of perceived absence that West Indian writers would fill, only to be critiqued (the way any surrogate would be) as both inadequate and excessive.[14] The strange paradox of the Caribbean writer as a surrogate for the absent imperial confidence of the English writer only illustrates the unique position of the Caribbean writer vis-à-vis England: familiar, close, and uncanny.

The trouble with the uncanny is that when the familiar and the foreign are mixed, the emphasis may lie on the one aspect or the other, depending on the perspective of the viewer. By way of discussion of an organization dedicated to the very West Indian literature of which Lamming has come to be considered foundational, the Caribbean Artists Movement, I would like to contextualize the sense Lamming introduces in his Paris speech of the West Indian's uncanny relation to the English, his presumption of intimacy with Britishness. It is this intimacy that forms the background to the agonistic development of black affinity beyond the borders of the English Commonwealth and Lamming's contorted wrestling with Baldwin in *The Pleasures of Exile*.

The archive of the Caribbean Artists Movement (CAM) provides a lens through which to see the drama of West Indian intimacy and distance in the English landscape.[15] The history of CAM is told in great detail by Anne Walmsley, who collected papers, interviews, and recordings related to the group for her book *The Caribbean Artists Movement, 1966–1972.*[16] At one level, it is nothing less than the story of the consolidation of an idea of Caribbean literature. If one important branch of West Indian literary nationalism had grown out of the migration of important writers in the late 1940s (George Lamming, V. S. Naipaul, Sam Selvon, Andrew Salkey, and others), then fifteen years later, CAM would bring Caribbean writers together in a gesture that confirmed the existence of a set of artists formed by the Caribbean experience. Andrew Salkey, Kamau Brathwaite, and Trinidad-born lawyer, activist, and publisher John LaRose brought writers and artists together in dialogue about West Indian aesthetics (Orlando Patterson delivered the first CAM paper on this very topic) and Caribbean cultural forms (Gordon Rohlehr delivered the second paper, on Calypso).

Rereading the CAM archive, another melody rings in counterpoint to this first. The Caribbean Artists Movement consolidated West Indian literature in England, but it also dramatized the complexities of West Indian literary identity at this time, a decade after Caribbean writers were supposed to have created it. For one thing, there were some notable absences from the group that suggest that "Caribbean Artist" was not the most ready-made appellation for writers like Lamming himself, who was not to be a part of the group, or Sam Selvon, or Wilson Harris.[17] In an interview with Anne Walmsley in 1986, Andrew Salkey explains this in terms of personality: "You know, the writers you've mentioned are supreme individualists. . . . Each of those persons you've mentioned—Sam, Wilson, and George, are very self-sufficient persons. I'm not, really, I tend to lean and to be a person solaced by others and so on. I like community, I depend on the warmth of persons, the acquiesce [*sic*] of persons and so on. But those people are pretty rugged and strong you know."[18] There was already a sense, one way or another, in which the writers who are considered the "founders" of a certain kind of Caribbean literary nationalism thought of themselves as having a different kind of relationship to "Caribbean literature" when it was organized as such.

Rereading the archive also makes it clear that the founders of CAM considered strengthening Caribbean artists' relationship to the British establishment a goal equal in importance to creating community among Caribbean artists. In a letter to the British poet Edward Lucie-Smith and to the West Indian critic Bryan King, Kamau Brathwaite (then known as Edward) wrote excitedly both about building a Caribbean community of letters and about showcasing that group to the British cultural establishment. Brathwaite wrote to King: "The more I stay here in England, the more it seems to me that our writers and artists are missing a wonderful opportunity to communicate with themselves and with British and Commonwealth artists around them. . . . There should be a link-up with Commonwealth and British writers and artists: it is time they really got to know what we are doing and what we are worth."[19] Two weeks later he repeated his vision to Lucie-Smith, writing that he had been "toying with the idea of getting a group going through which WI writers and artists here in Great Britain could meet each other and (perhaps even more important) meet other Commonwealth and British writers and artists in the hope of getting some wider discussion going than seems to me to obtain at present."[20] It is striking, given the later development within CAM of a vision of strong Black British identity, that CAM's inception conforms so much with a Commonwealth notion of West Indian colonial belonging. Brathwaite, soon to be the inventor of the Caribbean-Africanist poetics of "nation language," is here clearly enlivened by the idea of a dual-purpose CAM that would bring the West Indies together and bring it closer to England.

As it turns out, Brathwaite was wrong in his presumption that the British were as interested in his project as he was in sharing it. Indeed, the CAM archive dramatizes the way West Indian writerly relationships with England were elastic: how the English establishment pulled away at the moment when West Indians made claims on an intimacy that they presumed was theirs (Lamming's notion that the West Indian writer was "familiar" to the white Briton notwithstanding). Francis Pike from Faber wrote to Brathwaite in September 1967 congratulating CAM on its first conference and making a donation to the organization. By then Brathwaite's first collection of poetry had been published by Faber, and it seemed an establishment connection was secure. But talk of getting fellow Faber poet Ted Hughes to attend the conference came to nothing. Brathwaite seemed to believe that the British artist Roland Penrose would chair a session at the CAM conference, to which Penrose wrote to say he was "rather appalled to find that you expect me to take the chair at the Caribbean Artists Symposium. I did not realise in my short phone conversation with Mr. Andrew Salkey that I had committed myself so definitely. I was not aware of the time or date and unfortunately on Friday June the second, I shall not be in London."[21] Penrose was, therefore, "quite unable to help . . . in what I consider is a highly interesting and admirable activity."[22] Louis James, the English critic who was an integral part of CAM, said in an interview with Walmsley that "the English establishment was so entrenched" that it was impossible for CAM to make inroads.[23]

It is, on reflection and certainly in retrospect, not surprising that West Indians' presumed intimacy with Britain would not be enthusiastically affirmed. But one of the notes that the CAM archives strikes that *is* somewhat surprising is the difficulty of defining West Indian identity in the first place. In a letter to Brathwaite in 1967, the literary critic Gordon Rohlehr, who was then writing a thesis about Joseph Conrad at the University of Birmingham, wrote about the idea of the West Indian artist, the problems with defining a single aesthetic, and the primacy of the individual imagination. Sounding a skeptical note about grouping artists under the rubric "Negro," Rohlehr writes: "One hears constant talk of 'defining' identity, as if identity is definable. It makes more sense to speak of 'expressing' identity, since in any case the possession of identity is one of the prerequisites of expression. . . . Don't worry too much about finding names for the West Indian experience. For to name, to use terms like 'creole negritude' is to define and limit."[24] Again, I admit to some surprise encountering this letter from Rohlehr, whose masterful essay on Caribbean poetics, "The Problem of the Problem of Form" (1985), would become a foundational text of Caribbean literary criticism, so defined. But all the CAM archive was confirming for me was what Lamming's early essays had established. The coming into being of such a thing as "Caribbean literary criticism" or Caribbean literature per se occurred only through the procedures of calling the existence of those entities into question. Indeed, Kenneth Ramchand's jaundiced view of the politics of publishing in Britain at the time suggests that a wariness about how a rubric of black artistic identity might be instrumentalized lingered among some West Indian writers a decade after the '56 Paris Congress. In his reply to Brathwaite's invitation to join CAM, Ramchand—then a doctoral student in literature, later the author of the foundational critical text *The West Indian Novel*—wrote: "That the WI writer is left out of the present Heinemann-Leeds scramble after every African writer is a welcome indication that our men have ceased to dazzle by raw material or as phenomena: the West Indian writer is free to be a writer (who, importantly for his society, comes from the West Indies)."[25]

Veronica Jenkin wrote that she hoped the group would not become "self-consciously 'Caribbean.'"[26] Salkey told Walmsley that CAM members "didn't want to go on protest marches, and they didn't want to be arrested by the police, and so on."[27] There was, into the late 1960s, a sense in which the Caribbean relationship to the metropole inoculated against the development of a separate West Indian identity, even at its moment of conception. The anxiety here is couched in terms of an opposition between creativity and identity that is strikingly dissonant against later literary developments (and resonant with Lamming's speech in Paris). One need think only of Brathwaite's *Rights of Passage* (published in 1967) or of Linton Kwesi Johnson, progenitor of dub poetry (whose interview with Walmsley credits CAM with making him into a poet), to see why the picture that the CAM archive paints is such an important and eccentric document of West Indian relationship to Englishness.

Out of reading this archive in tandem with Lamming's essays, two things emerge clearly. First is that any self-conscious attempt to define subaltern artistic unity, be it Negro Artists and Writers in 1956 or Caribbean Artists in 1966, seems destined to run up against contention. This contentiousness, this fraught reckoning and its procedures of disavowal, should therefore be accounted for as part and parcel of what it means to forge black unity. Rather than undermining the results of the attempt to create affinity the difficulty of the attempt is precisely what creates the affinity. Second, the reason for the specific difficulty of Lamming and Baldwin's connection—a connection, let me emphasize, that I am drawing out of two instances of textual missed connections that I find particularly tantalizing—is that Lamming's relationship to the African American writer is mediated by his experience of himself as British. (Baldwin's difficulties with Lamming I will come to momentarily.)

The Pleasures of Exile lays out the terms in which Lamming experiences intimacy with Englishness, the threats to that intimacy, and the surprising oppositions he creates that serve to illustrate and produce that sense of British closeness. Writing the book quickly in the autumn of 1959, Lamming was working through the paradoxes of his experience as a migrant who had not realized he had migrated, as an exile in a place he thought was home. This state of affairs nevertheless produces pleasure. Lamming's writing on Baldwin in *The Pleasures of Exile* is part of a larger context in the book in which he struggles in complicated ways with America. Recalling through extreme opposition the experiences of Caribbean-born writers a generation earlier, such as Claude McKay in *Home to Harlem,* Lamming describes moments of misalliance while spending time in Harlem. And Lamming's colonial affections are made more striking, not less, because his careful parsing of his engagement with Englishness still allows him to claim that "the West Indian novel, particularly in the aspect of its idiom, cannot be understood unless you take a good look at the American nineteenth century—a good look at Melville, Whitman, and Mark Twain."[28] Lamming can claim this (white) American heritage even as he is unable to detect Baldwin's literary and cultural kinship contemporaneous with his own writing.

He introduces the section on Baldwin by summarizing the wide scope of the writer's undertaking in *Notes of a Native Son*: "He tries to examine and interpret his own situation as an American Negro who is also a novelist drawing on the spiritual legacy of Western European civilization. Baldwin, you will notice, has made the canvas wider. Not just colonial vis-à-vis England, but American and Negro up against the monolithic authority of European culture."[29] Lamming goes on to quote from the section of Baldwin's "Autobiographical Notes" in which Baldwin is confronted in a unique way with the edifices of Western civilization and first names himself a "bastard of the West."[30] Baldwin speaks of having to "appropriate these white centuries," saying that he was now "unfitted from the jungle or the tribe."[31] The similarities between Baldwin and Lamming's formulations here are striking. Baldwin writes in familial terms of his relationship to products and structures of European colonialism and American white supremacy just as Lamming does in *The Pleasures of Exile*. For Baldwin it is the discourse of illegitimate birth; for Lamming it is a narrative of relation-through-marriage. In both cases, the writers see themselves as possessing a confounding and upsetting intimacy with and distance from the symbolic centers of Western art, thought, and life. Furthermore, the disavowal inherent in Baldwin's "jungle or . . . tribe" reminds me of Lamming's reading of *The Tempest*, during which—most critics have not noted this—he proceeds to *distance* his own narrative consciousness from Shakespeare's savage Caliban, though he had begun the project by identifying with him.

All of this is to say that it comes as a great surprise when, after grudgingly congratulating Baldwin on the beauty of his prose ("That is very well stated"), Lamming charges Baldwin with an attenuating anger that he thinks stems from Baldwin's "feeling of inferiority, both personal and racial, when he is in the presence of these monuments."[32] We move from Baldwin's erudition, compromised by his anger, undermined by his sense of inferiority, and then almost entirely effaced by what Lamming goes on to say is "Mr. Baldwin's timidity."[33] Why, if Baldwin is writing in such a similar vein to Lamming, in effect exposing the ways the African American writer has a similar relationship to the history of whiteness in the world that the Caribbean writer has to colonialism—why would this be the moment of disconnection for Lamming? It is a complicated moment, where Lamming reveals the difference it makes to be colonized from afar over and against the compression of US segregation:

> But there is a great difference between Baldwin and a comparable West Indian. No black West Indian, in his own native environment, would have this highly oppressive sense of being Negro. . . . The West Indian,

however black and dispossessed, could never have felt the experience of being in a minority. For the black faces vastly outnumber the white or expatriate white. This numerical superiority has given the West Indian a certain leisure, a certain experience of relaxation among white expatriates; for the West Indian has learnt, by sheer habit, to take that white presence for granted. Which is, precisely, his trouble.[34]

Lamming's ambivalence is marked here: he is implicitly critical of West Indian complacency vis-à-vis the bourgeois colonial status quo—the West Indian is "in trouble." And yet the "leisure" Lamming imagines the West Indian possesses in the face of his majority status in his own island (as against Baldwin's anger) betrays something like a strange appreciation for the particular form Western hegemony took in the Caribbean islands. It also belies the fact that he himself, at the time of his writing, is in fact a minority writing from majority white Britain. In a set of essays dedicated precisely to the confounding facts of his migration, the moment of considering a fellow minority black writer induces a form of amnesia or dissociation in Lamming that is the ground of his separation from Baldwin.

Vexed Relations

I have been alluding to mutual misrecognition, so let's look at the other side of the gaze. James Baldwin attended the 1956 Congress of Negro Writers and Artists and wrote about it for *Encounter* in an essay he called "Princes and Powers." Published as a missive from France in an American publication, Baldwin's piece was not formally a part of the Congress proceedings. And yet in its prickliness, in its polyvocality, and, more than anything else, in its skepticism about the very project of global black artistic unity around which the Congress was conceived, "Princes and Powers" might well have been published alongside all the other essays in that *Presence Africaine* special issue. As it is, it makes a fine companion piece.

Baldwin registers his skepticism by striking an early ironic note, juxtaposing two images—the Paris streets on a day in early fall and the cramped lecture hall where the Congress took place. "It was one of those bright, warm days which one likes to think of as typical of the atmosphere of the intellectual capital of the Western world," he writes, drawing a picture of Paris at its most fantastically beautiful.[35] He rhapsodizes about the state of generalized cheer prevailing in the streets of Paris that day. Even the bread lines were picturesque. And then he lurches by means of a paragraph break into the rather more frenzied scene inside the Congress lecture hall: "The conference was to open at nine o' clock. By ten o'clock the lecture hall was already unbearably hot, people choked the entrances and covered the wooden steps. It was hectic with the activity attendant upon the setting up of tape recorders, with the testing of ear-phones, with the lighting of flash-bulbs. Electricity, in fact, filled the hall."[36] This distinction between inside and out persists throughout the long piece: the pleasant warmth of the Paris streets as against the strangling heat indoors. The fantasy of Paris at peace with itself (Algeria was burning in 1956, after all) is counterpoised against the reality of an unbearably close fraternity (equally fantastical in its evocation of a mythic underground). Baldwin will reflect throughout on what it means to be within a fold and outside it—who is Western and who is not; who is American and who is not; who belongs to which tribe. Each of these questions is advanced in different ways throughout the essay, with Baldwin maintaining the poet-prince's prerogative toward studied distance. Maintaining it, at least, except when bursts of irritation erupt, a sign of some other affect roiling beneath a surface indifference.

One notes as well in the opening to Baldwin's essay those apparatuses of perception—earphones for translation, camera flashes for lighting—that highlight the difficulty of unaided apprehension. As Brent Edwards has noted about an earlier moment in black Paris, diaspora could only take place in translation. We might add, given Baldwin's note here, that what is momentarily lit by the flashbulb goes unnoticed in natural light. The discrepancy between illuminated moment and what is left in the dark is another haunting gap between black subjects at a gathering. These gatherings, whether in Paris in 1956 or London in 1968 (as we will see) become referendums on recognition for Baldwin, always. Who can see him? What do they see?

The question of being American infuses all of Baldwin's meditations in this essay. And Americanness is wed to a discourse of singularity, which is itself then aligned with a discourse of prophecy. At the end of the Congress's first morning session, still overwhelmed by the sheer density of putative kin who surround him, Baldwin writes, "I was spewed forth with the mob into the bright courtyard," sounding like Jonah coming out of the whale. His discomfort with being one of many is less extreme, perhaps, than the righteous man of yore compelled to separate himself from the sinful masses. But a felt sense of elevated difference (one can just about see him dusting himself off on the sidewalk) matches Baldwin's career-long self-mythos as the prophet. Baldwin is here the seer from a privileged prospect, surveilling all. And not just he but *the American Negro* per se occupies this place on high, this crucial difference vis-à-vis the West, that prepares him to do nothing less than grasp and reconstitute the world.

Outside he is introduced by Richard Wright to the other official US delegates to the Congress—Wright was accompanied by five others. Baldwin is taken by the unlikeliness of the auspices of their company: "It seemed unbelievable for a moment that the five men standing with Wright were defined, and had been brought together in this courtyard by our relation to the African continent."[37] American blackness and African blackness, it seemed to Baldwin, had very little in common at bottom. For one thing, Baldwin saw the principle of hypodescent governing racial blackness in the United States running up against its limits of legibility on the world stage. One of the US delegation, John Davis, was asked to explain why he considered himself to be a Negro. We presume from the context that Davis was light-skinned. Identifying as black the way that John Davis was understood to be doing was, according to Baldwin, "scarcely coherent for an African," and as a result, the cultural and subjective experience of the so-called one-drop rule "remains a closed book" to Davis's African interlocutor.[38] Furthermore, Baldwin perceived a difference in cultural outcome between European colonialism and US segregation. Africans, he decided, could imagine overthrowing the machinery of their subjugation. African Americans had to find a way to work within the system: "We had been dealing with and been mangled by, another machinery altogether. It had never been in our interest to overthrow it. It had been necessary to make the machinery work for our benefit and the possibility of its doing so had been, so to speak, built in."[39] The arch tone to which Baldwin has intermittent recourse throughout the piece gestures precisely at the structural difference he analyzes between colonialism and segregation, and his sense of their different artistic outcomes. Irony—change the joke and slip the yoke, as Ralph Ellison advised—is the cultural consequence of existing within a system of extreme internal paradox. (Of colonial paradox, however, of which there is plenty, Baldwin has less to say.) Aligned now with the small group of other Americans at the Congress, Baldwin is impressed by a sense of their specific, separable cultural gifts: "The American Negro is possibly the only man of color who can speak of the West with real authority, whose experience, painful as it is, also proves the vitality of the so transgressed Western ideals."[40]

But who is this "African" to whom Baldwin persists in referring throughout the piece? Parsing the difference he feels so acutely from his black fellows during these days of heady discourse requires an inattention to other kinds of difference: "For what, at bottom," Baldwin asserts, "distinguished the Americans from the Negroes who surrounded us, men from Nigeria, Senegal, Barbados, Martinique—so many names for so many disciplines—was the banal and abruptly quite overwhelming fact that we had been born in a society, which, in a way quite inconceivable for Africans, and no longer real for Europeans, was open, and, in a sense which has nothing to do with justice or injustice, was free."[41] Baldwin's conflation of colonial blacks here is nearly total. It is registered in this passage as the interchangeability of "Nigeria, Senegal, Barbados, Martinique" and later when he renders Africa a "country."[42] Given Baldwin's claim that America is uniquely free, his earlier anger at W. E. B. Du Bois—one of the unironic moments in the essay—becomes comprehensible. Du Bois had planned to attend the Congress as a delegate but was not granted leave to travel by the US government. In lieu of attendance, he sent a letter denouncing the American government's racial injustice and saying that the American writer who was granted leave to travel could only be doing so because he acceded to the government's official ideology. Chafing, perhaps understandably, at what he felt was a personal accusation, Baldwin used Du Bois's letter to set up the misperceptions between African Americans and blacks everywhere else. Du Bois's "extremely ill-considered communication," Baldwin wrote, "increased and seemed to justify the distrust with which all Americans are regarded abroad."[43] This was a particular problem, Baldwin argued, since it was the US black who was best positioned to revitalize Western culture and who was therefore needed to travel abroad, who was required by those in the black diaspora—and indeed by white Europe and America as well—to embody the dynamic force of wrestling with internal paradox, of irony.

Let me say this: in a few short years, Baldwin would be much less sanguine about American freedom. By the time he left Paris to tour the US South, the gap between openness and justice that in 1956 seemed to him beside the point had become insupportable. Baldwin's return to America and support of the civil rights movement would be accompanied by a set of writings increasingly harsh and incisively critical of US racism. It came to him forcefully that freedom could never be accomplished in a nation, by individuals of any race, as long as whiteness was hegemonic. To sustain white hegemony meant mutually-assured destruction. "We cannot be free until they are free," Baldwin writes in the first essay of *The Fire Next Time*, an essay framed as a letter to his beloved nephew.[44] He continues: "I know what the world has done to my brother and how narrowly he has survived it. And I know, which is much worse, and this is the crime of which I accuse my country and my countrymen, and for which neither I nor time nor history will ever forgive them, that they have destroyed and are destroying hundreds of thousands of lives and do not know it and do not want to know it."[45] This was six years after "Princes and Powers." But in the *Encounter* essay, Baldwin is still of the mind that America is something special. And as an American, he is the son of the Western father, albeit a father who does not recognize him—a son imbued with special qualities that stem from his youthful vitality, and an independence of spirit matching the mythic independence of America itself. The conjoining of rebel will with the edifices of Western culture was what, in Baldwin's mind, created the particular vitality of the black American, who was neither beholden to European centuries nor, ripped away as he was by the Middle Passage, in a position to avail himself of the equally longer centuries of the Yoruba or the Ashanti or the Ewe or the Dogon.

Baldwin's assessment of the openness of American culture relies on decoupling culture from politics. He is cranky throughout the essay when he feels that "culture" falls out of view of the Congress participants. Of Cesaire's speech, for instance, he notes that while the audience reacted with "the most violent reaction of joy," he himself felt "stirred in a very strange and disagreeable way."[46] Cesaire's indictment of European colonialism was strong enough to be (unsatisfyingly, alas) "unanswerable."[47] But it did not to Baldwin's mind provide a vision of the "culture," "synthesis," and "reconciliation" of the West and Africa with which it purported to deal.[48] Baldwin notes in a parenthetical aside that the other disadvantage of the speech, apart from its being unanswerable, is that it was "very little concerned, at bottom, with culture."[49] (We remember Lamming: "Politics is the only ground of connection.") Note as well, however, Eileen Julien's perceptive reading of Richard Wright at the Congress, whose speech did not excoriate European colonialism in the manner of his prominent Antillean fellow-writers Cesaire and Fanon. Julien notes that Wright's "almost perfunctory acknowledgement that colonialism was violent and evil, and his eagerness to pass over European culpability to the supposed next phase are surely not unrelated to the fact that he, like James Baldwin, had found a haven in France from the nightmare of American racism."[50]

So here is the state of affairs at this point: as Baldwin himself reports, much of the contentious debate over the course of the Congress surrounded the role of the black artist as Western subject. Whether it was Alioune Diop rejecting as a false choice that of the colonial black African "assimilating" to European culture or throwing it over, or George Lamming noting that the Caribbean writer speaks the same language as his British colonial master, several prominent speakers at the Congress drew attention to the paradoxical constitution of black colonial subjectivity. By claiming the dilemma of hybridity as uniquely American, Baldwin was in fact drawing attention to the structural *sameness* of the position vis-à-vis Western subjectivity of multiple blacks in that crowded room. "Princes and Powers" gives us a spectacle of everyone claiming a uniquely paradoxical relationship to the West. This is not just diaspora as difference; it is diaspora as *disavowal*. This is diaspora made through the coming together of people mutually claiming to have no relation to each other. It is, therefore, the claim of separateness that constitutes the connection.

Once Baldwin comes to Lamming's speech, he more or less says this. Writing approvingly of Lamming's "refusal to be intimidated by the fact that he is a genuine writer," Baldwin summarized the main point of "The Negro Writer and His World" appositely:

> [Lamming] was suggesting to the conference a subtle and difficult idea, the idea that part of the wealth of the Negro experience lay precisely in its double-edgedness. He was suggesting that all Negroes were held in a state of supreme tension between the difficult, dangerous relationship in which they stood to the white world and the relationship, not a whit less painful or dangerous, in which they stood to each other. He was suggesting that in the acceptance of this duality lay their strength, that in this, precisely, lay their means of defining and controlling the world in which they lived.[51]

Baldwin likes this because it sounds just like him. He identifies with Lamming's skepticism toward black ideologues more concerned with their own power than with the difficult and fine points of how to live in the West. He resonates with Lamming's skepticism and sensibility more generally, writing approvingly of Lamming's concern with "the immensity and the variety of the experience called Negro," with Lamming's understanding of "this variety as wealth."[52] Indeed, Lamming does ruminate on the difference between the Nigerian writer and the British West Indian from the perspective of his reception in the metropolitan center. I have described how he gets there. Baldwin's sense of how he gets there is a little different. This is how Baldwin summarizes Lamming's speech:

> He cited the case of Amos Tutuola's *The Palm-Wine Drinkard*, which he described as a fantasy, made up of legend, anecdotes, episodes, the product, in fact, of an oral story-telling tradition which disappeared from Western life generations ago. Yet "Tutuola really *does* speak English. It is *not* his second language." The English did not find the book strange. On the contrary, they were astonished by how truthfully it seemed to speak to them of their own experience. They felt that Tutuola was closer to the English than he could possibly be to his equivalent in Nigeria; and yet Tutuola's work could elicit this reaction only because, in a way which could never really be understood, but which Tutuola had accepted, he was closer to his equivalent in Nigeria than he ever could be to the English.[53]

In other words, Baldwin attributes to Tutuola, the Nigerian writer, everything Lamming had attributed to himself, the West Indian writer. Those authoritative-looking quotes—"Tutuola really *does* speak English. It is *not* his second language"—are accurate to a degree. Lamming really did say "He does really *speak English*" (even if the emphasis is slightly different from Baldwin's memory). It is just that he said this in exactly the opposite way than Baldwin remembers it.

We have to allow for the exigencies of note-taking and mishearing (remember those headphones and microphones, that crowded compressed room spewing Baldwin out). We have to allow as well for the gap between listening to a speech and composing an essay out of it—the necessary mutations that time permits, the failures of memory. But even granted those allowances, this mishearing is significant. It is not that Baldwin is being willfully inaccurate. It is that his imagination in this setting, like Lamming's, is oriented toward a kinship based on difference. For Baldwin here, Tutuola and Lamming are interchangeable precisely because neither of them is American. Baldwin senses a kindred spirit in Lamming, yes. But this kinship emerges through a radical erasure of precisely the thing that unites them: a paradoxical, agonistic sense of belonging to the West. And, painfully, an abjection of the "African" subject whom both writers construe as marked by ineffable separateness.

I have found only one other critic who has been interested in marking the error Baldwin makes in his reporting on Lamming's speech. In "Baldwin, Paris, and the 'Conundrum of Africa,'" Akin Adesokan is as compelled as I am by the maneuvers through which the Caribbean subject becomes the African subject in Baldwin's version of Lamming's text.[54] Adesokan is exercised as well—more to his own point than to mine—by the frank mistakes Baldwin introduces into his text (who keeps referring to a language he calls "Youriba," meaning, presumably, Yoruba) and by the arguably more alarming fact that they go unremarked in the most recent reprinting of "Princes and Powers" in the Library of America edition of Baldwin's *Collected Essays*. Adesokan's elegant reading of the meanings of these misreadings overlaps in places with my own. But our readings also track separate, complementary, trajectories. We agree that the 1956 Congress presented an occasion when African diaspora culture was being forged out of contest rather than agreement. (Adesokan reads this primarily as working within the tradition of black artistic "competitiveness"; I have chosen to frame this as disavowal. The two terms are related, of course.) But while I am interested in the way Baldwin runs roughshod over global black differences in order to retain a delineated sense of the black American subject, Adesokan is interested in the particular way the *African* subject is excluded from Baldwin's view. For Adesokan, the Lamming anecdote, but also Baldwin's comments about E. L. Lasebikan, the respected Nigerian scholar who spoke about "Youriba" poetry, as well as Baldwin's comments about Cesaire, suggest that Africa functioned in Baldwin's imagination differently than the Caribbean did. To Adesokan's mind, Baldwin wrote approvingly of Lamming for the same reason he indicted Cesaire: Lamming represented the possibility of black literary identity that did not exclude the West. For Adesokan, Baldwin was interested in charting a "literary history," one in which the bastardized, westernized black subject created art not out of political opposition but with the creative use of the traumas of history.[55] And he wanted a literary sensibility, not a political one. Adesokan makes an important note as well of Baldwin's anthropological vision of the African writers. Baldwin's description of Lasebikan's dress and manner, Adesokan writes, "give or take a few words ... could have come from an eighteenth-century account of an encounter between an 'English gentleman' and 'a noble savage.' So settled is its regard of its subject as an absolute other, and so adroit the ethnographic gauge of its register, that the dress worn by the speaker in question, because it is visually arresting, acquires a value in alterity which the imprecision of the writer's choice of descriptive words does not undermine."[56]

Adesokan is absolutely correct in this assessment. And I agree as well that Baldwin's production of Lasebikan as a "Mohammedean" in a "red velvet toque" serves to "exemplify the gap that supposedly separated continental Africans of the time from the blacks in the diaspora."[57] I would only note that Baldwin's approval of Lamming's speech does not necessarily imply an alignment with Caribbean subjectivity, nor does it suggest that Baldwin supported a notion of undifferentiated diasporic subjectivity. His alliance with Lamming is based, remember, on an important misunderstanding of what Lamming actually said, which mistake demonstrates a crucial *missed* attempt at sympathy. If Adesokan is interested in how Baldwin aligns himself with and approves of the Caribbean writer, then I am interested in how that approval is partial and contested. We both agree, however, that the relationship between the US black writer and the Caribbean one at this moment in Baldwin's writing relies on leaving out altogether any possibility of a sophisticated African writer.

A bit more than a decade after the Congress of Negro Writers and Artists, in a humbler setting and with the more modest provenance of a grassroots gathering, Baldwin found himself in another theater of West Indian–US relations and with a similar dynamic in play. A recording of Baldwin speaking at a meeting of a Caribbean students' organization, the West Indian Students' Centre, is another example of agonistic diasporic fraternity, this time not alongside Lamming—though at least one of Lamming's compères was in attendance. Rather, this time Baldwin faces Lamming's younger heirs, and they are a little less British and a little bit more black.

Horace Ové's film *Baldwin's Nigger* records this event—a meeting of the West Indian Students Association in 1968 at which Baldwin appeared as a guest speaker. Baldwin was invited as a now eminent writer and activist to share his thoughts on the relationship between West Indians and African Americans. One senses he was there to inspire, to bestow of his grandness, style, and wit—but things got testy. Underlying what must have been framed as an amiable compare-and-contrast set of musings about American and Caribbean paths toward black progress were various tributaries of difference, rivers that skirted around the pillar of Baldwin himself and made of him a figure of sometimes opposing political imperatives. For those in the audience who were moving toward a radical black consciousness—witness the leather jackets, the Afros, and berets—Baldwin appeared a besuited, bourgeois intellectual of the "Negro" ilk, problematically interpellated at the very level of language into the white power structure. He needed redemption. For the erstwhile "brown" West Indians who had come to discover they were actually black by the reckoning of British racial calculus, Baldwin was a prophet, an emissary from the more vivid racial landscape of the United States who could consolidate what they were only now beginning to learn about the operations of imperial racism.[58] At one point, a well-spoken and light-skinned Jamaican woman precedes her question to Baldwin with the remark "when I lived in the Caribbean I never thought of myself as black," and she is booed. *Baldwin's Nigger* is a document of a changing of the guard in the Caribbean community in Britain. Indeed, arguably the film documents a move in the category of migrant identity in Britain from West Indian to Black British. The session also shows the ways the language of black agitation differed between America and Britain, despite the overlapping goals of black resistance in both locations, and despite West Indians' admiration for figures, such as Baldwin, who were on the vanguard of struggle in the United States. The breach between a more radical and separatist idea of black identity and an older sense of capacious Britishness in which the black colonial belonged (and that we witness in Lamming's essays and in CAM) was being played out in this film, and Baldwin became a lightning rod for its dramatization.

Baldwin's Nigger is Ové's first film, and it is done in a style similar to the Free Cinema aesthetic that had emerged in British filmmaking in the 1950s. This is to say that Ové's camera, like Lindsay Anderson's in *O Dreamland* (1953), which films an amusement park in Margate, or Tony Richardson and Karel Reisz's in *Momma Don't Allow* (1956), which wordlessly films dancing at a north London jazz club, captures the West Indian students' meeting with a minimum of obvious style and obstruction. The arresting title announces itself in black and white on the screen with no fanfare beyond its inflammatory epithet. It bobs in white letters over a black background (literally bobs, like a buoy in a black sea) and repels and intrigues the viewer simultaneously. Who is Baldwin's nigger? When possibly might James Baldwin have had occasion to possess one? Indeed the first sign of tension between the West Indian and American approach to race is signaled in this title. How on earth would one even sound the name of this film in America? That word after *Baldwin's* is charged in the Caribbean, yes, charged in Britain, but does not in either place have the brutal force of US segregation behind it—the spectacular violence that renders it virtually unspeakable, in most contexts, to the black American's ear.

The next title card announces innocently: "A Film Recording of a Discussion at the West Indian Students' Centre London." In apposition, the following intertitle: "In this documentary James Baldwin and Dick Gregory talk about the black experience in America and relate it with that of the Caribbean and Great Britain today." All right, so not quite a trip to Margate, but these descriptions of the film's events sound innocuous enough. They do not quite register the friction of the proceedings to follow, nor do they do anything to explain the vividness of that pair of words with which the viewer is first met, the provocation of the film's title. This kind of irony was a feature of Free Cinema—a sense of discomfort, foreboding, and looming threat is the tonal overlay to scenes of putative jollity. Here Ové juxtaposes horror (the film's title) with bureaucratic description (the last two intertitles sound like the minutes of an administrative meeting). And in this way we are alerted to the fact that his lens is not absent style or intent and that the meeting therein will not be business as usual.

For the most part, Ové trains his camera on Baldwin, centered in the frame and for almost all his speech rocking back and forth with his hands invisible, pressed against the table below him in apparent support. The very first image is of Baldwin standing and speaking, in medias res. There is another man seated at that front table, to the left and lower down in the frame. We see only his forehead and hair. We surmise as the film proceeds that he is one of the eponymous West Indian students, as we eventually see his face and discover that he is not Dick Gregory. Perhaps he introduced Baldwin to the gathered audience? Perhaps here, now abstracted, was the figure who would have provided the contextualization to the evening's events that Ové saw fit to edit out: the customary introductory remarks, the welcome and encomiums of the distinguished guest speaker. As it is, the beginning of the film renders the student a fuzzy shape at the edge of the scene, centering America prominently in a sea of Caribbean. The camera zooms in on Baldwin. The student's head is cropped out, and for several minutes we do not see it again, until Ové pans out again and shows him reclining slightly to the left, self-conscious of the camera, seated and therefore lower than Baldwin and listing slightly away from him. In that first wide shot we also see seated beside the student Andrew Salkey. Salkey is looking all eminent himself with his Marxist beard and serious, impassive face staring out at the audience. (He is not *at* the table-podium, but he is beside it, up front.) Perhaps Salkey gave an introductory speech too? We know that Salkey loved Baldwin: he wrote two poems for him decades later, when Baldwin died—that is, after London, after Salkey had moved to America and become a professor at Hampshire College, where Baldwin himself briefly taught too in the 1980s. For the duration of the film, the camera makes this movement from tight shot to wide—closing in on Baldwin's face and panning out to the others. To this lateral movement, Ové eventually adds cutaways, swoops that pass from Baldwin to the West Indians listening to him. There is a mixture of rapt attendance to Baldwin and something like disinterest.

What does Baldwin say? He begins his speech with an anecdote. Like Lamming's "Negro Writer and His World" in Paris, the story dramatizes an encounter between two men in England, one of whom is Baldwin himself. Also like Lamming's speech, the story revolves around the ambivalence of cross-ethnic encounter, this time between two black men from different nations. Here is how Baldwin begins:

> I'll tell you a story from me. Many years ago when I first came to London, I was in the British Museum, naturally [eyebrows arch; audience laughs knowingly]. And one of the West Indians who worked there started up a conversation with me. And he asked me where I was from. And I told him I was from Harlem. And that answer didn't satisfy him. And I didn't understand what he meant. I was born in Harlem. . . . And I could see, though I didn't understand it, that he was growing more

and more disgusted with me, that he was growing more impatient. My mother was born in Maryland, my father was born in New Orleans, I was born in Harlem. He said "Yes but before that where were you born?"

The crowd erupts into laughter. He continues:

> And I had to say "I don't know." And I could see that he did not believe me. And I had to explain that if I were originally from Dakar or wherever I was in Africa, I couldn't find out because my entry into America is a bill of sale. And that stops you from going any further. At some point in our history I became Baldwin's nigger. That's how I got my name. Now that really cannot be considered my fault. It can't be considered the fault of the cat in the British Museum either that he doesn't know that I can't find that out.

At this point, the camera pans away from a close-up of Baldwin to a close-up of Andrew Salkey. The sound of Baldwin's voice is juxtaposed against the image of Salkey looking at Baldwin with a great, sad, sidelong stare. Here is what Baldwin says to close the anecdote, while Ové closes in on Salkey's skeptical-seeming gaze:

> I tell you that story to dramatize the nature of the distance created, created deliberately. Because when I became Baldwin's nigger, it is also important to point out, I was handcuffed to another man from another tribe whose language I did not speak. We did not know each other. And we could not speak to each other because if we could speak to each other we might have been able to talk about what was happening to us. And if we could have figured out what was happening to us we might have been able to prevent it. We would have had, in short, a kind of solidarity which is a kind of identity which would have made the history of slavery very different. . . . Well that didn't happen and here we are.

Here we are. In London, or in Paris, trying to figure out a language and the terms for a connection whose power is profound enough to compel persistent attempts at its definition. The fact of always having to ask the question is itself a kind of answer.

A few aspects of the anecdote Baldwin shares stand out as curious. Note that in the story Baldwin's interlocutor is West Indian. But this is a particular kind of West Indian—the kind who does not appear to understand about the slave trade. Who is this West Indian who, by virtue of the line of questioning he follows with Baldwin, we are meant to assume thinks he knows "where he came from?" For me, listening to this anecdote there are two absent presences, both of whom I can imagine as substitutes in the story. For it is possible, I feel, to imagine that Baldwin's questioner was in fact white. Imagine that the security guard was a white British man seeking to place Baldwin securely in the cradle of an Africa he imagines to be hermetic and safely at a distance. The story then takes on a meaning similar to that of Lamming's story in "Negro Writer and His World," in which the imaginary white British reader experiences a feeling of uncanny kinship to the West Indian writer based primarily on a sense of the *difference* between the West Indian from the Nigerian, whom he imagines to be further away. (*He is a Negro, yes, but a Negro with a difference.*) But imagine that Baldwin's interlocutor was black, was from a nation in Africa. Do the questions of origin take on a different valence here? Is the slave trade repressed on the other side of the Atlantic? It seems unlikely that Baldwin would have forgotten that his questioner was white British, since this would have given the story an entirely different meaning. But it seems equally unlikely, to me at least, that his questioner would be West Indian. For this would put the West Indian in a fundamentally different relationship to Africa and to "the West" than Baldwin, and such a difference, on the basis of the archival gaps to which Baldwin alludes, is difficult, historically, to justify, given that the West Indian is subject to the very same losses that Baldwin lays out. Here we are again, like Paris in '56. Fraternity is denied.

Clearly, though, the facts of Baldwin's story are less important than the rhetorical effect to which the details are put. The point of the story is that the same forces of imperialism that created the "Americas" and the "West Indies" deliberately imposed ethnic barriers in the Middle Passage. Baldwin uses the ethnic differences of the Middle Passage as a metaphor for the ethnic differences between modern Caribbean and American blacks. The cauldron into which variegated African ethnicities were put to create the entity of racial blackness, Baldwin is saying, itself became a stew of conflicting identities.

For Baldwin here, as in Paris a decade earlier, the crucial sign of his own felt difference is *America*. Witness his halting introduction of that provocative sign into his speech: "One of the most terrible things [he stammers: pause] One of the most difficult things. [pause] Because one wants to resist it but also to use it. [pause] Whether I like it or not I am an American. . . . I was formed in a certain crucible. My school was really the streets of New York. My frame of reference was George Washington and John Wayne." The way Baldwin cannot finish a sentence until he gets to the simple declaration ("I am an American.") points to his sense of its painfully catalyzing effect in conversations about diaspora. America is the three-hundred-pound gorilla in the room. And while Baldwin knows enough to joke about it, the wry references to John Wayne and George Washington are, if anything, confirmation of the discursive might of US iconography. Everyone can laugh at that quip precisely because everyone has been living in a world in which John Wayne and George Washington are legible. And indeed the same forces of cultural hegemony rendering white icons culturally available ciphers for black people all around the world who are simultaneously cut off from the power to which these icons refer—this same hegemony is what Baldwin now realizes he has access to, and it is one source of the stuttering embarrassment of bringing America into the conversation at all. At one point Baldwin says of himself: "I'm well enough known to be an ornament."

There is a cut. The film moves on to the question-and-answer section of the session, and the very first question is a crystallization of the conflict I have been describing: "Why do you call a man Negro? Why don't you just call him a black man? There is no country after Negro, you know that?" (This last question is half declaration.) The questioner's accent is Caribbean, and he is nervous, though committed to an adversarial line of questioning. One imagines he worked up his courage ahead of time and will barrel on through, despite Baldwin's bristling request that he repeat the question. For his part, Baldwin initially takes the question in stride but then visibly braces as he warms to his theme. The question of language, he says, is not answered in a day or two but takes time. Soon he is angry:

> It was not I, nor any black man in America, who invented the word Negro. It is not I who wrote that on my birth certificate. It is not I who invented that language. I understand the [principle] of your question. And indeed there is no country called Negro. I know that. But you must understand too that I cannot change my vocabulary overnight. I may agree with you. But we've been called, we've been called and we've called ourselves American Negroes for nearly four hundred years. Now do you suppose that because it angers you that suddenly an entire nation is able to change its vocabulary? Your generation, not mine, will call itself black.

Baldwin's anger marks territories of differentiation between West Indian and African American experiences. His allusion to the inheritance of language, however, is nothing if not a reminder of Lamming's double-edged inheritance. Black writers divided by a shared language, bound to their distinct sense of polity and belonging by differing habits of thought, nevertheless share the idea that language forms an intimate bond to culture in powerful and ambivalent ways.

Ceremonies of the Soul; or, Sycorax Breaks In

I have been speaking about brothers as if there were no sisters. The mutual disavowal I have described between Baldwin and Lamming is indeed one of fraternal agony. But the contentiousness of diasporic brotherhood evolves in relation to the silenced female black subject, who is—again, in a structure of full disavowal—everywhere and everywhere not named in the history of subjecthood in the West. In my final section of this chapter, I do not wish to offer a compensatory narrative of female voices, as the fraternal struggle here is gendered in such a specific way as to render such a gesture false. Rather, I want to clarify that this mode of masculine agonistic intimacy operates precisely in that register of male contest, identification, and desire that usually excludes women or disavows them. I do want to say, however, that it is possible and useful to read a moment when feminine disavowal breaks through, as it does in a classic Lamming moment. I do end here by way of reminder: the structure of exclusion of female voices comes with a dub side. These brothers are in wary, side-eyed contest; their sisters have been working all along.

Lamming and Baldwin's perceived status as bastards of white hegemony implies the extremely convoluted familial logic of slavery and its aftermath that Hortense Spillers explains in her classic essay "Mama's Baby, Papa's Maybe."[59] It is a genealogical arrangement whereby the black father is disappeared ("legal enslavement removed the African-American male . . . from *mimetic* view as a partner in the prevailing social fiction of the Father's name") and the white father—in slavery's curious and inevitable doubling of fatherhood—remains "a mocking presence," endowing neither name nor fortune; and black motherhood is simultaneously denied and foundational.[60] Maternity cannot endow cultural inheritance in Western society, yet in representations of black Western subjectivity, it is precisely the case that matriarchy (in often monstrous figurations) is determinative. ("The African American male has been touched, therefore by the mother, *handed* by her in ways that he cannot escape.")[61] Thus, any discussion of black subjectivity and relation, according to Spillers, implies a simultaneously absent and overwhelming matriarchy as both scourge and wound. In such a situation, the female "breaks in upon the imagination."[62]

Toward the end of his famous reading of *The Tempest* in *The Pleasures of Exile*, Lamming writes: "We ask ourselves why a Duke should debase himself to speak in such a way [cursing Caliban's mother]. The tone suggests an intimacy of involvement and concern which encourages speculation. But we could not speak with authority on the possibilities of this defect until we had heard from Sycorax and Miranda's mother. They are both dead; and so our knowledge must be postponed until some arrangement comparable to the Haitian Ceremony of the Souls returns them to tell us what we should and ought to know."[63] According to Lamming, a ceremony must be arranged to bring forth these missing and cursed feminine voices. Throughout his career, Lamming has returned several times to a Haitian vodou ritual he names the "Ceremony of the Souls." By the terms of this passage, he relates this "Ceremony" to the reclamation of suppressed female knowledge. He begins *The Pleasures of Exile* with a description of this ritual, literally inaugurating the book with these words: "In the republic of Haiti—one corner of the Caribbean cradle—a native religion sometimes forces the official Law to negotiate with peasants who have retained a racial, and historic, desire to worship their original gods."[64] A ritual he observed in the suburbs of Port-au-Prince four years previous to his writing, he says, involved a drama of truth-telling from the dead to the living:

> This ceremony of the Souls is regarded by the Haitian peasant as a solemn communion; for he hears and sees, at first hand, the secrets of the Dead. The celebrants are mainly relatives of the deceased who, ever since their death, have been locked in Water. It is the duty of the Dead to return and offer, on this momentous night, a full and honest report on their past relations with the living. . . . It is the duty of the Dead to speak, since their release from the purgatory of Water cannot be realized until they have fulfilled the contract which this ceremony symbolises. The Dead need to speak if they are going to enter that eternity which will be their last and permanent Future.[65]

In a 1965 speech published as "The West Indian People," Lamming again returned to the "Ceremony of the Souls," describing a ritual "at which all the celebrants are relatives of the Dead who return for this occasion to give some report on their previous relations with the living. These Dead are supposed to be in a purgatorial state of Water, and it is necessary for them to have this dialogue with the living before they can be released into their final eternity. The living, on the other hand, need to meet the dead again in order to discover if there is any need for forgiveness."[66] For Lamming, it is not important to "believe in" Haitian vodou for this ceremony to be what he says is "a very awesome encounter."[67] And indeed, it is perhaps not important to believe in Lamming's rendering of the ritual—I have yet to find in descriptions of Haitian vodou practices of the dead the name "Ceremony of the Souls" or the activity as Lamming describes it.[68] Both in this essay and in *Pleasures*, the "Ceremony of the Souls" functions as a symbol for Lamming, invoking the "question of the Sea" for black people—the way the lost and missing of the Atlantic crossing produce subjectivity in subjunctive and interrogative moods.[69] Colonialism functions as the Law, the official Law against which vodou practitioners must devise rites of subterfuge, such as the elaborate ceremonial drawings, *veves*, chalked in dust and erased when the authorities arrive: "The worshippers stand to welcome their protectors, the police, and in the same moment their feet have erased the signs of invocation they had made in the dust."[70] In *The Pleasures of Exile*, Lamming uses the ceremony as a paradigm for his reading of *The Tempest*, Shakespeare's play becoming a kind of map of the colonial project as it relates to human experience and the vodou ceremony becoming a prospective intertext. Arguably, *The Tempest* functions as a kind of masking in Lamming's text, too. He still has not found that ceremony whereby Sycorax or Miranda can "break through." Rather, the ritual of court testimony he goes on to describe invokes a subject close to Lamming's own writerly persona who is a special witness, "claiming extraordinary privileges."[71] This witness says:

> I am the chief witness for the prosecution, but I shall also enter the role of the Prosecutor. I shall defend the accused in the light of my own evidence. I reserve the right to choose my own Jury to whom I shall interpret my own evidence since I know that evidence more intimately than any man alive. . . .

Involvement in crime, whether as witness, or an accomplice, makes innocence impossible. To be innocent is to be eternally dead. And this trial embraces only the living. Some may be corpses but their evidence is the evidence of a corpse who has returned to make the unforgivable apology.[72]

The ritual of testimony here combines with the ritual of resurrection. This is a court case for "the living," he says, even if some of those living will have to be recalled from the dead, or like Caliban, the imaginary. Testimony is often considered a moment of power for the autonomous subject. The individual finds a voice; the victimized tells his or her story. But in Lamming's combination of the ritualized forms of testimony and resurrection, power is undermined. Any involvement in colonialism, Lamming claims, makes "innocence impossible." To be colonized by language is to find oneself complicit with the accused; it is to find oneself in the unthinkable situation of "defend[ing] the accused," testifying on his behalf. Although doing so in the "light of [one's] own evidence" grants a certain autonomy to the colonized, notice that the person who is resurrected in this scene is not a Caribbean soul but an English corpse, returning to say "Sorry, I knew not what I did."

Lamming reads the religious celebrant as enacting a ceremony that resists colonial domination, but he cannot in fact escape the colonizer in his writerly rendition of the ceremony. And he never escapes the masculine, having cracked open a space for the possibility of a feminine voice. His subjectivity, like the witness claiming extraordinary privileges, puts him in the position to tell his own story, but always with the perspective of the colonizer hovering nearby—and it is the gendered terms of the colonizer that Lamming appears to accept. It is for this reason, I would argue, that *The Pleasures of Exile* does not have the moment of catharsis that is typical of ritualistic writing, proceeding instead through a series of deferred epiphanies.

Gordon Rohlehr's aforementioned essay "The Problem of the Problem of Form" gets at what I am trying to understand of the procedure, and limits, of Lamming's use of Haitian ritual in his essays. Rohlehr writes of a "compulsive Caribbean drive to realise a complex, multi-faceted, flexible sense of shape," arguing that the Caribbean's "oral tradition has always been concerned with matters of energy, its containment in the shaped process of ritual enactment, and catharsis. Any aesthetic based on the oral tradition seeks naturally to address itself to these considerations: energy, containment, catharsis."[73] But Lamming points to the oral tradition in *Pleasures*; indeed, he initiates the book with these traditions and gestures to their ritualistic forms, but then he does not avail himself of their cathartic payoffs. There is no "movement of ritual enactment . . . towards climax and catharsis" here. Rohlehr writes that Caribbean writers from Lamming on "realized . . . that there is an aesthetic, a trope, a shape locked up in the religion and fully relevant to their contemporary quests. What they seek to do is to discover and release the shape of the hidden paradigm."[74] What Lamming does in his essay is to dramatize the search for such a form and then also make clear the limits of this form in the face of English discourse. By inhabiting the various positions in the courtroom, or by making the mark of the cross in the street and then erasing it again, Lamming made clear the ambivalences of Caribbean writing in its metropolitan hotbed in the 1950s: its sense of debt and honor to the English language squeezed up against the resisting consciousness in search of the formal inheritances of creolized religion.

What does it mean to achieve freedom of form in the face of this ambivalence? And why am I closing by suggesting that this freedom is gendered? Chapter 4 deals specifically with spirit possession, which, as will become clear, is not confined, is not limited to, the specific remit of the feminine. But I think there is something about the unnamed feminine in Lamming's work here that allows the trope of spirit possession to function as the disavowed feminine—as that which "breaks in upon the imagination"—in a way that Lamming is not fully able to handle or reckon with. Ceremonies must be found. They are what Lamming was looking for, too, in the 1950s and what he could not quite find because the intersubjective imagination of his writing at this time, at least in the examples I've read here, was overdetermined by the masculine and the imperial, both of which compelled him into dramas not of reconciliation but of retreat.

THREE

ANDREW SALKEY AND THE QUEER DIASPORIC

I must learn to wait and wait and wait . . .
—Andrew Salkey, *Escape to an Autumn Pavement*

The Negroes are of marvelous respectability.
—Alexander Baron, *The Lowlife*

Harryboy Boas, the narrator and main character of Alexander Baron's 1963 novel *The Lowlife*, puts forward his observation of the marvelous respectability of the Negroes while watching his east London neighborhood of Hackney transform in the midst of massive postwar Caribbean migration to Britain.[1] Here on his doorstep was the so-called *Windrush* generation, that signal arrival at the east London docks of the vessel bearing some hundreds of Caribbean shipmates, the first breaking of the wave that changed everything from the demography of major British cities, to academic sociology, to immigration law.[2] To be sure, as Harryboy notes, Hackney continues to be a place where "all sorts live," where the Jewish community mingles with "Cockneys . . . with the stamp of markets on them." However, the large Edwardian houses that were once impeccably kept by "superior working-class" families, have been turned into tenements. The streets, still clean, are far more crowded. And, as Harryboy notes with a tinge of pleasure, "Negroes have come to live, more every month. . . . Every Sunday morning they all go to the Baptist Chapel in the High Street. You should see the men, in beautiful pearl-grey suits and old-fashioned trilbies with curled brims, the big women full of dignity, and the little girls in white muslin and bonnets. It slays me."[3] The marvelous respectability of the Negroes who have come to live in Hackney suggests that while Harryboy's neighborhood may have lost some of its luster, the incoming black residents are not arriving overly rumpled by their transatlantic journey. Indeed, if an influx of black residents has become the proverbial index of a community's decline, then something slightly different is happening in Harryboy's Hackney: these incoming Negroes are providing the neighborhood with a new measure of dapper propriety.

Let's say as a beginning to my discussion of what I will characterize as the *queer diasporic* that those men in beautiful suits are a metonymy, a sign for a figure and a structure of belonging developed out of class angst and nonnormative eroticized desire. The closeness of queerness and dandified self-presentation is only part of what I will explore here—though it is a fascinating part. For as Monica Miller has told us, "a well-educated, well-traveled black man will forever be out of place, queer even if he is heterosexual."[4] And indeed the relationship between bourgeois black coloniality, dapperness, and gender nonconformity informs Harryboy's wry pleasure in those lovely trilbies. White working-class *ressentiment* during the postwar period of West Indian immigration to England illuminates the intimacy of black middle-class colonials with certain styles of Englishness, even as colonial performances of black masculine style introduced the possibility of queer pleasure in those "beautiful pearl-grey suits." That an image of West Indian men just disembarked from the *Empire Windrush*, jauntily posed at the docks, has been included in a recent book called *One Hundred Years of Menswear* is one of those ironies to which we have become accustomed—though hopefully in the context of this chapter it will appear freshly unusual. The laboring and maligned black body is temporarily enshrined as a symbol of sublime masculine styling, cosmopolitanism, and self-care.[5]

But apart from this concordance of colonial self-styling and nonnormative gender presentation, there is another queer element to the idea of diaspora I explore here, and to which Harryboy draws our attention. His working-class suspicion/desire vis-à-vis these crisp arrivants elicits in *them* a set of responses to being watched. "Dignity," after all (of which the black women are supposedly full) might be another shading of hauteur—itself a performance of self-containment necessitated by the violent intrusion of surveillance. And those hats and suits, coverings for days and nights spent walking, are fit armor. Stemming from desire but not limited to it, the queer diasporic as embodied by the black London migrant (in this chapter's example) names an insistently eluding relationship to community, an extravagant embrace of urban anonymity, and indeed a refusal

FIGURE 3.1. Jamaican immigrants arriving at Tilbury on board the ex-troopship *Empire Windrush*. ©DOUGLAS MILLER/GETTY IMAGES.

of any attempt to confine a subject to the limits of identity. The enclosures of surface presentation—clothing—are the most vivid features of this version of the queer diasporic in *The Lowlife*, but this is not where things end. My readings arise from what I consider to be a paradigmatic novelistic instantiation of this formation—the Jamaican novelist Andrew Salkey's novel *Escape to an Autumn Pavement* (1960). Through this queer little novel, first forgotten but now revived, I inaugurate the deterritorialized belonging that is the second half of this book. The queer diasporic becomes a structure for understanding how it can be possible to belong while rejecting the strictures of conventional relationality.

Recent queer theory's antirelational impulse is instructive here. This turn toward describing queerness as antisocial, nonproductive, and radically antiteleological can loosely be described through a critical trajectory from Leo Bersani's *Homos* (1996) to Judith Halberstam's *The Queer Art of Failure* (2011), with Lee Edelman's *No Future* (2004) arriving as a particularly strident clarion call for queerness as social refusal.[6] Heather Love's *Feeling Backwards* (2007)—also sometimes identified as part of this critical line—articulates a wistful pessimism about the likelihood of finding positive representations of queer relationships in historical novels, a wistfulness that harmonizes particularly well with what I find when I look back to Salkey as potential fountainhead of contemporary queer Caribbean literature. Critical wistfulness presumes a desire to find queer history that Caribbeanists are generally okay with claiming—such has been the tedium of the "West Indian homophobia" discourse against which such research sets itself. Further, Love's interest in finding something useful to do with the less-than-stellar models for queer lineage in early twentieth-century fiction invites a critical attention to a novel like Salkey's that is very enabling. Love writes:

> As we consider the history of queer representation, it is crucial that we recognize how central the failure of community is in such representations. Such a recognition in turn asks that we expand our sense of what counts as a relationship ... and suggests that we might need to rethink what counts as legitimate or significant political emotions. We know that "hope for a better form of existence" counts as political, but what about feelings of loss, despair, anger, shame, and disgust, feelings represented so richly in many twentieth-century queer texts? Can we begin to think about mobilizing emotions like these?"[7]

With a main character like the one with which we are presented in *Escape to an Autumn Pavement* it is necessary to find a way to make sense of a sort of jaundiced hopefulness alongside all those feelings of "loss, despair, anger, shame, and disgust"—to make some kind of sense, that is, such that we understand this negativity as also enabling attachment. I find that we only need follow Johnnie Sobert, the Jamaican-born London-migrant protagonist of Salkey's novel, in order to discover how his refusals are also attachments. When at one moment he explicitly invokes his anti-social impulses, he posits them as two forms of attachment in conflict with each other, rather than as a rejection of attachment altogether: "two anti-social emotions," he thinks to himself about his stressful erotic entanglements; "to be of service to one, carnally; to be at ease with and to be affectionate to the other."[8] As I will show, Johnnie does not go on to choose either of those paths. He suspends a decision about himself and his loves and the novel imposes an ending in which he, and the reader, "must learn to wait and wait and wait."[9] I want to argue that it is in this deferral that the queer diasporic inheres. A belonging in which the unit of measure is as much time as space is the sort of belonging Johnnie Sobert models for us.

Diaspora, then, lends to the queer refusal of lineage, futurity, and community a strong countervailing impulse toward an embrace of potential, a better that must be to come. When Johnnie suffers his own impatience—"wait and wait and wait"—I see this not only as a critique of his present circumstances but as an emphatic orientation toward the future, what the late performance critic Jose Muñoz might call a utopian formation; that is, a set of desires "always directed at the thing that is not yet here . . . moments that burn with anticipation and promise."[10] This is different from nationalist teleology or conventional reproductive futurity because its potency lies in the holding of the moment that is to come, not in arriving at it. Formally, in Salkey's novel, this impulse expresses itself not quite so pleasurably as in several of Muñoz's texts, which burn with "queer relational bliss" (James Schuyler's poem "A Photograph") or the "queenly identification" in the stomp of performer Kevin Aviance, his "sway-back walk" that appropriates high glamour while rendering the gestural trace of "black and queer racialized survival."[11] No, in *Escape* we have a cranky first-person narrator who is nearly unwavering in his sullenness and a narrative that never "goes anywhere," so to speak, structured around Johnnie's doubling-back, flitting between choices he does not want to make, and ultimately embracing a kind of suspension that similarly leaves the reader up in the air. But one senses that for Salkey pleasure is not precisely the point of this novel. In relation to Muñoz's readings of works often characterized by rather striking beauty, and by a recovery of pleasure from the snarls of oppression, I see Salkey's novel as most similar to those photographs by Kevin McCarty of empty punk stages. The novel's tripartite scaffolding presents three phases of Johnnie's passages through London, traversals that are mostly devoid of classic novelistic development. The barrenness of the plot, however, and the austere presentation of London spaces characterized by their being stridently inhospitable to Johnnie's joy, defies cheaper renderings of exoticized Caribbean-esque "sheebeens" (see Colin MacInnes).[12] Along the edges, though, especially when Johnnie is walking the streets, there are glimpses of possibility—like the "small shimmering light bulbs" edging the barren stage of McCarty's photograph of the Catch One nightclub in Los Angeles.[13] These glimpses of what might be possible, coupled with Johnnie's critique of what is, including his complete refusal to identify with anything—this is the point of the novel, its importance to the Caribbean literary canon, and why I choose it to define the possibilities of belonging I name the queer diasporic.

Perhaps because diasporic subjects have been habituated to belonging where they should not, to connecting to people with whom difference is pronounced, any antirelational principle in the context of the queer diasporic does not end in a grim cul-de-sac—neither in Salkey's novel, nor in the queer of color theory that helps to inform my reading of it. Muñoz, for one, proposes an expansive utopianism that is hopeful even as it celebrates elusiveness. Through the only quasi-lovable protagonist of *Escape to an Autumn Pavement* and his increasingly attenuated presence within a complex network of relations in postwar, post-Windrush London, I offer a mediating space between queer anti-relationality and heteronormative or homosocial community. *Escape to an Autumn Pavement* provides a model for diasporic belonging at the center of a transformative moment in British history when the queer bourgeois migrant subject cuts across racial, class, and sexual identities to illuminate the implications of these identities and ultimately to reject their strictures.

To render the refined but powerful difference offered by Salkey and his character, it is necessary for me to trace the gendered, sexual, and communitarian alternatives (ultimately unsatisfying alternatives) to the queer diasporic in 1950s Britain. These present quite clearly within the domestic sphere of postwar Britain because the implications of racial commingling in the wake of massive colonial migration (from the West Indies especially and at first) gave rise to discourses in a wide variety of contexts — newspapers, academic sociology, popular film, racist sloganeering — in which domesticity was a key concept. The body politic was represented both as a home to be protected and, simultaneously, as suffused with the violent and eroticized intimacy of physical proximity. The colonies were outstaying their welcome and things were getting close. And the convergence of discourses around homosexuality and West Indian migration meant that both figured in postwar legal and media contexts as issues in which nothing less than Englishness was at stake. Black male colonials were the wrong color, white male homosexuals were problematically gendered, and these figurations laid side by side described a false choice between racial masculinity and gendered nationality that Johnnie Sobert rejects. In his rejection, as in the modes of theoretical queerness informing my analysis, Johnnie presents a potent possibility, a queering of the migrant communal formations that developed during the Windrush era, and a model of proto-queer Caribbean subjectivity beyond that era.

Johnnie's life in London is the affirmation of refusal. He refuses conviviality. He resists the community of other West Indian subjects, the vibrant transnational "Caribbeanness" being created in the crucible of migration documented in such archives as CAM (of which Salkey, we remember, was a founding member) and represented in more famous novels by Sam Selvon[14] and George Lamming.[15] He embodies the black colonial flaneur belonging to no one country, to no one person, to no single erotic affiliation, and he does so in a way that exceeds even the companionable homosocial vagabondage of Claude McKay's novels a generation and a half earlier.[16] Indeed, at one typically rash moment of conjecture, Johnnie apparently refuses hope: "I knew that the future was a myth."[17] Though Johnnie quickly reverses himself on that point — the novel could be said to be structured by Johnnie's thought reversals — his refusals are nevertheless striking, and they stem from his reading of migrant communities as exhibiting exclusionary features of the nationalism he has fled and has been working assiduously to avoid in migrancy. His encounters in his compatriot Larry's barbershop, for instance, betray the peculiarly sharp loneliness that accompanies compulsory intimacy: "Larry and Ringo [another Jamaican habitué] seemed distant, almost completely outside my own tight, neurotic world. They were acquaintances; but they really didn't touch any part of my immigrant experience. I could patronize them; feel like being with them; even suffer them in a nasty, pompous way; but I couldn't truly, honestly, have more than a passing interest in their affairs."[18] Apart from Johnnie's profound inclination toward introjection, he diagnoses the scene itself as formally brittle, bereft of all but the most mannered and perfunctory workings of communal recreation. The performances of national bonhomie not only ring false; they lack even the compensatory conviviality of humor we see in Selvon's portrayal of the most cynical migrant interactions. And when Larry eventually lambastes Johnnie for living with a man, it is confirmation that Johnnie's desire for men, and his domestic arrangement with one of them, are dismissed on national as much as on supposedly moral grounds: "Can't you see that you doing something that is not your duty to do? Your duty is to feel sorry for your own people, not to try to compromise. As a matter of fact, that's what I really notice is wrong about you.... Look like you sell out to the other side."[19] Larry eventually apologizes for his rant. But the turns his speech takes are revealing, particularly the slippage throughout between the indictment of Johnnie's choice of mate by turns because he is white and because he is male. Selling out to "the other side" is sometimes whiteness, sometimes queerness, and the uncertainty this vacillation creates reveals a conflation between the terms.

Yet, despite Larry's notion that Johnnie's queerness makes him, in fact, *too English*, Johnnie does not have access to the emerging space for homosexuality within the national boundaries of Britain, either. This is in part due to race, as I will discuss shortly. It is also because Johnnie's most vibrant erotic feelings are constituted by subsumed rage, not respectable domesticity. My reading of Johnnie's relationship to his working-class neighbor Gerald Trado—one side of the rooming-house quadrangle that Johnnie forms with Gerald's wife, Fiona, as well as with his eventual cohabitant Dick Snape—is that its sublimated erotic violence is the most revelatory of the specific class dimensions of the queer diasporic, defined as it is by black colonial bourgeois subjectivity and white English working-class resentment. In post-Windrush Britain, as questions about which subjects had access to the category of Englishness became more urgent, England was increasingly figured as a domestic family in which black subjects were problematic, potentially explosive interlopers. Following this metaphor and extending it,

Salkey represents the simmering erotic entanglements of Johnnie's rooming house as a dysfunctional family in which the animus between male subjects across race and class enables the development of a striking diasporic figure: solitary, simmering, with free-floating rage, boredom, and eros that attaches at will and then retracts. The possibility of this form of subjectivity—what makes it different from the strictly anti-relational queer subject—is the novel's end. Johnnie has left the flat he has shared with Dick, having already left the rooming house that was the site of that whole other sphere of eroticized and hostile intimacy. His eventual disappearance on the last pages of the novel is, for me, the "then and there of queer futurity," to quote Jose Muñoz. This is a futurity that in its conjoined locatability (the city sidewalk) and open-endedness (an unspecified escape; a set of affective and sexual choices perpetually suspended) eludes the normative logic of telos and reproduction but embraces the potential, the then and there, of some goodness that must be coming. Fiona had once accused Johnnie of aimlessness, asking him what he *really* wanted to do and saying: "Nobody bothers to take the journey that you've taken from the West Indies for sheer pointless escape. If you escape, there's always a plan at the end of it somewhere."[20] As it turns out, Johnnie embodies a powerful form of Caribbean diaspora precisely because the apparent pointlessness of his journey *is* the plan.

The queer diasporic as implied by the novel's ending is mirrored in spectral presences and refusing voices I found in London archives, as I began searching for others like Johnnie. I lay some of these fragmented voices out throughout the course of this chapter and suggest why forms of archival disappearance may also be read as queer diasporic incorporation—a refusal of the project of the archive and a space-making within the limitations of the British body politic. These archival voices function uncannily like Johnnie at the end of the novel. It is Johnnie, after all, when fuming about both Dick *and* Larry's imposition of a homosexual identity onto him, who thinks: "They made me know that truly 'whole people' whatever that means, were tagged, always have been, pigeonholed, easily classified, easily lumped in a bundled mess, conveniently distributed to a waiting mob of diagnosticians, analysts, observers, recorders."[21] In lieu of that mob of analysts, queer diasporic voices await readers who, as Omi'seke Natasha Tinsley has argued, are willing to suspend any determination of gender, sexuality, and indeed, place in favor of reading both landscape and sexuality as ongoing processes, processes in which desire and identity are often fugitive, hidden, and at some level invisible.[22] Anglo-queer theory has often relied, Tinsley notes, on "an Enlightenment-inspired bifurcation between the invisible and the visible . . . in which invisibility and privacy are linked to oppression."[23] Our disappeared Johnnie merges with London pavements and, at least as far as Salkey's novel suggests, he is in some measure freer than he ever could be otherwise.

Salkey and the Queer Diasporic

In the development of a modern corpus of Caribbean literature, Andrew Salkey has, until very recently, been overlooked. Yet the enormity and scope of his work; his centrality to the community of artists in London; his descriptions of the fairly pervasive though little-analyzed phenomenon of Caribbean middle-class angst; his considerable contribution to several important archives, including CAM and the Bogle-Louverture Press—all these are argument enough for more serious consideration of Salkey's work. Aspects of his corpus, especially his early novels (*Escape to an Autumn Pavement; The Late Emancipation of Jerry Stover* [1968]; *The Adventures of Catullus Kelly* [1969]), have even greater salience now than ever. To a critical moment when Caribbean cultural studies has begun more seriously to consider sexuality as a central part of the familiar analytical matrix nation-race-gender, Salkey offers insightful, prescient fiction that manages all these terms. His work uses sex to think about a complex of issues relating to class, race, and national belonging. In Salkey's work, we find anticipated many of the issues that are in play in contemporary debates about sexuality, identity, and black queer desire: the effect of migration on the construction of the self; the politics of competing localities; the conjunctions and disjunctions of nationalism and sexual identity; masculinity and class in images of Caribbean nationhood. His novels also help us to see that alongside popular discourses against homosexuality and literary tropes of heterosexuality engendering the nation, there is a separate, distinct tradition of homosociality in Caribbean culture.[24] In Salkey's novels, and especially in his London novels, the society of men is privileged, and we recall that at least in the first wave of migration to England, men from the colonies outnumbered women to a great degree.

Salkey's representation of the educated middle-class colonial in Britain is unique among his literary peers. If we recall Lamming's claim that "the West Indian novel . . . has restored the West Indian peasant to his true and original status of personality," we will remember that many of the fictions of the West Indian literary renaissance of the 1950s—and certainly the ones that are still read and taught today—feature poor or rural characters.[25] Novelists were reckoning with the legacy of colonialism, concerned to discover the unique aesthetic contribution of the islands, and focused understandably on representing the denigrated creolized forms of the working-class black and Asian majority of the region. This made historical and aesthetic sense, though it did have some problematic effects at the level of reception, creating an almost uniform impression of West Indian characters and their relationship to the metropole. This has no doubt impacted Salkey's reception, concerned as he was not just with the poor Jamaican worker (as in his first novel, *A Quality of Violence* [1959]) but also with the confusions and motivations of a privileged class of men who found themselves in England abashed by their dual sense of intimacy with and distance from the "motherland."[26] Arthur Drayton's 1969 article "Awkward Questions for Jamaicans," in the *Journal of Commonwealth Studies*, reported on a panel at the University of the West Indies at which Salkey was asked to defend his portrayal of the middle-class in the sphere of English letters.[27] There was a sense that representing Jamaica's best and brightest as ambivalent drifters was a betrayal of the public mandate of the West Indian writer abroad.

As representations of the Caribbean homosocial, Salkey's early novels are also foundational. I will come to what this looks like in *Escape*, but the two other Salkey novels of the sixties also betray a deep skepticism about the possibilities of heterosexuality—male-female relationships being almost invariably marked by tawdriness or anaesthetized compulsion.[28] The novels feature sturdy and deeply affective ties between men. Among the lettered and bored Kingston set in *The Late Emancipation of Jerry Stover* and later in swinging London with *The Adventures of Catullus Kelly*, Salkey portrays male-female relationships that are strikingly at odds with the security of male-male alliances. Furthermore, the cynicism and torpor of Salkey's heroes demonstrate the insecurity of a certain kind of middle-class man, groomed for power but uncertain of his place in the nation, displaced in migrancy and displaced too in a rapidly changing homeland. It is telling that when I first began working on *Escape to an Autumn Pavement*, it was no longer in print. The work was "awkward," to use Arthur Drayton's term—pessimistic about the uses of community and bristling at the strictures of the nation. The characters went to London to feel free. These sentiments were mirrored in the rhetoric and the structure of the sixties novels each of which is marked by stilted, self-conscious first-person narration and jerky, meandering, nondevelopmental plots. Salkey's fictions were at odds with the cultural nationalist narratives of independence, and deeply strange at that.

As students and critics slowly began to rediscover this work, however— through online used bookstores and neglected sections of libraries— excitement began to grow.[29] The Jamaican writer Thomas Glave excerpted a section of *Escape to an Autumn Pavement* in his edited collection *Our Caribbean: A Gathering of Gay and Lesbian Writing from the Antilles* (2009) and subsequently spearheaded a reprint of the novel by Peepal Tree Press.[30] This long-neglected novel by Salkey is now benefiting from the queer trajectory in critical Caribbean studies. Not only is the novel's subject matter of literary historical interest but its very queer, thwarting structure now fits with an interest in uneven plot development, teleological skepticism, and refusal.

A brief account of the novel's plot, such as it is, may be usefully dispensed with at this point. Young Johnnie Sobert moves to England and haunts various London rooms—his drab bedsit in Notting Hill, the club he works at in Soho, Larry's barbershop, his gentleman's flat with Dick Snape near Leicester Square. Johnnie's traversal through post-Windrush London rooms is a claustrophobic mirroring of his impacted, thwarted thinking. When at the end of the novel he takes to the street, his disappearance is the logical extension of an increasingly attenuated character—thin and thinly drawn, all the better to elude capture by any constituting force of community. Johnnie has no time for incipient West Indian nationalism, those mandates encased in his mother's hectoring missives from home. He has no use for a conventional love affair with a woman. And he has no feel for how to be in his deepening and companionable domestic arrangement with Dick. His narration is full of abandonments and changes of mind, producing a frustrating, thwarted feeling in the story, unfolding as it does primarily in his own head. It is, thus, an unsettling and at times frustrating novel. But it is an apt way to experience the mind of a person defined by an inability to make progress, an allergy to settled social arrangements, and an unspoken, only slowly dawning awareness of his erotic desires. In the community of midcentury London immigrants, becalmed by ennui, Johnnie's most animating attachments are the powerfully negative, erotically charged, almost entirely interior animus he carries for his rooming-house neighbor, the working-class Brit Gerald Trado. Between them is a generative interclass hate. And in Johnnie's inability to fit into West Indian community in England, and his near embrace of life with Dick, is an implicit critique of the strictures and the pressures of migrant conviviality. Thus, Johnnie embodies a different version of diaspora from that captured by "Windrush London." Another form of diasporic belonging, one framed around Johnnie's queer suspended identification and his poorly defined, fuzzy-edged, and increasingly attenuated characterization, provides a model for belonging as escape. This, to recapitulate, is a future-oriented belonging, a feeling for a place that relies on the belief in a surely finer place to come. This is the queer diasporic.

At the center of a novel about a man's deferral of his sexual identity is a rather blunt naming pun. The other half in Johnnie's domestic arrangement has a name harboring both childlike (*See Dick run!*) and adult associations, and Dick Snape emerges less like a literary character and more as a function through whom Johnnie explores possibilities for himself. The name also allows for moments of sophomoric double entendre, as when Johnnie is on yet another unpleasant assignation with Fiona and thinks: "Anything to forget Dick for a while"; and then a few moments later, "Dick's on the brain, again."[31] These phallic and nominative incursions into Johnnie and Fiona's sex raise the question of how to define Johnnie's relationship with Dick, whose ambiguities gesture to the type of queer diasporic belonging that Johnnie models. Though Johnnie does not experience anything intensely libidinous with Dick, he cares for him—"Why should I like him as much as I do?" he once asks himself—and to that extent theirs is a modern, postwar, post-Wolfenden, "homosexual" plot line. The historian Matt Houlbrook might call what Dick and Johnnie have "respectable" homosexuality, with its restraint, middle-class air, and lack of overt sexuality.[32] Houlbrook argues that in the wake of more spectacular cases of queer male sexuality reproduced for public consumption during the fifties and sixties in England, forms of middle-class queer decorousness emerged, modes of cohabitation in reputable postcodes in which gay men were at pains to perform styles of dyadic living that mirrored those of bourgeois heterosexual coupling. (*Look, we're just like you!*) Though a reader cannot trust Johnnie's assertion that he has not slept with Dick, it really doesn't matter one way or another for their lives together to conform to this line of postwar homosexual domesticity. His ultimate inability to live out this domestic bliss is yet another sign of his queer refusal of conventional community.

Dick's relationship with Johnny is in the lineage of homosexuality as identity, which is why Dick forces Johnny to make a choice between him and Fiona, urges him to "make up his mind" about himself.[33] We know that Johnnie has deep emotional ties to Dick that he has to no one else. He tells Fiona that his "life with Dick is very uneventful. It's steady. It's relaxing and it's happiness nearly all the time."[34] When he first seeks his compatriot Larry's advice, he says he's "sure of it!" when Larry asks if he is happier living with Dick than with a woman.[35] And when he sleeps with Fiona after moving in with Dick, he feels he has cheated on Dick. The relationship illustrates the complexities of the homosexual-homosocial continuum. Dick and Johnnie show that it is entirely possible to be homosexual without necessarily having sex. The corollary is true of Johnnie and Fiona, who prove that it is possible to have heterosexual sexual intercourse without being straight.

To call *Escape to an Autumn Pavement* an early "gay" Caribbean novel, then, is to run up against some difficulty. What is interesting to me is not so much the novel's instantiation of the Caribbean literary tradition of gay male representation. It is, rather, the narratives of class and colonial belonging surrounding male eros and affection that provide a far richer and thornier set of representations and that underpin my sense of how the diasporic might be inflected with queerness. The novel works so well at doing this in part because it lays side by side two very different classed and eroticized relationships between men. The first and more prominent narrative involves Johnnie and Dick. The second narrative, briefer but no less important, involves Johnnie's intense relationship with Gerald Trado. The two men identify with and are repelled by each other in equal measure, hostile and interested, each fearful that the other might compromise his claims to Englishness. To my mind the pressures of masculinity and class are worked out most fully in the intense dynamic between Johnnie and Trado. This parade of homosocial anxiety is particularly well defined in the novel because it is laid alongside the rather staid arrangement with Dick, from which it is distinguished. Indeed, if *Escape* is one of the first novels by a Caribbean writer to narrativize male same-sex desire, it is fair to ask whether this is done more clearly through Dick, whom Johnnie loves, or Trado, whom Johnnie hates. One would be forgiven for imagining that *Escape to an Autumn Pavement* is "about" Johnnie's quest to make sense of his identity in London, a quest that is centered on a choice he must make between two lovers. The novel appears to set up the choice starkly between "heterosexuality," described always in terms of a suffocating, pathological enclosure, and "homosexuality," defined as a situation of settled, quasi-contented domesticity. However, neither of these plotlines actually provides any true moment of crisis or narrative drama in the novel. I would argue instead that the most intense—if apparently divergent—plotline is reserved, by far, for Johnnie's working-class nemesis, Trado.

Johnnie's entrenchment with Trado forms in the wake of a heated encounter surrounding Trado's books. Early in the novel, when Trado summons Johnnie to his room to berate him about late rent, Johnnie coolly sizes up his collection of little magazines and novels. His apparently casual assessment of Trado's tastes is meant to contrast with Trado's effortful acquisition of culture and to mark out a crucial class and culture difference between the two men:

> Sexy boy Trado is sprawling in an armchair. Quite obviously reading *The Observer*. Quotes Ken Tynan the way a Jamaican peasant quotes the Bible. . . . Carpet by mantlepiece a trifle threadbare; just the spot where jolly Trado takes his stand after a hard night at the pub and lays down the law on anything *The Observer* had already made clear to him the Sunday before.
>
> In the left-hand corner, a delightful tortoise-shell cat, curled protectively against the thick Sunday-newspaper atmosphere. Multicoloured cushions. Ubiquitous Penguins, little reviews, Thomas Manns, Evelyn Waughs, and precious back numbers of *Horizon*.
>
> Oh, man! Am I not glad I'm a bloody waiter!
>
> All protective colouring. All that keeping up with the dead literary Joneses—museum bait.[36]

"Sexy boy Trado" sprawled in his armchair is simultaneously a figure of scorn and passion for Johnnie. He knows that Trado is engaged in a project of self-improvement, acquiring culture for class mobility. Johnnie's more secure intellectual status means that he recognizes the modernist slant to

Trado's collection and can be dismissive about Kenneth Tynan. The phrase "protective colouring" applies equally to both men: Johnnie disguises his pain at migrant and racial exclusion with nonchalance, Trado his British class inferiority with books. The analogy Johnnie draws between Trado and a Jamaican peasant is telling. In England, Johnnie is finding that his race and colonial background place him in a much more complicated relationship to British workers above whom he is educated. All Trado's conspicuous learning is supposed to be pitiable to Johnnie, who, effortlessly bright, need not show off. (He is of course, as a narrator, showing off to us.)

When Trado tries to racially humiliate Johnnie, insinuating he might run off without paying the rent, Johnnie's normally distant, ironic self-commentary explodes into one of the only scenes of real passion in the novel, no less intense for occurring entirely in Johnnie's mind. At first he admonishes himself: "Ignore him. He's lonely. He's anxious. He's insecure. He's bisexual. He's unhappy. He's anything. For God's sake, just don't do anything stupid. Hold on, boy!"[37] However, in the next moment Johnnie is recanting: "Can't let his jackass get away with all this! Might as well jump him and be over with it. Surely, it's the only way to deal with a crap hound like Trado. Of course, there's no use in behaving like a *civilized chap*. No use behaving the way my mother would want me to, responsibly and politely; the way she would be proud of; the way a *little gentleman* is brought up to behave; the way up to the bloody stars! I'll just mess his face about a bit; and as I'm about it, I might as well smash his little library-cum-castle of a room."[38] The appeal to middle-class colonial values as a safeguard against violence shows how closely Johnnie's class identity plays into his physical and sexual repression. And all this intense feeling around books is one of the most distinctive aspects of the hostility and angst between working-class and colonial characters in the postwar era. White workers sometimes found themselves striving for an Englishness that educated black and brown colonials already felt at ease in having. In Alexander Baron's *The Lowlife*, the postwar British novel I invoked at the beginning of this chapter, the protagonist, Harryboy, is another in the line of the working-class autodidact and he muses on the fate of such a man when he meets another, his upstairs neighbor Vic. When the two characters happen upon each other in the local library, Harryboy notes: "Among the uneducated (which frankly is what you would call the general population where I live) the serious reader is a lonely person. He goes about among the crowds with his thoughts stuffed in him. He probably dare not even mention them to his nearest pals for fear of being thought a schmo. There's a hunger in his eyes for someone to talk to. He watches, and from time to time when he sees someone likely, he makes his signals. His situation is very much like that of the nancyboy."[39] Baron's riff on the similarities between the reader and the homosexual resonates with Salkey's novel of a few years earlier. Johnnie Sobert would recognize the sense of lonesome singularity that comes from having "thoughts stuffed in him," working his way through the crowds of London streets looking for someone likely. And Gerald Trado would recognize the loneliness of the serious reader among the less educated. What is telling in *Escape to an Autumn Pavement* is that Johnnie and Trado do not, like Vic and Harryboy in *The Lowlife*, bond over their shared love of books. There is no meeting of the minds in Salkey's novel, only an intensely felt subterranean desire and violence that is acted out, unsurprisingly, through the medium of Trado's girlfriend, Fiona. The difference is racial. Trado does not feel that he can afford to bond with Johnnie, insecure as his own class status is. And Johnnie has only his felt intellectual superiority over Trado to guard against the racist insults he suffers from him. Intellectual bonding would eliminate Johnnie's sense of academic security, the only inheritance of his colonial upbringing that he seems to believe has had some positive effect.

This anxiety around the working-class boy who becomes educated was in the air in late fifties and early sixties Britain. Richard Hoggart's *The Uses of Literacy* (1957), one of the first works in what became the influential movement of British cultural studies, used the grammar school system (of which he was himself a beneficiary) to think through the implications of class mobility—and indeed to reflect on what he came to see as the cultural losses of working-class economic gains. "The valuable social changes of the last fifty years," Hoggart writes at one point, have arrived with "accompanying cultural changes [that] are not always an improvement but in some of the more important instances a worsening."[40] Hoggart focuses mainly on the undoing of the family structure and the deleterious effects of "new mass culture," but he also spares a thought for what he calls "the uprooted and the anxious," those working-class scholarship boys and autodidacts who move into greater literacy without an accompanying sense of social ease or prestige. The similarities in description between Hoggart's nervous working-class reader and Johnnie's mockery of Gerald Trado are uncanny. Hoggart talks about the "ostentatious adoption of protective co-louring" that some middle-class aspirants take on, lacking the poise either of the securely middle class or the brilliant and earnest working-class man who makes it through mobility unscathed.[41] He (somewhat phobically) describes a situation of feminization that mirrors Johnnie's attempt to psy-chologize Trado's sexuality ("he's bisexual") when he writes of the smart working-class boy being separated from "the lads" and his tendency to be "closer to the women of the house than to the men."[42] Hoggart writes: "Such a scholarship boy has lost some of the resilience and some of the vitality of his cousins who are still knocking about the streets. . . . his sexual growth is perhaps delayed."[43]

There are the others, too, not the scholarship boys but the ones who never made it to grammar school and who nevertheless strive for intellec-tual improvement, men like Trado. This kind of man "cannot face squarely his own working-class," is sometimes "ashamed of his origins," and conse-quently "provides himself with a mantle of defensive attitudes." "He tries to read all the good books, but they do not give him that power of speech and command over experience which he seeks. He is as gauche there as he is with the craftsman's tools."[44] Indeed, a passage in Hoggart's almost anthropological description of the working-class reader sounds uncannily like Johnnie Sobert's judgmental assessment of Trado's books. Summing up the naïve reading choices of the self-taught worker, Hoggart writes:

> I have in mind the reading of cultural publications which is from one aspect improper, which is inspired by too strong and too vague an ex-pectation. It is my impression that this kind of interest in serious pub-lications is more common than is generally thought. . . .
>
> For some people the late *John O'London's Weekly* obviously met a strong felt need, one stronger, I think, than it could have legitimately claimed to meet. Others are proud of reading J. B. Priestly and writers such as him, because they are "serious writers with a message." Others have learned that Mr. Priestly is a "middlebrow" and only mention him in tones of deprecation. They tend to read bitterly ironic or anguished literature — Waugh, Huxley, Kafka and Greene. They own the Penguin selection from Eliot, as well as some other Penguins and Pelicans; they used to take *Penguin New Writing* and now subscribe to *Encounter*. They know a little, but often only from reviews and short articles, about

Frazer and Marx; they probably own a copy of the Pelican edition of Freud's *Psychopathology of Everyday Life*. They sometimes listen to talks on the Third Programme with titles like, "The Cult of Evil in Contemporary Literature."[45]

It is interesting to discover that a character in a middle-class West Indian writer's novel would make assessments about working-class intellectual striving similar to those of a British-born academic drawn from the ranks of those he analyzed. But this convergence only amplifies the sense that shifts in working-class culture were visible not only as improvements but also as anxieties. And, while it is beyond the scope of my current project, this convergence of West Indian fiction with British cultural studies at its very inception in *The Uses of Literacy*, bears noting. The shared concerns and modes of inquiry between writers from abroad and British intellectuals developing new models to ask questions of British culture is a fascinating one, a convergence that helps to contextualize the fact that Jamaican-born Stuart Hall eventually emerged as the leading cultural studies critic of England.

There is one last, silent eruption from Johnnie during his weird tête-a-tête with Trado. Interrupted again, Johnnie thinks: "Hit him! Hit him murderously hard and be done with it. Bash whatever little brains he has left and feel like a man afterwards. There's only one way to get out of this with any satisfaction, and it is done with a touch of violence. Not enough to land in prison. Just enough to restore the balance of power. That's all. Drive him a nice one in the mouth, and two swift ones in the guts."[46] Having, of course, not done any of these sexually violent things, Johnnie climbs the stairs to his room where he has the following elliptical thoughts: "Door knob feels like Trado's head. Cold. Round. Easily destroyed. Wrenched off and discarded at the back of the house."[47] We get nothing else in the novel that approaches such intensity of feeling or evokes as much physicality or tactility as we do in these passages. Johnnie's assignations with Fiona (the aforementioned "Mrs. Trado") are strikingly disembodied. In contrast to the imagined feel of Trado's skull, the squash of his guts, Fiona's body is never imagined, and it is not even really felt. (When they first make love on Hampstead Heath, Johnnie recites poetry to himself in order to mimic the rhythms of sex: he drowns Fiona out with words.) The particular battle Johnnie has with Trado is homosocial to the extent that it maps beautifully onto what Eve Kosofsky Sedgwick describes in *Between Men* as "murderous ressentiment."[48] By fantasizing about "jumping" Trado, Johnnie can imagine breaking out of the confines of middle-class colonial respectability—experienced here as a feminized, ersatz version of robust English masculinity. To jump out of civilized confines is also to jump into physical intimacy with English masculinity. Johnnie is understandably enraged and confused: this is a fairly complicated reversal of the expectations of colonial British masculinity. His fantasy of pounding on Trado is the closest we get to action in a plot eccentric with digressions, pauses, and climactic punctures.

Trado is an irritant because no one else makes Johnnie feel as feminized and with no one else are his claims to Englishness as compromised. But Johnnie also identifies with Trado's ambivalent relationship to Englishness. The modern ideal of gentlemanly English conduct, forged along with empire in the eighteenth century, has a difficult relationship to the masculine body. On the one hand a proper English man was vigorous. He exercised control and intellectual mastery over his body. Deviations from this ideal—whether into unmanly foppery or Creole sexual licentiousness—deeply complicated a man's relationship to his Englishness. And there was always this danger; that attention to the physical ideal could veer into the unsafe territory of vanity or excess. A further complication occurs when this ideal is transplanted to the black colonial. Johnnie's school and his overbearing mother have trained him to aspire to a modern, bourgeois version of the English gentleman. But in an island colony where class distinctions must be closely guarded and, as Johnnie is always reminding Fiona, where there is little actual capital or money, Johnnie has also been taught to distinguish himself from those who work. The working class has tended to be associated with a threatening, deeply compelling version of masculine physicality. This is the conundrum Johnnie finds himself in: having been trained to contain physical expressions of rage, he has also been trained out of one of the most obvious expressions he could use to demonstrate superiority over Trado: violence. It is little wonder the abortive pounding Johnnie delivers takes on the force and frustration of unconsummated sex. Identification is often soluble with desire.

In a classic homosocial substitution for beating Trado to a pulp, Johnnie sleeps with Trado's woman. The Johnnie-Fiona-Trado triangle involves the novel's protagonist in one of the least savory heterosexual unions ever described in Caribbean fiction, one defined by a marked misogyny that, while inimical to the queer diasporic in its most expansive glory, cannot be overlooked in Johnnie Sobert's particular instantiation of it. Because of this reflexive sexism, and because Fiona functions primarily as a route through which to observe the classed and sublimated erotic dynamic between Johnnie and Trado that I find more interesting, I choose not to linger on Salkey's portrayal of Johnnie and Fiona. I will only briefly note that Johnnie's images of feminine corporeality are almost uniformly debasing and disgusted. Fiona's talk is likened to "albumen" exploding over everything; her perfume is sickeningly overwhelming. And when he does finally leave Fiona in order to set up a bachelor pad with Dick (though he later cheats with her), it is, he tells her, "to be rid of your overpowering passion and depressing sexuality."[49] It is at moments like these that we are tempted to imagine Johnnie is simply gay. But the application of the label misses the point. For one thing, misogyny does not equate with gay male desire. And for another, Johnnie is not unaware that he might be "that way," to invoke the Jamaican circumlocution. As the novel proceeds, the possibility is constantly in play, though Johnnie denies this at various times—most violently when Dick asks him gently but directly to make up his mind about himself, and Johnnie screams back, woundingly, "Look, I'm no *queer*!"[50] The point, it seems to me, is that Johnnie chafes at romantic enclosure, both when it is gynophobically represented by Fiona *and* when it is settled and happy, as it is with Dick.[51] By contrast, the agitation of his feelings around Trado are some of the most animated in the novel and direct the reader toward a queer dynamic contoured by particularities of class and colonial subjectivity operating during this period in British and Caribbean history.

Visualizing Intimate Hostility in Postwar Britain

In many popular representations of immigration in midcentury Britain, interactions between working-class subjects and middle-class migrants evince a complex stew of identification, repulsion, and desire that simmers and then boils over. Much of this conjoined admiration and anxiety around black bourgeois masculinity came out in so-called issue films that were contemporaneous with Windrush, Salkey, and shifts in the British class structure. An actor such as Bermuda-born Earl Cameron, for instance, who featured in several of these films, or Sidney Poitier, who performed, a bit later than the period under consideration here, in that classic film of black colonial reform *To Sir with Love* (1967), evinced a fine gentility and beauty that was at once threatening and unthreatening. So lovely to look at; so scarily like what we English are meant to be, yet so very black. The stakes, these films suggest, of the new commingling of the colonies and the motherland, were not just the very familiar fear of black men taking away white women, but the queerer, less well noted anxiety around the diminution of working-class claims to normative Englishness after a decade of gains in this direction. Caribbean colonials may have thought themselves arriving in a homeland to set themselves up, but all these filmic representations suggest that mass black arrival into the motherland had the status of catastrophe. And it was catastrophe of a very particular kind. Murder and riot feature heavily in representations of cross-race, cross-class interaction in postwar England. The violence is at once shocking and inevitable: built into the structure of the genre—either setting off the action or providing its dénouement—alarming in its implications, and yet resonant, as well, of Johnnie and Trado's interior explosions.

Popular films, such as Basil Dearden's *Pool of London* (1951) and *Sapphire* (1959), or the television movie *Flame in the Streets* (1961) directed by Roy Ward Barker, contrast West Indian migrants who in one way or another have a relationship to England that British working-class men, or families, perceive to be more settled or comfortable than their own.[52] These are often transitional families whose liminal class position creates insecurity that blooms into rage. There is rage, however, on both sides. And filmic narratives of cross-class racial encounter are often domestic narratives that allow for the contradictions of intimacy, desire, and hostility to be observed at the full intensity of their interiority for both British and West Indian characters. Dearden, who was one of the major British directors for Ealing Studios, made dozens of films of various genres for the company and several films that directly addressed "social issues," from youth delinquency to homosexuality and race relations. *Pool of London* and *Sapphire* dealt directly with the black presence in England, and with the ensuing complications of race, class, and sexuality. The screenwriter Ted Willis, who wrote *Flame in the Streets*, was also prolifically involved in the production of social issue films during this period. Both Dearden and Willis were recognized for their work on these films: *Sapphire* was judged

Best British Film by the British Academy of Film in 1960, and Willis won the Academy's award for best screenplay in 1962. As examples of popular entertainment with the imprimatur of the British cultural establishment, these films showcase the status of race as a "problem" at this moment and the complications that ensue when popular forms attempt to address or even propose solutions for it. The films all include a crucial plot point, moment, or juxtaposition in which members of the English working class feel their survival is contingent on the fate of black migrants. The rational temper of British culture is threatened, though ostensibly not by the black figures who are at the center of the plot but by the irrational prejudice that victimizes them. In each film, there is a character who represents a magnanimous tendency toward racial equality (Dan and Pat in *Pool of London*) or sound English good sense at the silliness of race prejudice (Superintendent Hazard in *Sapphire* and Jacko in *Flame in the Streets*). And these sensible characters are counterpoised against violent and irrational white characters—workers—whose extreme views result in raging outbursts, senseless riot, or murder.

Attempts to cordon off racial hysteria (many of the most violent racist perpetrators in these films are women) from the mainstream of English experience, however, are undermined by the films' class details. By positioning working-class characters alongside or against respectable black figures, these movies suggest that the more extreme forms of racism are the responses of a class and racial structure that is more thoroughly tense and difficult than can be inoculated by shots of intense violence. As Anne McClintock has written about an earlier period in British colonial popular representation, women and working-class subjects "at home" were important staging areas for racialized colonial relationships "abroad."[53] To the extent that, say, prostitutes and factory workers already occupied the lower regions of the great family of man, British imperial ideology had a ready-made template for organizing human categories that handily allowed for the incorporation of abject racialized subjects while preoccupying them all with disputes as to who most deserved to lay claim to an English gentility that could never be secure.

Thus, the emergence of a particular figure in postwar British representation of race relations: the genteel West Indian immigrant man. This figure crystallized a knot of anxiety around images of domestic order, throwing into disarray settled hierarchies equating physiognomy with

FIGURE 3.2. Film still from *Pool of London*, 1951.

moral achievement. And there was enough anxiety to go around: from the workers in the films, who were often portrayed as the most violently upset by changes wrought through immigration, to the supposedly more moderate bourgeois subjects, generally represented by figures associated with the law, who saw things more rationally but were concerned, too, about the implications of a changing social order. In the latter category were proxies for the liberal-minded filmmaker and the educated moviegoer who were exercised by issues of race. And in the casting of Earl Cameron, who appeared in *all three* of these issue films, there was the perfect embodiment of male Caribbean gentility.

Cameron played the kind of unthreatening black masculinity that would show up white prejudice as irrational and unfounded. It meant, however, that he played a version of West Indian respectability denuded of the fierce intelligence or culturally mandated confidence associated with the "outstanding" men of his generation who went overseas.[54] In *Pool of London*, his Johnny (another Jamaican John!) is so kind as to be naïvely drawn into a diamond theft plot. He must be saved from his own quiescence by the white friend who has gotten him into trouble in the first place. Even in the more complex characterizations of Dr. Robbins in *Sapphire* and Gomez in *Flame in the Streets* (here Cameron is able to show a moment of uncharacteristic frustration with his life, in a speech reminiscent of Walter Lee Younger in *A Raisin in the Sun*), Cameron's role in these films was to justify white characters' belief in the fundamental goodness of the mainstream of black migrants to England. This put Cameron in the curious position of playing characters whose distinguishing feature was their decency, whose job it was to act as a foil to more volatile and active characters; whose job, indeed, was essentially to stand still while others reacted *to* him. Providing for, shall we say, a somewhat limited dramatic palate, these circumstances meant that while satisfying a liberal desire for a certain black masculine type, Cameron's performances simultaneously revealed liberal qualms about other, potentially more frightening, types of black masculinity.

In this context, as I hope is becoming clear, *Salkey's* Johnnie takes on more interesting features. He is class secure (at least vis-à-vis Gerald Trado) but he is not good, not very respectable. Nevertheless, his cross-class intimacy with Trado harmonizes with the way these films represent working-class desires in complicated relation to black subjectivity. In *Pool of London*, for instance, Cameron stars as the upstanding Jamaican sailor who enjoys the camaraderie of life on the sea, usually feels lonely during calls at port (implicitly because of the racism he endures within European boundaries), and is beginning to hanker for a more settled life. His best friend on the ship is Dan MacDonald, a white sailor with a slightly indeterminate accent (he is played by the American-born actor Bonar Colleano, who worked professionally in England until his early death in a car crash), who is crooked to Johnny's straight arrow. It is Dan who gets entangled with an ill-fated plot to steal diamonds and smuggle them for sale in Holland. Johnny is the moral compass of the film; he sets the standard for respectability, fair dealing, and gentlemanly behavior. Everyone can vouch for him, and everyone likes him. But Dan becomes the moral center of the movie because it is he the film follows as he makes the choice to do the right thing, turn himself in, and save the unwitting Johnny from being implicated in the diamond heist.

Pool of London is set up to turn the expectation of black malfeasance on its head. The opening of the film contrasts monumental images of

London's landmarks with ominous string music. Some threatening incursion is arriving at London's docks, but this time the threat is not from uncertain and unfamiliar black faces. Earl Cameron's first shot in the film shows him smiling and at ease, affably helping Dan by taking his excess cigarettes through customs for him. Cameron is physically graceful, with settled, chiseled features, and the baritone voice and clear intonation of Paul Robeson. In contrast, Colleano's Dan MacDonald is slight and shifty. He is a man on the make, constantly coming up with schemes to evade the law and to get more than he can reasonably afford to expect as a young sailor. With Dan's slightly American provenance—a rat-a-tat-tat line delivery and a GI-style jacket—it is not he who represents the thwarted class mobility at odds with black respectability that we get in the Salkey and Baron novels. Indeed Dan *needs* Johnny and could not manage his schemes without the upstanding and loyal friend to carry off some of the legwork. But the film's weekend jaunt through London affords many views of the peculiarities of class and race in postwar England, with nods to the complexities of ethnicity thrown in. (The ship's Scottish engineer stays aboard for the entire weekend to read a collection called *English Verse*. He turns to Johnny at one point and declares, "This city looks like a jewel from afar, but close up it's all grime.")

On the first night out, Johnny accompanies Dan to a theater, waiting for him in the entryway. Pat, the beautiful and kind blonde girl selling tickets at the window, invites Johnny to watch the show through the back door while he waits. When the theater steward sees Johnny there, he angrily orders him away, shouting: "We've got enough of your lot paying for their seats." It is unclear which is more galling: a black man potentially cheating to see something he cannot afford to pay for or the fact that an increasing number of black people can actually afford to pay. Either way, the steward's reaction is miscalculated. Pat (played by Susan Shaw) jumps to Johnny's defense, spurns the steward, and eventually spends the evening with Johnny. Their impromptu date further associates the gentlemanly Johnny with refinement and class, juxtaposing him against Dan. While Johnny is out with his beautiful, polite, and very feminine date, Dan goes to pick up his girlfriend, Maisie, a rougher sort of girl whose relationship with Johnny is spiteful and selfish. Johnny pays for Pat's coffee and shields her from the rain. Meanwhile Maisie's sister opens the door to a dark house loud with screaming children. Maisie and her sister yell at each other over the din, cynical about their chaotic house and hard-drinking father: "Fat lot he'll care by closing time," is how Maisie responds when her sister invokes him.

This portrait of a working-class home coupled with the characters at the heart of the diamond heist plot constitutes a critique of settled notions surrounding English respectability, while simultaneously reinforcing classed assumptions about what happens when subjects attempt to get above their stations. After all, the masterminds of the ill-fated diamond heist are one Charlie Vernon and his brother, the former of whom is described as a man who "got the idea that the world owes him a living." Trying to buck up his brother's courage for the heist, Charlie eventually lambastes him: "You were going to be a big shot, your own boss, with everything you ever wanted, and what are you now? An ex-clerk with a pension you can't buy fags on." Charlie is, of all unlikely professions, an acrobat, and he describes his nervous older brother as "the respectable one of the family." The film suggests that British respectability is far more contingent than might be admitted and also perhaps less common. Respectable fair dealing cannot be relied on to get ahead and must be compromised when the promises of English fairness—that right living will result in just reward—are not forthcoming. When Johnny and Pat amble up to the Greenwich meridian, the central geographical location of London prompts a mirroring set of thoughts on the contingency of race. Johnny asks why London should be where time is first measured; then he asks why one man should be born black and the other white. But unlike those of Charlie Vernon, Johnny's musings do not lead to any action that violates these arbitrary rules.

When Johnny goes on an uncharacteristic drunken bender after failing to get up the courage to meet Pat on his last night in London, he finds himself in an after-hours bar, languishing. After his ne'er-do-well drinking buddy steals his money, he breaks, screaming that everyone in the bar, everyone in London, is "pushing me around." He punches a bar patron and is eventually thrown out of the bar, screaming. One of the men who throws him out of the bar says, "They're all the same," as Johnny lies in the gutter. But the point of *Pool of London* is precisely that the English tendency to misread race for class (in both senses of that word) blinds them to more nefarious tendencies in their midst. The film sets Johnny up as a good guy who is victimized by unsavory British elements. He remains an itinerant figure, unthreatening to the British fabric because he does not plan to try and weave himself into it. Despite his blossoming feelings for Pat and his halting declaration at the Greenwich Observatory that now he does want to "come back to the pool," the last shot of the movie is Johnny on the *Dunbar* waving to Dan on the shore. Dan stays to turn himself in and do the right thing; Johnny is on the boat out to sea.

Dearden's next movie with Earl Cameron made things even more complicated, primarily because Cameron played a character no longer so easily separated from the texture of British life. He is, rather, a settled, prosperous doctor who has always lived in Birmingham. Filming in lurid color, Dearden deliberately left behind the documentary-style black and white of *Pool of London*: "My idea is to throw all this [the somber winter background] into contrast with the sudden splashes of colour introduced by the coloured people themselves. The things they wear, the things they carry, their whole personality."[55] In addition, the wider variety of black characters who come in and out of the plot relieves Earl Cameron of the burden to represent blackness, though his import as a singular figure of colored goodness remains. There is more to say about *Sapphire*, a tantalizingly strange and undertheorized film, than I can manage here. Suffice it to say that it turns on the racially indeterminate body of the murdered titular character, whose corpse occupies the first shot of the film, thrown on a bed of leaves, white makeup chalky against her bright red hair. The punishment visited on a young woman who dares to transgress her racial identity is an old narrative and Dearden's film does not update it so much as contextualize it in a British setting, where passing narratives do not have the long tradition they do in the United States. Like classic American films of melodrama and passing, such as *Imitation of Life*, *Sapphire* is staked on the thematic of surface versus interior: the puzzle when these two elements do not apparently match; the crisis and betrayal that results in their being judged not to match.[56] A familiar play on black race as "natural," ineffably revealing, beneath the artifice of white passing proceeds alongside a prevailing interest in portraying British good sense in its wake. And so *Sapphire* includes discursive asides from legitimate sectors of British society—Superintendent Hazard; Sapphire's doctor, Burgess—who argue the coolly rational position that physical differences do not matter (judging the character of person based on color is as absurd as judging a policeman by the size of his feet, one character opines).

But the thematic conflict between surface and interiority is followed through from victim to aggressor and, in an interesting turn, moves from black woman to white. The murderer turns out to be Mildred Farr, the sister of Sapphire's white boyfriend, David Harris. Mildred is a neglected wife, a mother of twins whose sailor husband stays on the sea to avoid his duties at home. She is prickly about having to live with her parents and has grand aspirations for her young daughters—dance lessons and elocution. Her neat and orderly appearance belies a talent for murderous rage. When Millie finally confesses to the murder, her composed exterior falls away, and she screams with fury, recollecting the moment when Sapphire told her she was pregnant. Sapphire was so happy, so confident. Mildred's sense of powerlessness in the face of this joyful freedom brought to the surface her darkest parts. Not just Millie but the entire Harris family come to embody putatively imperiled white working-class values in a film populated by wealthy blacks, respectable white professionals, and West Indian gangsters. And it sets up white working-class mobility as hinging on the most intimate choices of a more prosperous black girl.[57] Earl Cameron, meanwhile, as poor Dr. Robbins, Sapphire's brother, presents as the reasonable mourner.

Finally, in *Flame in the Streets*, Cameron is allowed a moment to explode—though not before putting in his time as a decent, hardworking family man. If, in some ways, this film is the least artful of the arc of "issue films" creating the Cameron type I have been discussing, it is important in another sense. It is here that the themes of interracial domestic intimacy and imperiled British working-class positionality conjunct most forcefully. The film is oriented, after all, around a labor union drama. Cameron plays a hardworking warehouse foreman who has the opportunity to take on the supervisor's position permanently. One strand of the film puts his diligent quietism (his wife wishes he would stand up for himself more at work) against the idle threat of three white workers in the warehouse. At the beginning of the movie, when Cameron's character Gomez gives orders about work to be done in the warehouse, one of the black workers jokes agreeably, "He commence to talk like a real foreman now." Meanwhile, when the white supervisor Mitch asks the three white workers who have been hovering in the restroom if they ever do any work, one of them responds, "We're only white trash, mate," leering at Gomez's brown supervisor's coat. The question put to the film's flawed hero, the white union man Jacko Palmer, is: "Would you like to take orders from spades?" That question becomes intertwined with another one that Palmer and his wife have to answer by the end of the film: Would you have a black man as a son-in-law? Though Jacko supposedly has "as many principles as a monkey has fleas," neither of these questions can he answer easily or directly.

The film translates labor politics into domestic politics very early on. In the opening scenes, Mitch brings up the problem of Gomez's possible promotion by saying that white workers would resent this black worker's increase in pay.[58] If workers are beginning to expect the accouterments of middle-class life, then Mitch is concerned about the precariousness of their consumption and the way this consumer fragility is measured, however unfairly, against the achievements of blacks.[59] These struggles around the fate of the working-class home become focalized through two interracial couples, Cameron's Gomez and his white wife, Judy, and Jacko's daughter Kathie and her Jamaican romantic interest, Peter. Taking place over the course of Guy Fawkes Day, the brewing tensions, punctuated by the staccato clap of firecrackers, imply that racially inspired domestic strife has the potential to pull apart the body politic. But since the bonfires of Guy Fawkes also unite, the riot at the film's conclusion provides a catharsis, allowing Jacko and his wife the kind of redemption that distinguishes them from the "yobs" who start the trouble. It is true, as the critic John Hill suggests, that the three Teddy Boy figures who punctuate the film with senseless violence are "the dramatic counterpoint to reason." In this sense they are ideologically problematic, relieving "good" British racists from the burden of their own impulses to violence. But not really, since the film gives Nell several scenes of vitriolic and irrational displays of hatred, showing that it is possible for even "decent" working-class figures to explode, if not attack. The Teddy Boys are not "devoid of context or motivation," as Hill suggests.[60] Their presence in the warehouse where Gomez works places them in economic competition with him, providing them with both context and motive. And while it is true that by the end, the film emphasizes their almost languid idleness, the direction that the first thrown rock gives their anger in fact connects them to Nell. The film does not so much separate the good working-class people from the bad as suggest that a passion that surfaces in relation to black success and romantic freedom connects the groups to each other. That moment of ecstatic stasis that critic Ian Baucom describes in the British riot zone is fully illustrated in the final scenes of the film, when all the constituent actors are gathered together around a dangerous and unifying fire.[61]

Uniting this trio of filmic explorations into classy black masculinity set against working-class anxiety is a set of circumstances around gender, education, and attenuating colonial relationships occurring at the time the films were made. For one thing, masculine expectations in the decolonizing Caribbean were as ambivalent and complex as they were in Britain, though historical and cultural differences elucidate the dynamics we see in British films of racial and class encounter. A first group of black, educated, middle-class men emerged at the turn of the twentieth century out of the exhibition prizes to high schools reserved for the few. Gaining a scholarship to Queen's Royal College in Trinidad, say, meant that a boy could move from a poor rural or working-class family into the intellectual culture of the colonial and brown elite within the space of a few years. Unlike the scholarship boys of 1950s England, these West Indian scholarship boys had behind them the support of an entire class of people who fully expected their personal success to lead to larger-scale social change. These boys, then, worked not just on their own behalf, experiencing the isolation of particular intelligence, but also on behalf of an ethnic and cultural majority who perceived the waning days of empire and the dawning of a new day of leadership by their own sons. They were "exemplary figures in a society which otherwise provided very limited opportunities for the vast majority of its citizens," as Ivar Oxaal has written; symbols of an "embryo meritocracy" whose mettles were tested in the fires of English examinations.[62] Accounts by famous examples of these men, such as C. L. R. James and Eric Williams, emphasize not their alienation from a class culture but rather their mastery of an entirely new one. Meanwhile, increased access to education in Britain created class fractures within families, with "scholarship boys" off to grammar school and university developing different expectations and terms of reference from those of others in the family. Improvements in wages and lifestyle led to better living conditions among many working-class families but also to a sense of nostalgia and resentment for the particularities of cultures that were being lost. If the improvements of life for the worker in Britain involved a necessary sense of what was also being lost, then black middle-class subjects, seemingly already familiar with the genteel cultures to which the British working class was only now gaining access, could become a symbol for all the barriers that still stood in the worker's way. There were barriers to the good life even as the old one was fracturing, and the colonials seemed to have a head start.

The educated black West Indian man may have had a sense of himself as embodying vigorous intelligence, but it is worth noting that perceptions of Caribbean masculinity often deviated from or complicated this sense. Marcus Collins's account of the perceptions around West Indian men in Britain during the postwar era works through the sociological and autobiographical literature of the period and describes the contradictory associations around West Indian men during this period.[63] Just ahead of the massive wave of midcentury migration to England, the Moyne Commission report (1938–1939) represented a version of West Indian masculinity that was attenuated to the point of social crisis. According to the report, West Indian men managed to be both patriarchal and inattentive to their duties as heads of households. The image was of the "unscrupulous and improvident father . . . evad[ing] his responsibility toward his children and probably unmarried mother."[64] This image would have laid the groundwork for other stereotypes that West Indian men met once in England. They suffered from prejudices that they were "work shy" and, puzzlingly and simultaneously, that they worked too hard, threatening the union structure and creating problems for established white workers.

After the losses suffered from bombardment and on the battlefields in World War II, there was a sense in which British national interest lay in restoring a strong home front. Changing gender norms in Britain in the wake of the war appended to the demands of heroic masculinity the somewhat contradictory necessity for masculine domesticity. The model man on the home front during wartime combined elements of the public school code—fair play, "decency"—with the physical vigor of sportsmanship, thus creating a composite of emotional reserve and bodily strength that could be mandated for middle-class as well as working-class men. Having men return to orderly homes, and having men be a part of the running of orderly homes, became one way of ensuring the restoration of the home front. Surveying the historiography around men and domestication, Martin Francis writes that during the years of reconstruction following World War II, "social and cultural authorities sought to make marriage and the home more attractive to both women and men through the promotion of 'companionate marriage,' in which teamwork and partnership were to replace unquestioned patriarchal authority as the basis of domestic life."[65] This model of companionate marriage, which had emerged in the late Victorian era as a model for middle-class society, increasingly became available to working-class people as well. Stephen Brooke has written about 1950s sociologies of working-class communities in which men were a far greater presence in home life than at earlier points in history.[66] He quotes Ferdinand Zweig's *The Worker in Affluent Society* (1961) as observing a "new man" emerging from the more prosperous of the working classes, one who was "softened" by his association with his wife and feminine values.[67] In *Family and Kinship in East London* (1957), Michael Young and Peter Wilmott write about "a new kind of companionship between man and woman" that was emerging as "the old style of working-class family [was] fast disappearing."[68] Companionate marriage also became a litmus test for the civility of black migrant men, many of whom were thought to be morally deficient in their treatment of women and unaware of the modern domestic imperative for companionship and equality. The sociologist Sheila Patterson argued that for a majority of West Indian migrant families, "the Anglo-American ideal of love and marriage" remained unattained.[69] This image went on to be reflected in the numerous domestic dramas portrayed on film during the 1950s and 1960s. The pressure point of the social and economic change in relation to black immigration was the working-class home. It was in the context of the domestic scene—neglected mothers, interracial lovers, working men with responsibilities at home—that filmmakers chose to represent the conflicts around race and class.

I began this chapter with *The Lowlife*, a novel that I think nicely encapsulates some of the issues around postwar migration and class that I have been discussing—and with the additional perspective of a Jewish narrator. Two families move into Harryboy's boarding house during the course of the novel. The first is a white family: the wife, Evelyn, stays home to take care of the rooms and their son, Gregory; the husband, Vic, is a low-level business clerk studying for exams to rise in the company. Though Evelyn's family is from the suburbs, she and Vic could no longer afford to live there and were forced to take the rooms in a house she feels is beneath her. Evelyn is particularly keen to distance herself from the neighborhood, insisting that their situation is a temporary drop in fortune. The other family that arrives is the de Souzas, a West Indian couple. The wife, Milly, also stays home to look after the house, but her husband, Joe, works at the ironmongery. All the other tenants agree that the de Souzas are "lovely people," but Evelyn refuses to speak with them and will not allow Vic or Gregory to enjoy their company.[70] For Evelyn, a black family in the boardinghouse is incontrovertible proof that it is a place beneath her family's status. She begins to look for new housing immediately.

Baron takes pains to describe the lengths to which the de Souzas go to be good neighbors, buying a washing machine for everyone in the house to share, changing their habits and doing whatever is asked of them to make everyone else in the house happy. Evelyn's recalcitrance is portrayed in unequivocally unattractive terms, so that the de Souzas, with their "good nature" and bronze sculptured handsomeness, are the ones seen to be classing up the joint.[71] Ultimately it is the de Souzas who move out, not Evelyn and Vic. The West Indian couple is able to get a deposit together with a cousin to buy a house in Stoke Newington. Describing the source and quality of Evelyn's rage at hearing the news, shifting from Harryboy's consciousness to Evelyn's, Baron is able to point to a constellation of feelings that black success incites in the struggling white Briton:

> It choked Evelyn that the de Souzas could get a house before her. This black man, this work man, who came home in overalls and grime, had got a house! They were all as bad as each other, the workpeople who lived down this street, with their cars, and their holidays abroad, and their washing-machines, and buying drinks all round on Saturday night at the pub on the corner. They poured out money like water, these unions were always getting more for them, and Evelyn, the daughter of a decent middle-class family, had to go without, to trudge up and down the market saving pennies, to live in a mean flat below her proper level.[72]

Evelyn shifts from particular hostility to generalized resentment in her thoughts, cursing the de Souzas and then moving on to all the "workpeople who lived down this street." It is a network of related, though curiously nonintersecting, offenses that these uppity black people commit: to their egregious acquisition of equity is added the problem of their frivolous consumption. To their grime is added their weekend conviviality. To their economic frivolity, their socialist investment in workers' unions. And it is true that Evelyn has no affection for any of the working-class people in her new neighborhood, white or black. (Her own family, middle class as she calls them, is too close to the working class for comfort.) But her language suggests there is a special kind of resentment reserved for black uplift. The unions, which also feature in *Flame in the Streets* as a traditional working-class institution that could begin favoring black workers (though in reality did not), is singled out for the particular unfairness of her new status. Earlier in the novel, Joe de Souza had offered a theory as to why Evelyn and others did not like him and his wife: "Joe said, 'I tell you why, Mill. We got too much life. We are not liked because we have too much life in us.'"[73] Evelyn's bitter reverie suggests, however, that it is not so much life as capital that liminal class occupants such as Evelyn find difficult to bear in their new black neighbors.

At the end of *Escape to an Autumn Pavement*, Johnnie wanders the street with two assessments reverberating in his head. Larry has told him that he has sought out his relationship with Dick because he is in search of a nation: "You want an identity like. You want to feel that you have a nation behind you, a nation that you call your own."[74] His coworker Biddy's voice tells him that now that he is living with another man, apparently loving another man, he's "finished as a man."[75] In these voices, Johnnie hears the conjunction of masculinity and nationality, and he wonders whether his two friends might be right: that he is not manly enough, not grounded enough, to know his way in London. The crisis of Johnnie's national identity in connection with his sexuality seems to turn on his choice between Fiona and Dick. Johnnie feels unmanned and deracinated, and it is tempting to see those two things finding their fullest expression in Johnnie's being gay. This interpretation is clearly in play—not just in this novel, but in Caribbean cultures where legal and social injunctions against homosexuality circumscribe national boundaries and create sexual out-groups. What I am suggesting with my reading of *Escape* and the larger context of British postwar representations of race, class, and sexuality, however, is that in Salkey's novel the most potent pressure point in the nexus of national and sexual identity is not at the homosexual but at an even less straightforward, less easily defined point in the relations between two men—that aspect of the queer diasporic in which erotic relations between men resist identity. That point is at that place where desire and identification are not sexual per se but intense, hostile, and evocative of sexual intimacy. For Johnny, it is at those moments when envy and resentment flare into violence and anger with Trado that we have the fullest, most generative sense of identity in crisis. In this way, Salkey's novel is so crucial for understanding Caribbean subjectivity in relation to England because it demonstrates how intimate is the violence that flares between colonial and British men; how confounding are the expectations of middle-class

West Indian men in the midst of the old colonial status quo and the new emerging nation-state. And the novel is crucial for our understanding of the complexities of Englishness because it throws into relief working-class desires and vulnerabilities vis-à-vis colonial ones.

Following the imperative of deferral, Johnnie absolves himself from the cares of identity and absorbs himself into London. "I'd make them wait for their answer," he thinks.[76] And then again: "I knew I had to wait."[77] In my next chapter, I will think through more thoroughly the messianic temporality that Johnnie's waiting and waiting implies. For now, the emphasis on Johnnie himself as a figure eluding identity allows me to think through Muñoz's "then and there" of utopia if in a slightly more discordant key. For Johnnie, like Muñoz's figures, understands that "the world is not enough." This phrase encapsulating felt insufficiency applies to the structure of queerness, as Muñoz tells us—indeed, that phrase is a definition Muñoz offers for queerness. And it applies equally well to the structure of diaspora—a formation defined by a sense that whatever ground is beneath one's feet could never be the only place one belongs, could never be enough. "The here and now is a prison house," Muñoz tells us. "We must strive, in the face of the here and now's totalizing rendering of reality, to think and feel a *then and there*." Queerness as a horizon of possibility is "a modality of ecstatic time"—a reading of the past critiquing the present with a vision of the future.[78] The horizon we see in Salkey's last pages might look like a tepid vision of futurity, one that is foggy rather than struck by eros or joyfulness. And yet I enjoy the vision of our irascible Johnnie making everyone wait, waiting for himself, and stomping the streets until some more satisfying London might emerge—a London in which the hodgepodge family of queers-colonials-whites are at home with their manifest and difficult affiliations, and domestic bliss is measured not by tepid dyadic structures or even, indeed, by mere bliss.

Postwar England and the Irruptive Black Queer

What is the relationship, then, between class formations, sex, and elusive identity, especially in the wake of the robust sexual conversations that characterized midfifties and early sixties England and in the wake of the Wolfenden Report, which changed the character of British homosexuality? And how did the emergence of the legal homosexual subject intersect with the increasing interdiction of the colonial black immigrant? Do we see here as well a class dynamic that creates a set of tense intersections between white racial formations in England and black British identities coming into shape?

I have been demonstrating, primarily through class and masculinity, that several curious nuances of the *Windrush* story have remained unexplored. I would like to end my consideration of diasporic belonging here by noting some implications of the coincidence of the arrival of thousands of black migrants in Britain throughout the 1950s and 1960s with the explosion of debate around the legal status of homosexuality and prostitution in the wake of voluble discussion in newspapers and reporting, often salacious, of men being caught having sex in public. Whether it was a wave of "dark strangers" from the colonies preoccupying parliamentarians and their constituents or the spate of high-profile arrests for public indecency that whetted everyone's appetite for scandal, there was a sense that something was amiss in postwar Britain, and it was taking place out in city streets. In exploring this milieu, what appears to be a curious trade-off emerges between the legal incorporation of one formerly abjected subject—the white British homosexual—and the delegitimization of the black colonial British subject, who became, after the blatant audacity of having laid claim to British citizenship in the wake of World War II, and through successive immigration laws, a "coloured immigrant." This trade-off belies the shared subject positions of the homosexual and the black migrant: they have a strikingly similar relationship to the laws and discourses that governed their status in 1950s and 1960s England.

Weirdly, though, the sources that might have documented the intersecting discourses between sexuality and race actually enact a separation between black and queer—a discursive marking characteristic of these texts that is symptomatic of the political culture of which they form a part. The logic of homophobia and anti-migrant racism relies on similar language. In the most prejudicial accounts of sexual and racial alarm, homosexuality and exponentially increased West Indian presence in Britain become indices of the nation's decline. The fact that these discourses do not then explicitly intersect argues for the particular role of blackness (and the particular image of black men) in white English prejudice. In the 1950s, publicity around "indecency" arrests was most prominently associated with privileged white men—Rupert Croft-Cooke, Lord Montagu and Michael Pitt-Rivers, Peter Wildeblood, and Guy Burgess and Donald McLean—arguably consolidating one vision of male homosexuality as a sort of "excess of civility," a condition of European modernity to be parsed out from the potentially destructive atavism of black colonial masculinity.[79] This particularity of black abjection provides a basis for understanding why policy decisions resulting from simultaneously occurring discussions of sexual indecency and colonial immigration pulled in different directions. In 1967 the Sexual Offences Act was passed, decriminalizing homosexual acts between consenting adults and therefore significantly removing legal barriers to gay sexual expression. By 1962, successive laws had been passed to curtail immigration from the West Indian colonies, and in 1971 the Immigration Act radically constrained black movement to the metropole, limiting untroubled migration to those with white ancestry.[80] Since homosexual men were figured largely as white, and troublesome migrants were figured mostly as black and brown, the sad, blunt truth about this period in British history is that sexual freedom, aligned with whiteness, trumped black freedom of movement and access to metropolitan citizenship.[81] Furthermore, such citizenship as was being made available to black migrants by the sociologists and advocates studying their settlement unwittingly reproduced the colonial asymmetry they were ostensibly working against. Black queerness registered, if at all, as vulnerability, creating either an association with degeneracy that needed to be purged or a mandate for migrants' rescue.

In Race Relations discourse, a field of study that emerged in the wake of West Indian and other colonial migration to Britain and that included studies by such scholars as Michael Banton, Sheila Patterson, Ruth Glass, and the community advocate Edith Ramsay, black men had a curious position in the affective matrix of postwar Britain.[82] They were either predatory on English heterosexual formations, desiring the white women who symbolized normative domesticity and then wreaking havoc on that domesticity; or they were defenseless prey, abandoned by the national institutions that should have kept them safe, unhoused and apt to be swept away by the city streets and corrupted by decrepit, malingering English men. In these discourses, black queerness emerges as an unmarked presence, an excess to figurations of migrant blackness in the London landscape. The black queer was somehow nowhere in the voluble discussions of homosexuality in the mid-1950s that crescendoed around 1957, when the Wolfenden Commission was charged with reexamining (and eventually proposing overturning) the sexual indecency laws. And yet in another way, the black queer was everywhere, suffusing popular and academic discourses around "colonial immigration" that were as voluble as those on the homosexual. This queer figure is not necessarily easy to find: he lurks and sidles in these documents.

And it is for this reason that Andrew Salkey's novel *Escape to an Autumn Pavement*, in which the black queer lurks and skulks but only because he is the *center* of the action, not at its margins, is such an intriguing text. It takes place in the close quarters of a boardinghouse, where a liminal working-class couple must cope with a West Indian couple who seem to be above them. Salkey's novel adds to this compression the complication of various conflicts around masculinity. As with all of the cross-class encounters I have discussed in this chapter, Salkey's take place in the realm of the domestic, and it is largely in the crucible of the boardinghouse that these intimate hostilities must be worked out. With class, there is no finer way to distinguish difference, it seems, than in the space of the home.

Metaphors of otherness pervaded discourses of postwar Britishness, when the nation reconstituted itself around abjected categories of difference in the wake of war and the decline of empire. Homosexuals and immigrants were thought of as possessing partial citizenship. They had claims on Britain, yes, but were not considered entirely trustworthy stewards of the rights and responsibilities of nationhood. Homosexuals and racial others were threatening to the British body politic because at a moment of intense, postwar vulnerability these figures pointed to an inherent potential for national deviance, an intrinsic tendency for the nation to fracture rather than to cohere around readily agreed-on norms. Popular reports of queer urban culture and prosecutions of homosexuality in the 1950s took on a tenor of national guardianship in which the homosexual man was positioned on the outside of the boundaries of Britishness. Houlbrook writes: "The operations of the law, in this schema, were imagined as protecting the national community against what was variously termed a 'disease,' a 'plague,' a 'canker,' and a 'foreign' invasion. . . . Called into being through a 'dialectics of discovery,' the spectacle of the queer urban culture established the abject outside of Britishness."[83] Similar evidence exists for the ways black migrants were discursively placed outside the boundaries of Britishness. Kathleen Paul's work on the governmental archive around postwar immigration cites a 1953 parliamentary working party paper on the "problem" of Caribbean immigration to Britain that fretted about how "an influx of coloured people domiciled here is likely to impair the harmony, strength and cohesion of our public and social life and to bring discord and unhappiness among all concerned."[84]

The sense of the English nation as imperiled by the unnatural tendencies of blacks and homosexuals is clear in texts hostile to them. For writers who were sympathetic to at least one set of these abjected figures—the Race Relations scholars who attended to postwar black migrants—working against national hostility meant delineating an acceptable black subject, which had the effect of demarcating black from queer. Black men are not associated with homosexuality—or at least, they are not themselves portrayed as homosexuals in the field of race relations. Black men have to cope with the threat of degeneracy, living in cramped and insalubrious urban spaces. But their actual or potential attraction to other men is not explicitly registered. And yet, if a certain politics guided the establishment of lines between racial and sexual categories, which lines established greater freedoms in one region and fewer freedoms in the other, then the texts themselves demonstrate that the borders were less fixed, the boundaries murkier than the politics would have it.

Between the 1947 publication of Kenneth Little's *Negroes in Britain* and the establishment in 1958, after the Notting Hill riots, of the Institute of Race Relations and its journal *Race*, there was a decade of intense work to document the lives of black people in Britain.[85] The fruits of this labor appeared throughout the 1950s and 1960s: among them Anthony Richmond's *Colour Prejudice in Britain* (1954) on Liverpool; Michael Banton's *The Coloured Quarter* (1955) on London's docklands neighborhood of Stepney; Ruth Glass's geographical study of migrant settlement in London, *London's Newcomers* (1960); and Sheila Patterson's *Dark Strangers* (1963), a large sociological study of the Caribbean community in Lambeth.[86] Banton's study of Stepney is the most explicit on the issue of homosexuality. Part of this candor may be attributed to the particular context he is describing: sailing communities were male-dominated and traditionally laissez-faire. Throughout the late nineteenth century and in the years leading up to *Windrush*, West African and West Indian sailors had arrived for work and stayed in Stepney, which had already become home to Jewish migrants from Europe. By the early 1950s, black workers (some of them erstwhile sailors adversely affected by the 1925 Coloured Seamen's Order) had set up in particular streets, often scrambling to get by in poor housing and neglected bombed-out areas.[87]

Banton is intrigued by the domestic partnerships of black workers and white women in Stepney, seeking to dispel the myth that many migrants lived on the earnings of their prostitute girlfriends. This myth is not entirely dispelled, and Banton puts another in its place—that of the damaged girl in thrall to the amoral man.[88] And because of his preoccupation with these alliances, Banton misses opportunities to probe more fully into alliances being formed between men. For instance, briefly, toward the end of his book, Banton writes: "A number of white homosexuals come round the cafes and public houses of the coloured quarter looking for coloured 'friends.'"[89] These homosexuals are positioned outside the community of black migrants. They are a white, foreign element to be amused and tolerated, like the middle-aged woman Banton mentions just before, "performing a burlesque of jitterbugging with a coloured man for her partner." No sooner does Banton refer to these prowling men than he lets them fall from sight.

And yet Banton's imagery of black masculinity implies a more capacious practice of sexuality than the heterosexual partnerships he documents. Single men roam freely; those who are attached often have flexible arrangements with their domestic partners. And there are men living in disreputable all-male hostels who feel the need to lie about it: "There are many men's hostels in Stepney, and they introduce a distinctive element into the population—decrepit old men and irresponsible younger men as well as law-abiding but shiftless persons.... They are not popular with the coloured men, partly because their fellow lodgers are so obviously the least respectable of the native population and the hostels are looked down upon by the other people in the neighbourhood. Most of the immigrants are sensitive to the criteria of 'respectability,' and many will give a friend's address rather than reveal that they are staying at a hostel."[90] That Caribbean men are ashamed about their involvement with these spaces on the margins of Stepney's fragile respectability suggests that migrants are aware that there are ramparts to be held against absolute cultural exclusion. If these defenses are erected against queer sexuality—and the intensification of the language here suggests that they might be—then Banton's work helps to explain the sense of competing exclusion between queer and black communities we find debated later, so much at the fault line of black British representation in the 1980s and 1990s.[91]

We learn more about the association of men's hostels with degeneracy in the papers of East End borough councilor Edith Ramsay, deposited at the Tower Hamlets Local History Archive.[92] Rowton House (later Tower House), on Fieldgate Street, and the two Salvation Army Houses on Middlesex Street and Whitechapel Road were certainly considered disreputable. In a 1961 memo about the Men's Salvation Army buildings, Ramsay's veiled language, like Banton's, implies sexual taint, but leaves specifics unsaid: "These two hostels are extremely uncomfortable and sordid. This is at least in part due to the type of men, outcasts and social failures, who use them. The Hostel in Whitechapel Road takes 300 men. They can only be said to attract derelicts to Stepney, without doing anything effective to help the men."[93] Another document has Ramsay referring mysteriously to "the moral problems that arise" at Colonial House on Leman Street. Suggesting that the hostel is only indifferently maintained by the Colonial Office, Ramsay writes that the "token recognition of responsibility" the CO takes in providing the house only, ironically, promotes these unnamed moral issues that "need not be described, though their gravity should be stressed."[94] Ramsay's concern for migrants' moral welfare is legible in the longer history of British colonialism in which institutional and economic power conjuncts with the power to save. But the particular inflection of the language of sexual indecency here (the moral problem that dares not speak its name) adds a complication. For in Ramsay's view, the British government's housing provision actually *introduces* forms of sexual vice that, presumably, black migrants would be able to avoid were they properly accommodated. Following the logic of her analysis, the government is not simply derelict in its duty; it is directly contradicting its principles of colonial improvement. Sexual indecency here is structurally British, colonial migrants its victims.

A letter exchange in the Ramsay archive only intensifies this sense of queerness as colonial victimization by introducing the anxieties of a separate British figure, differently positioned from Ramsay. An Oxford-based Christian worker named Kenneth Leech wrote to Ramsay hoping to gain access to the neighborhood, putatively to minister to those on the outside of respectable society: "I think there is a tremendous need of Christians who will mingle with the café population," he writes, singling out "homosexuals" as being "the most glaring case [in] which there was such a need."[95] Throughout the correspondence, there is a now-familiar toggle between blackness and homosexuality in Stepney, such that the two categories are spoken about as if they could not coexist in the same figure. Writing to Ramsay about various gatherings around Stepney clubs, Leech argues:

> You say that there has been a remarkable decrease in homosexuals in the last few years, and it would be interesting to hear further details of this. But what has struck me as marked during the last eighteen months or so is the increase both in very young girls and also of white teenage boys who are around the cafes in Cable Street in the very late hours. My own experience in 1958 and 1959 was that very often one saw few white male youths about in places like Howard's Cafe and the Bruno, but this has changed of late. I have talked about this to various friends who could be classed as cafe drifters and they agree. Of course, few or none of these may be homos [sic] but I think some are.[96]

That Leech is anxious about white boys around Howard's and Bruno's suggests these are traditionally migrant cafes—and that white presence at these places is legible to him mainly in sexual terms. The missing signifier here, blackness, suggests that foreign men are simultaneously overlooked and treated as an ever-present background to these problematic scenes. Leech's concerns about white loitering outside these cafes also mark the patrons inside as possessing a kind of shifting, unhinged, and unlabeled sexuality. They are vulnerable to these predators but also highly corruptible themselves.

Ramsay is aware of there being homosexuality in Stepney.[97] But she is not inclined to think of black migrants in her borough as requiring salvation primarily from their sexual vices. Instead, she consistently writes about them as neglected—her motivating terms familial rather than erotic, with the British government positioned as an insufficiently attentive parent and the connections between men understood primarily as the expedience of poor housing. This means that in her private correspondence she is frank about homosexuality (and wary of Oxford do-gooders who wish to base their charity on its repudiation) while in public memos she speaks in the veiled terms of the Race Relations sociologists, making it difficult to know for certain whether, when she refers to the "sordidness" attaching to colonial rooming houses, she is actually referring to homosexual activity (which would have been considered sordid by the terms of local borough memorandum writing). That said, Ramsay does sometimes make references that suggest she thinks about black migrants' domestic arrangements in moral terms and that they embody the duality—victims, victimizers—that makes the black queer figure such a shifting, mobile target in Leech's imagination. Colonial seamen on short stay in a male hostel in London, for instance are—in the same sentence—both "a danger to the area" and impressionable subjects who "learn much that is evil and little that is good from their stay."[98] This ambivalence in postwar British representation of black male migrancy positions these men as both victims and threats; integral to a set of unspoken problems and also unwitting prey to them.

In the work of Ruth Glass and Sheila Patterson, perhaps the most well known in the field of early Race Relations studies, these ambivalences of representation sometimes turn on vignettes of queer, undecidable meaning. If anything, these ambiguities are heightened at the moments when Glass and Patterson describe their black male subjects most vividly, in novelistic gestures of characterization and dialogue. For instance, Ruth Glass's study *London's Newcomers*, characteristically, does not explore homosexuality per se. But at one point she relates an amusing anecdote that reads on multiple levels. At Paddington Station, she strikes up a conversation with a Guyanese railway clerk who talks about his smooth transition into British culture: "'I belong to the YMCA, you see. I go three or four times a week, I'm very keen on it. That's where I make my friends. Most of them are English. Real friends, I get on with them very well.'"[99] Glass continues:

> He paid £2.10 for his room in Paddington, to which he regularly invited his friends. Although he lived fairly near to Notting Hill, he had not been involved in the disturbances. "I didn't see anything, not even at night, going home from work, or at the YMCA. As a matter of fact, I've never met any trouble at all, all the time I've been in England." At this several West Indians standing nearby laughed derisively. One said: "He walks around with a placard saying 'I'm not to be touched by kind permission of the High Commissioner.'" But the railway clerk insisted it was true.[100]

The railway clerk's location for cross-cultural exchange is the YMCA, with its homosocial associations, and the erotic overtones are compounded by the sheer pleasure he seems to have while there ("I'm very keen on it").[101]

These connotations are not lost on the eavesdropping West Indians, whose apparently harsher experiences of settlement are reflected in their bitter laughter. Their derision touches on other presumed differences between themselves and the rail clerk. One man's mockery taps into cultural codes of supposed homosexual fastidiousness and social aspiration. He suggests ironically that though the rail clerk is a mincing, particular type, his patronage by the British high commissioner makes him open to touching by certain others. Glass includes this tableau in her study without remarking on these sexual overtones, which allows room for multiple meanings and semantic slips to resonate beyond the pages of the book. This both marks the limits of her ethnographic study and leaves open several possible interpretations. The ambiguities of a scene like this on the terms of traditional race relations scholarship signals the discursive limitations of the field, though, simultaneously, this openness becomes the very basis of apprehending the image of the black queer in London during this era.

Another example of the discursive limitations imposed on sympathetic studies of black migration to Britain during this period is the work done by Philip Mason, director of the Institute of Race Relations (IRR). An IRR letter sent out in 1959 to do a quiet study of black migrant criminality missed an opportunity to gather information about black queer practices. (In fact, a letter from the Home Office demonstrates the difficulty of performing any analysis within the category of race when the government felt it "desirable to avoid giving the impression that statistics of this nature are collected on the basis of colour.")[102] In the wake of the 1958 Notting Hill riots, Mason canvassed several local London police stations asking superintendents to report the incidence of black migrants involved in the following categories of offense: brothel keeping; living on immoral earnings; and dangerous drugs. (Curiously, Mason also requested the number of migrant suicides. No police station reported more than one suicide; most had none.) Having not asked for statistics on homosexual offences, none were offered. In an example of how perceptions of black criminality are formed, Mason delimited the kinds of crimes he expected black migrants to be involved in—or at least, the kinds of crimes that mattered. Black migrants were problematic, according to the IRR, in this kind of sexual way: female prostitution. Their involvement in queer practices did not create any concern or interest in the IRR. But if you are looking for touts, then you'll probably find them. And in Philip Mason's attempt to cast his net wider for evidence of migrant despair—suicide—he chose a category that was not particularly revealing. We will never know what we might have discovered about black queer male practices had Mason asked different questions. And we can only speculate as to whether evidence of queer sexuality would have been construed as a sign of migrant adaptation (love, relationships) or maladjustment.

Sheila Patterson's work on Brixton in *Dark Strangers* shows her keen interest in cultural differences around (hetero)sexuality and cites Caribbean researchers on these issues. But Patterson underplays the role of religion in migrants' attitudes toward sex. She writes that "West Indian attitudes to sex and procreation remain relatively untouched by puritanical teachings or northern hypocrisies."[103] This is clearly untrue, not least because the emphasis on procreation itself has puritanical and hypocritical overtones in these communities. However, Patterson is illuminating on a number of matters. She draws clear class lines between working-class Brixton and the more upmarket Notting Hill area. As she does so, the values attached to these landscapes shift unexpectedly. Middle-class, professional migrants are supposed to be drawn to west London, but Patterson also writes that these areas are the preserve of "the more lively and antisocial, café-society elements so sharply painted by Samuel Selvon (1956) in *The Lonely Londoners* and by Colin MacInnes (1957) in *City of Spades*."[104] The judgment in that loaded description suggests Patterson's desire for migrants' inclusion into respectable British culture. This investment in respectability means it is sometimes difficult to disentangle Patterson's opinions from her subjects'. She writes disdainfully of short-term relationships between black men and white women without actually quoting any statements from what she calls "the group"—the Caribbean community—itself.[105] She also writes of "a small minority of white people, mostly unattached men and, in later years, teenagers, who were regulars at the various local coloured clubs and shebeens. This was usually because they found the atmosphere more easy-going and uninhibited, and could drink, dance, or gamble in peace. In the teenagers' case the main attraction seems to have been jazz. These contacts were not socially approved by the settled local population, which regards the coloured clubs as a major neighbourhood nuisance."[106] The scene she describes in the clubs—jazz playing, teenagers, gambling, and dancing—looks suspiciously like the scenes described in the works of Colin MacInnes, whom she had earlier distanced from Lambeth.[107] Patterson helps us to maintain a complex idea of the class variations of West Indian migration, but she also helps us to see how widespread would have been the opportunities for "unattached men" to be together, and how lacking in respectability such venues became.

Sheila Patterson's work on Brixton does not take us into the neighborhood's White Horse pub, the one that an observer cited in Houlbrook's study claimed was "full of prostitutes . . . with coloured men . . . and perverts of a very low type."[108] These Race Relations studies were being produced throughout the 1950s and early 1960s, when scholars and local government officials such as Edith Ramsay and Phillip Mason were working against oppressive discourses in calling for good housing, employment, and educational policy to smooth colonial integration in the metropole. But they were also largely uninterested in exploring how homosexuality expressed itself in the communities they studied. They sought to counter what they saw as growing, uninformed sentiment about black migration and focused on questions of housing, since normative domestic migrant subjects made potentially more suitable British citizens. Certain areas of London were "zones of transition" that placed queer Britons and black migrants in similar geographies.[109] But these subjects' relations to the state were often analyzed as if you could control for one group or the other. Inevitably, things were more complex and tangled than that.

Following archival trails for evidence of black participation in postwar British queer culture often ends in ambiguity or apparent dead-ends. Certainly, Caribbean people are to be found everywhere in London, including the middle of sexual experimentation in clubs and cafes in Notting Hill and Soho, though their presence is often vague and shadowy. Established lore has it that the Colony Room, a Soho landmark and center of artistic London during the 1950s (Francis Bacon and Lucian Freud were habitués) was so named because its owner Muriel Belcher's female partner was from Jamaica.[110] Significantly, we only ever see her first name, Carmel. And though memorialized in Michael Andrews's group portrait *The Colony Room* (1963), on permanent exhibition at Pallant House and shown at the Tate in an Andrews retrospective, we cannot see her face. She is to the extreme right of the painting, racially indefinite, impossible to make out.[111]

The National Archive in Kew, London, houses official documents on the policing of migration and sexuality in the mid-twentieth century, papers archived in files of the War Office, the Royal Air Force, and the Metropolitan Police. Houlbrook's history of queer London makes prodigious use of the archive of discipline and punishment to enlarge on the culture of sexual subversion during the first half of the twentieth century. But these sources prove shadowy and unverifiable when it comes to identifying black involvement in the queer scene during this time.[112] For instance, war provided both greater opportunity for and greater scrutiny of homosexual encounters, and since male homosexual acts were still illegal, documenting their existence was often done by the same mechanisms that prosecuted them. But many documents relating to sexual offenses have been redacted and remain covered under various exemptions from the Freedom of Information Act.[113] In the case of Caribbean soldiers and airmen, when a lead does appear, it is difficult to ascertain the race and nationality of the offender. A list of court-martialed soldiers in an Army and Royal Air Force report on homosexual offenses from the early 1950s notes that on December 1, 1953, two men were convicted of "buggery" in Jamaica.[114] But were these men native-born Britons stationed in Jamaica or were they Jamaican? Were they involved with each other or with Jamaican locals? Were they white? Though I cannot say, it is also the case that the colonial West Indian island has historically functioned discursively as a space of racial otherness, against which racial normativity was constructed. The fact of these men's conviction in Jamaica does not secure in the archival record black gay sexuality, but it gestures at one set of geographical and discursive boundaries to be found around racialized queerness.

Despite this lack in Britain's official repository of archival information, I found one first-person text of queer West Indian identity, though Richie Riley's interview is also paradoxical and irruptive in some of the ways I have demonstrated about texts of queer blackness throughout this piece. The Hall Carpenter Archive, named for lesbian novelist Radclyffe Hall and sexologist Edward Carpenter, stemmed from the larger project that aimed to set down the history of homosexual lives in Britain. Riley was interviewed during 1994.[115] He agreed to be part of a project that is explicitly about collecting narratives of gay men and women in Britain during the twentieth century—and then he proceeded not to mention homosexuality, male lovers, or identify himself as gay at all. Riley's testimony indicates his keen awareness of the disciplining force of the archive and the multiple exclusions to which he is subject as a black, Caribbean-born man in Britain. The way he steers the conversation, employing a poetics of delicacy in refusing to label or pin down his sexuality, empowers him and provides valuable lessons to the researcher of queer Caribbean lives decades later.

Riley was a founding member of the late 1940s dance group Les Ballets Nègres. He was born in Jamaica in 1910, and he spent time with his parents in Cuba, where he first danced with his friend and cofounder Berto Pasuka.[116] At the urging of Pasuka, who had gone before, he moved to London in 1946, as soon as he could after the war. Riley tells fond, exciting stories of his time in the Ballets Nègres, particularly their debut season in London in 1946 and the European tour that followed. His memory of the sensation that this multinational, mostly black dance company caused in major European cities is matched by his pride at what he remembers to be the superior technical skill of his dancers. His assured vision of the group, his pride in their taking over in metropolitan centers, matches his mannered speech and his implicit association at this time with British and European culture. Riley's faltering memory is sure about dancing on the Champs-Élysée, which he throws in with a curious mixture of casualness and emphasis. One of his first anecdotes involves friends at the Slade School.

Riley mentions three times that he suspects that he and his friend were mistaken for "African dignitaries" at public events in London.[117] The first time, when they went to the opening of an exhibit at the Victoria and Albert, the long line led Riley to suggest entering the museum through the Slade School entrance next door. Unbeknownst to him, this entrance backed on to a grand staircase that was reserved for VIPs. Because he and his friend were "very well turned out," the security guards waved them through, and Riley and his friend attended the event free of charge and without the wait. Building on the momentum of that story, he uses the phrase "African dignitaries" twice more in reference to D-day events when they were unwittingly saluted by officers and thronged for autographs in Hyde Park. Riley is carefully groomed, aware of himself as a spectacle, and conscious of the effect he has on the British public. But he does not mention the interpretation I believe to be in play, that the public's spectatorship exists in the context that I adumbrated at the beginning of the chapter—those dapper *Windrush* arrivants, Harryboy's trilby-topped new neighbors. The "African dignitary" is the beautiful black man gazed at and assessed for his looks, deemed to be out of place, sexually attractive but also fearsome. The connection between male dapperness and gender nonconformity is also in effect, though Riley waits until much later to broach the topic of drag.

Juliet Margets, the Hall Carpenter interviewer, asks some pointed questions, presumably to encourage Riley to open up about sexuality. "Can you explain to me how you met Quentin Crisp in one of the cafes in Soho?" she asks at one point. That yields reflections on the black artistic community in London, however, rather than memories of the white sexual demimonde as we might have expected:

> Now I first met Quentin Crisp when I went one evening to do modeling at the British Art Society and he was there, and that's where I met, first met Quentin Crisp and we chatted. And then afterwards, sometime after, I met him in Soho, and then discovered that he used to frequent this café in Soho where a group of us used to meet because it was a sort of a theatrical café. . . . All evening we would sit there drinking coffee . . . and people would bring in their latest poetry and we would talk, all the gossip of the theater, of the musical world, of that group. Now the classical musicians, musicians of that sort, we even had classical musicians and sometimes we'd have African drummers because there were quite a few African drummers in London in those days because they came on ships and they would leave the ship in Liverpool and find their way to London and then they would play drums to make a living. Speaking of drums and drumming.

And on the story goes. That digressive narration is typical of Riley's interview and is part of its instructing value: for one might feel thwarted on hearing this response if the goal is to discover more about black queer life in postwar London, narrowly conceived. Indeed Riley's digressions are counterpointed by his interviewer's increasingly (and understandably) leading questioning. And all of this is punctuated by recurrent breaks in the recording, mimicking the rupturing effect of Riley's idiosyncratic form of queer testimony and suggesting, offstage, the interviewer's attempt to regroup and take another tack. For instance, close to the end of the recording Margets asks this nested set of questions: "Who were the people who had the most effect on your life, you know, who were the big loves of your life? Or who were the people you've felt closest to? Like, did you keep up your friendship with Berto after he went to Paris, or did you become close to other people?" We had, in the course of the interview, already been made privy to the fact that Riley had been married. That moment of disclosure had been accompanied by choked pain (his wife had died suddenly) and uncomfortable silence. What, really, were we doing here in this gay and lesbian oral history? Now, as Margets seeks to uncover something in the friendship between Riley and Pasuka, we cannot help wishing that he finally would disclose in a typically coming out moment of queer testifying. But here is Riley's response: "Of course as I told you, I was married but I don't really . . . I cannot talk about her. We were very close together and after she died I really . . . didn't . . . get on with anybody else. Life became painting, dance studios, dance groups, and that took up the whole of my life, so to speak."

Riley's refusal to speak directly about the issue for which he is a respondent takes a different turn at the end of the recording. After a break in the tape, Margets begins a fresh section of the interview by asking Riley once again to go back in time, to explore his friendship with Berto Pasuka before they arrived in London. We discover that during his period in Cuba, Riley had done dance performances in which Pasuka dressed as his female tango partner. As we have now become accustomed to expect, we get this information rather circuitously:

> I had a girl, a beautiful girl who I did the tango with. And, strange enough, she was also my adagio partner. Well, adagio dancing in those days was very popular too. Adagio dance is a routine acrobatic dance of two, two persons and she was a brilliant dancer. She could roll—tie herself into a knot backwards, she could stand up, bend over backwards and touch her heel with her head and roll into a bulk, and she was very good. But she got married and pregnant, that put an end to her partner with me. Therefore, after that, Berto impersonated a girl and we did the tango together.

Therefore. Naturally. When Margets asked if audiences found it unusual to see two men dancing the tango together, Riley answers ambiguously: "They knew it was a boy doing it, but the makeup was so good, he didn't look like a boy, he didn't look like a boy in drag." That double disavowal— it wasn't a boy and it wasn't drag—says a lot about Riley's veiled exposition of his gay life. Riley is more forthcoming about gender transgression when recalled in the supposedly repressed first half of the twentieth century. It is in the present, in the 1990s, when the interview is taking place, and during the era of gay liberation, that he is reticent. The interview is suddenly illuminated by images of Riley and Pasuka performing drag tango. Margets had asked Riley pointedly if he had remained close to his friend after Les Ballets Nègres disbanded. Riley had said no. Now, however, it is as if Riley's bond to Pasuka is confirmed by the placement of this anecdote at the end of the recording. "I was trying to find, I actually have a photo of us somewhere doing the tango together and it's hard for anyone even now to realize that it was a boy."[118]

I had been looking in Riley's interview for evidence of gay Caribbean migrants in postwar London so that I could strengthen the historical argument this chapter makes about the political effects of the separate discursive realms around homosexuality and immigration in postwar Britain. What I found was an account marked by indirection and by a certain structure of disavowal that is also, like Philip Brian Harper's account of certain modes of African American speech in his essay "Eloquence and Epitaph," a kind of avowal. For when Riley answers Margets's question about his loves with the bombshell that he was married to a woman, this is not so much a refusal of queer subjectivity as an indication to wait. Riley knows that he is participating in a gay oral history project, and so in a certain way the intention of his testimony is clear.[119] However, he is speaking on his own terms. And so when we tarry, we get to the final moment of the interview: the extremely poignant sibilance of Riley shuffling through papers, searching for Pasuka's photograph, the wordless sound that becomes the interview's queerest moment of testimony. "I still can't find it . . ." These are literally the final words of the recording before it suddenly breaks off for good. They are fitting words to describe the open-ended effect of the archival search for black, queer subjects. What is found still waits, in a sense, to be found.

FOUR

BURNING SPEAR AND
NATHANIEL MACKEY AT LARGE

Over the course of this book, I have tracked different modes of diasporic belonging, each difficult and each complexly tied to particular locations. As I come to the end of the book, I discover that one of the most powerful modes of black belonging is metaphorized in the body's sway under spirit possession, an experience in which location, per se, is in deep flux. Spirit possession encompasses many things: religious thought; radically intimate and paradoxically freeing experiences of the body; sometimes agonistic relationships to powerful and unpredictable spirits; an extremely untethered relationship to normative time; and gendered expressions that can be incorporated into the expansive discourses of queerness I have described at other moments in this book. Spirit possession concludes the book as a structure of diasporic belonging, then, because it both enfolds earlier forms of belonging I have been interested in throughout and points to possibilities that, by definition, exceed the ground of any one location. One belongs, under a spirit's possession, neither to oneself strictly, nor to any one particular moment or place in time. Rather, for an eternal moment, a moment during which nothing but paradox reigns, a subject may be both *here* and *there*; may be, or rather will of necessity be, at once in the current moment, wherein she can be perceived by others, and in another time altogether, perceived only minimally. She will be in place—perhaps spinning—but she will float above that place in a way that enables a perception of expansiveness and travel. She will give herself over to another power; and yet that other power will work with her, alongside her, so that she may feel differently empowered—possessed of knowledge and understanding that she does not usually own. In the moment of possession the erotics, contention, and the suspension that I have described in the three previous chapters as proper to the structure of diasporic belonging are held together: a subject incorporates, contends, and hovers.

I will explore these ideas of possession through the work of Nathaniel Mackey and Burning Spear—generically and geographically dissimilar enough that even their pairing embodies the yoking of apparent oppositions that fascinates me about possession. Throughout an oeuvre marked by a striking and systematic recursion and seriality, the poet, novelist, and critic Nathaniel Mackey has delved deeply into Dogon burial rituals and into the multiple meanings of the Yoruba deity Legba. Mackey constructs a poetics around Legba and the Dogon mythological figure of the *andoumboulou* based on an understanding that these spiritual figures embody a broken enabling—an ability to articulate and to mean that stems precisely from a fundamental rupture or creak. Mackey's incorporation of the Dogon metaphor of creativity as a "creaking of the word" and the rhythmic "break" figured by Legba's limp, have compelled critics such as Brent Hayes Edwards and Fred Moten to reflect on the paradoxical articulation of the difference across diasporic "joins" and on the haunting "break" of conjoined meaningfulness and inscrutability of certain black utterance. In any understanding of diasporic cultural practice operating from Mackey's ideas one proceeds in the wake of these powerful critics. What compels me in particular, and indeed what moves me, is a return to the ritual of possession as such. Through a unique recuperation of Malian rituals of the dead, a recovery that plays with the not-uncontroversial tools of cultural anthropology, Mackey develops a critical poetics that both enacts and reflects upon his ideas of diasporic dispossession and repair. I will pair Mackey's essays here with the music of Burning Spear, which, nondiscursive, *performs* an aesthetics of spirit possession. I offer these two artists as a way to renew the considerable potential for possession to symbolize and to *mean* in African diasporic subjectivity and practice. Mackey and Burning Spear close the book while, in keeping with the character of spirit possession, directing the reader to possibilities of other openings, always other openings. And, too, to freedom. In the long history of black Atlantic dispossession, spirit possession, whether as embodied practice, aesthetic appropriation, or literary metaphor, provides a mode of reclamation. Mackey develops much of his aesthetic theory in relation to music, and references to Burning Spear are threaded throughout his work. Spear, for his part, is a transformative figure in popular music, arguably less well-known than his super-star contemporaries Bob Marley and Peter Tosh, and yet notable for the longevity of his career and for the overt spirituality of his music. His work, like Nathaniel Mackey's, is marked by forms of recursion and seriality—in repeated themes and refrains that appear across albums, yes, but even more strikingly in the musical tone, atmosphere, and rhythms of the work, which sustain a similarity of hue across decades. Bringing some of the principles and aesthetics of Rastafari to his music—strikingly the emphasis on chant, call-and-response, and the use of kette drums, all features of Rasta religious ceremony—Burning Spear has brought to the popular and world music sphere works that are sacramental. Yet the apparent aesthetic simplicity can obscure the difficulty of Spear's claims and the power of his technique. In contrast, Mackey's prolix, sometimes recondite, prose may account for why it has been, to my mind at least, understudied.[1] The questions became, then, how to read Spear's lyrical claims with a defamiliarized curiosity about the nature of possession; and how to read Mackey's many, interlocking essays and his long, serial work of fiction as containing a similar spiritual force. These questions arose precisely as it became clear that to put these two apparently inapposite figures together was to begin both to be offered their similarities (in relief) and to throw up, as a shadow against a wall, the features proper to each artist that are often least visible. Mackey and Burning Spear make difficult propositions about how we come to know the historical and affiliative forms of modern blackness. The work of theirs that I read here proposes that black expressive and religious practices very far afield might come to be intimately incorporated into a black diasporic subject's own practice and person. And if the whole canvas of black phenomenology can be rigorously, though not necessarily *systematically*, made available to you, then, I suggest, Mackey and Burning Spear provide models of diasporic belonging: they show how it is possible to belong in the diaspora in a way that feels almost entirely unbounded.

Of the many compelling accounts of spirit possession in scholarship from anthropology to religious studies to history, I find Judy Rosenthal's study of ecstasy and loss—*jouissance*—in the possessive rituals of West African Goroyodu most illuminating of the aesthetic paradigms I study here, and her insights will be threaded in throughout. For instance, though it will at first appear as if Nathaniel Mackey and Burning Spear metaphorize and produce very different possessive effects—something like the difference between paucity and abundance; possession's paring down versus its amplification—Rosenthal has pointed out that Gorovodu's possession revolves precisely around the simultaneous effects of subjective amplification and attenuation. And so the differences between Mackey and Spear resolve through Gorovodu's example, and around an effect that I call the *waver*, channeling Mackey and (counterintuitively, as I will show, Frederic Jameson). A wavering, like the stammering that Mackey muses on in "Sound and Sentiment, Sound and Symbol," is a vocal, aesthetic, and epistemological distortion that is both surplus and deficiency.[2] The spirit's passing through the air, its passing through the body, shifts matter, bends it in barely perceptible increments, producing infinitesimal shattering and multiplication. The texts I consider here, Burning Spear's landmark LP *Marcus Garvey* (1975) and Mackey's essays on Legba and the andoumboulou collected in *Discrepant Engagement* (1993) and *Paracritical Hinge* (2005), as well as his novel *Bedouin Hornbook* (1986), deal in the traversal of that border between life and death, which is also the border between the material and the immaterial.[3] For both artists these crossings constitute an aesthetics of diaspora—diaspora itself being formed at that border between the nation and the imagination, landedness and dispossession, materiality and immateriality.

A word of explanation may be required for what might appear an unusual or even imbalanced pairing—that of Mackey's voluminous essays and Burning Spear's spare vocal performances. Comparing a single text to a body of work is a gesture toward the unusual calibrations required by the black archive. Sometimes one text has the comparative impact of a whole body of work. Sometimes one artistic gesture—here Burning Spear's *Marcus Garvey*—encapsulates the sweep of a career: Mackey's. This is not to privilege one iteration over another. It is not to suggest, for instance, that Burning Spear's artistic economy represents a condensed potency over and against Mackey's more graduated articulations. Nor, in the obverse, is it to suggest that Mackey's erudition and scholarly citationality represents work of greater intellectual power than Spear's supposedly folkish musical output. My instincts do not point in these directions, and my critical sympathies do not reside with either of those ideas. On the contrary, it is the one set of effects in the other that intrigues me: the lingering effusion of a Spear song and the crystallization of a single, strong poetic idea over the course of several of Mackey's enunciations. To pair these very different styles of working through and producing a particular version of black diaspora is not just to respond to the archive but also to replicate its effects. The historical archive of the black diaspora is by its nature fragmentary and generically confounding—neither of which suggests a principle of lack or deficiency. It is simply the way the archive appears to us, for reasons of history we can perhaps fully appreciate by way of allusion. It often happens, then, that compelling artistic and intellectual pairings are unexpected. A folk saying may generate and then have the weight of a critical theory—think of Gates's signifying monkey.[4] A dance repertoire may have the standing of a set of religious ideas—say, the Jamaican National Dance Theatre Company's signature piece *Kumina*. A religious artifact may stand in for a much larger historical archive—Robert Farris Thompson has shown how the carved divination trays found in Brazil testify to the continuation of Yoruba religious practices across vast temporal and geographical distances.[5] To be sure, these features are to be found in other archives as well. They bear notice now given my own critical practice, as a particularity of the archive with which I am engaged. The nature of my archive thwarts conventional ideas of what is systematic—which is emphatically not the same thing as saying there is no system of black diaspora criticism. It is to say, however, that to work in defining the culture and practice of black diaspora is to be confronted perpetually by the unexpectedly apposite—the surprising heft of the seemingly slight; the extraordinary interweaving of apparently far-flung experiences. I hope my pairing here replicates the effect of surprise I have constantly encountered in the corpus of New World black art.

But how did these texts in particular come to haunt me, and how do they haunt together? I heard the title track from Spear's *Marcus Garvey* as a set of repetitions, first as a snippet of an old Jamaican radio commercial ("Marcus Garvey words come to pass . . . Marcus Garvey words come to pass . . ."). I have no recollection of what was being advertised—maybe a documentary about Jamaican independence? Perhaps a reggae concert. Either way the lines lingered beyond the ad, and their fragmentary evocation returned over a decade later when I saw Burning Spear briefly mentioned in an essay by Nathaniel Mackey. Turning to the album *Marcus Garvey* meant placing myself—this is not unique to me, any listener places himself or herself—under the sway of a set of songs that will repeat in the mind. There is no being rid of it.

This return of Burning Spear in the midst of research on an African American poet pointed to a long-standing question about how to read Caribbean and African American art together. Mackey is particularly inspiring on this front, this attempt at crossing borders, given that the defining feature of his intellectual project can be summed up in the title of his first academic book, *Discrepant Engagement*. Mackey's intellect and imagination range widely and do not just range across but intentionally yoke traditions, geographies, and forms that have often been kept separate. The borders of his output are similarly permeable. His first novel, *Bedouin Hornbook*, emerged out of a poem, "Song of the Andoumboulou."[6] Mackey then quoted from the novel a year after its publication in his signature statement on black aesthetics, the essay "Sound and Sentiment, Sound and Symbol." And his novels and poems kept arriving intertwined with each other, and involving a novelistic narrator, N, who bears a striking resemblance to Mackey himself. *Bedouin Hornbook* became the first volume in what is now a four-volume work titled *From a Broken Bottle Traces of Perfume Now Emanate*.[7] Each new novel—the second is *Djbot Bhagustus's Run* (1993), the third *Atet A.D.* (2001), and the fourth *Bass Cathedral* (2008)—simply picks up where the last left off. Similarly, Mackey's two books of essays are characterized by intercitationality and by ideas worked through and developed in slight returns—a kind of propulsive recursion. This seriality is one version of Mackey's ongoingness. His narrator N.'s sentences stretch as if taking on a life of their own. They are as full of words as Burning Spear's verses are stripped bare of them.

But both artists are interested in how history might be considered a form of haunt—they produce the verbal and aural consequences of stalking historical phantoms—and this interest eventuates in one particular way of dealing with ghosts and spirits: the delineation of the specific qualities of religious deities and spirits of the dead such that a generalized and potentially problematic haunt might be worked with in the form of spirit possession. Burning Spear's *Marcus Garvey* appears to me to be animated by the spiritual through its repetition (the aesthetic element most analogically related to a returned spirit), its deliberately obscure phrases, its undulating moans and hums, and crucially, its espousal of an embodied philosophy of history. The phantom limb on which Mackey ruminates in "Sound and Sentiment" is the image of black diasporic loss and gain that recurs throughout his oeuvre. The absent limb represents what was broken

phantom limbs

off and left behind in the Atlantic crossing, but it also represents the memory of that absence in the West, so that absence is also a phantom presence. One thinks of Derrida's specter, departed at the moment of its apparition.[8] For Mackey and Burning Spear, the spectral might be harnessed, mediated through elegant and highly elaborated religious practices, into enabling, if difficult, metaphors of possession.

In *Bedouin Hornbook*, N. directs his missives to an unseen figure he calls Angel of Dust. She prompts her interlocutor from beyond the page and inspires in N. defensiveness, accountability, and music. She invokes N.'s reflection on memory and loss and induces startling formulations of global black culture. N.'s is a personal mythos of diaspora that weds Dogon and Yoruba cosmology to North African Islam and to a panoramic vision of the New World that encompasses the Caribbean and South America. Through N., Mackey circumvents the accustomed trajectories of the Black Atlantic. The uncanniness of his imaginative geography, however, brings him closer in one sort of way to Burning Spear, with whose geographies we are generally more familiar. For both Spear's work and Mackey's articulations are modified by a passing current that, in Spear's case, strips them down and, in Mackey's case, multiplies them. A wavering. Call it the spirit passing through.

For clarity, and for substance, I am distinguishing between spirit possession and haunt in the work of Mackey and Spear—but I do not want to do so without indicating some of the resonances, at the level of black Atlantic history, between these two structures. Haunt—generalizable, abstract, often frightening—is a powerful way of thinking about the relationship between contemporary African Diaspora experience in the West and the brutal histories, and ongoing structures, of race and capital that determine those experiences. In *Ghostly Matters*, Avery Gordon argues that a haunt is a "particular mediation."[9] Ghosts mediate between life and death, and they also signify a return, a repetition (a remediation), and in so doing they have the potential to become a remedy. Pheng Cheah's sense that there are good and bad haunts relates to this notion. The bad haunt of the colonial state constitutively infects the spirit of the postcolonial nation.[10] Cheah enlarges on this difference in many ways, evoking revenants that are "the traces left behind by any act of destruction, the indelible marks of the absence of what is destroyed but cannot be exorcised," heralding "an eventual return and reincarnation."[11] The memory of a native radical in the incipient postcolonial nation becomes an incarnation of native spirit, "a living past event that has been interiorized by memory so that it can be revivified."[12] Though the postcolonial nation will always be haunted by the colonial state, a salubrious native memory keeps hope alive.

What happens, though, if we shift the focus from nation to diaspora, as both Burning Spear and Nathaniel Mackey do? Does the inorganic haunt of the colonial state persist into the spectral imagination of diasporic sociality? One answer seems to emerge in Cheah's reading of the prosthesis (different from Berlant's, which I explored earlier)—the colonial *techne* that grafts itself onto popular nationhood, and the only potential resistance to that grafting: a form of national spirit possession whereby the popular will incorporates the haunt of the state (rather than the other way around). Cheah writes:

> The state can resist capitulation to transnational forces only if it is transformed from an inorganic prosthesis into a popular nation state. This is the hope we saw in Fanon, Anderson, Pramoedya, Ngugi, and others, who believe that popular rearticulations of the nation are not ideologies, but ethically imperative spectralizations of the state. However, the exclusionary dimension of popular nationalism can always be manipulated by state elites to hinder postcolonial national *Bildung*. There is a persistent flickering between death and life, ideology and the people's spontaneous will. The state is an uncontrollable specter that the national organism must welcome within itself, and direct, at once *for itself and against itself*, because the state can also possess the nation-people and bend it towards global capitalist interests.[13]

The postcolonial state as an uncontrollable haunt makes a great deal of sense. One imagines the moribund colonial nation undead and roving while the architects of postcolonial and revolutionary nationalism attempt, often futilely, to get on with their business. Cheah suggests they will not succeed without a form of spiritual reckoning.

But in the realm of diaspora, as described by Nathaniel Mackey, a different set of terms and emphases appear. For one thing, Cheah's prosthesis of state haunt might be transmuted into Mackey's phantom limb—an invisible prosthesis that is the mark of colonial wound in the diaspora. In this case, the prosthesis is not inorganic so much as immaterial and it belongs not to the retrograde state but to the body of the diasporic subject, as such and writ large, who may "step and move" in unexpected ways on its unusual and wavering dimensions.[14] And in the music of Burning Spear, I find not a call to popular statehood, not an interiorization of state ideologies, but rather that "persistent flickering between death and life" at the level of the individual herself who must decide whether to follow Spear into what Saidiya Hartman has called "the time of slavery"—that persistence into a realm in the present of the vivid and visceral losses of slavery. Recasting spectral nationalism in the context of diasporic subjectivity recuperates haunt from painful symptom of persistent historical injustice to enabling metaphor of wounded endurance. The aesthetic instrumentalization of spirit possession, I argue, streamlines this move even further. Burning Spear's music welcomes a set of spiritual encounters with figures from the past not so as to revive a moribund national project, but rather to imagine an alternative, diasporic framework in which timescales are in every sense different from the illusory teleology of independence and statehood. Meanwhile, Nathaniel Mackey's riffs on the phantasmatic—the deity Legba's phantom limb, Dogon myths and practices surrounding the *andoumboulou*—provide a critical practice of diaspora in which colonial history's routes take a back seat to the writer's expansive sense of spatial possibility. For what Mackey and Burning Spear teach us, if we imagine their work within the temporal and spatial frame of spirit possession, is that if indeed the diasporic subject does not belong easily within any nation, then at least to be diasporic is also to have access to this other way of being—at large in the world, possessed of its enchantments and alive to its temporal creases; audacious about the possibilities for attachments to multiple, far-flung sources of inspiration.

Conjuring Independence

The very first words on Spear's album are the resolution of a prophecy: "Marcus Garvey words come to pass / Marcus Garvey words come to pass." What follows is a couplet of economic distress: "Can't get no food to eat / Can't get no money to spend." So the first refrain is in tension with the next. First Spear proclaims that Garvey was right, that an idea of his had in some sense been effected, particularly coming after the music's heralding trumpet, suggesting success. Was Jamaican independence the accomplishment of Garvey's prophecy of black self-determination? But that notion is overturned: either the prophecy is being answered with an equal and opposite force of economic degradation, or the prophecy was never one of success but of precisely the privations Spear describes. Taking another turn, the next refrain is: "Come little one oh let me do what I can for you / And you, and you alone." This is curious and paradigmatic. Here, as is the case throughout the record, Spear's solo takes him inside and out of several subject positions. He is the scribe pronouncing prophecy fulfilled to the masses. He is then one of the masses struggling through the prophecy. He is finally the one who will soothe those sufferers. He becomes in that final turn, then, Marcus Garvey himself. He is Garvey come back to attend singularly to each of the sufferers ("for you / And you, and you alone").

There is one other thing: Spear becomes as if a priest. "Ketch them Garvey, ketch them," he sings at the end of the song. "Hol' them Marcus, hol' them." Translated from Jamaican patois, the lines read "Catch them" and "Hold them." Spear is now speaking to Garvey directly, who has been invoked by Spear and is now incorporated into the sociality of the song. He is there to be addressed. And he is both catching up with and capturing those who unjustly persecuted him. But in Jamaican patois, "ketch" also means to be spiritually possessed, to get "ketch up in the spirit," caught up in the spirit. Similarly, it is idiomatic to say that a spirit can "hol'" you, can grab hold of you and reveal itself to you without first asking permission. Like a priest, Spear invokes Garvey to hold us, to catch us up in his spirit. And in Spear's ethical structure, the justice of retribution, that is, redress (ketch them) is mirrored in the process of spirit possession (hol' them).

Marcus Garvey is a remembrance of Garvey in a moment of forgetfulness. And memory is connected to possession but is not its equivalent. The spirit is uncanny because it is that barely remembered being—"gone but not forgotten." Even the encounter with a spirit seemingly removed from one's own personal history can become a metaphor for the repressed memory of an event with which one is now implicated. M. Jacqui Alexander's account of the method by which the historical figure Thisbe, a slave woman in Trinidad who was executed as a sorceress, chose to confound the normative method of archival research and reveal herself to Alexander spiritually as Kitsimba—a woman who traversed the very locations young Alexander did herself—is one powerful example of this connection. Alexander's rigorously articulated questions about embodiment and spirituality on a West Indian slave plantation came to seem "entirely inadequate to the task of knowing Kitsimba, who was waiting to be discovered." Learning about Kitsimba through spiritual work, Alexander came to know this figure, whom she at first considered a subject of objective academic inquiry, with a specific kind of intimacy: "I could no longer continue to conduct myself as if Kitsimba's life were not bound inextricably with my own." Indeed: "Kitsimba walks with me," Alexander asserts. "She lives in springs, in water—that is, everywhere."[15]

Why would this intimate and spiritual form of memory be required at the moment of *Marcus Garvey*'s production? Three decades after Garvey's death, his dream of politically autonomous black nations was ostensibly coming into being. Certainly, there had been no mass repatriation of global blacks to a state on the continent. Except—crucially—in the minds and imaginations of those who followed Rastafari, Garvey's vision of repatriation had by and large been abandoned. This may not have been a failure in a Garveyan sense since what were emerging instead were the very black states he longed to bring into effect. Beginning with Ghana in 1957 and followed successively by Nigeria (1960), Jamaica and Trinidad and Tobago (1962), Kenya (1963), Barbados and Guyana (1966), and so on, the Union Jack was being brought down, and new symbols of black nationalism were being unfurled.

Yet for many black people in these new nations, not much was changing in daily life. The hopes for greater equality, shared citizenship, and cultural inclusion after British colonialism were beginning to fade. These diminishing hopes were equal to the way independence was being worked out in the West Indies. Independence was being brokered through legislative channels with colonial elites bartering with British state functionaries and in this way consolidating rather than diffusing oligarchical power. Furthermore, as Deborah Thomas has argued in the case of Jamaica, national "culture" was being explicitly forged out of bastardized materials, poaching from and then disenfranchising the black masses.[16] Not attending to slavery's ghosts, the new coalition of politicians, almost all of them middle class, worked to create a national culture that was ostensibly inclusive but jettisoned the dance and music emerging out of creolized Africanist traditions. Blackness, the racial sign of the majority of the nation's population, was to be subsumed in a discourse of hybridity, phenotypically represented in the "brown" (that is, light-skinned) chief minister, Alexander Bustamante, and the first prime minister, Norman Manley—cousins on opposite sides of the political aisle.[17] Indeed, the coat of arms of the new nation featured representations of the one set of subjects whom it was impossible to find in Jamaica: the Tainos killed off centuries before by the depredations of colonialism. Under the banner "Out of Many, One People," these Arawaks (as they were called) were conveniently "hybrid"—which is to say, physionogmically "brown" in Jamaican racial signification—and also, conveniently, annihilated. They could not complain about being pressed into the service of an illusory democratic ideal. And their co-optation meant politicians did not have to reckon with the trouble of representation in the contemporary era, with those problematic black subjects whose faces were presumably unseemly as symbols of state. Equally, the new politicians' creation of what Thomas calls "creole nationalism" (evoking the historic connotations of creole both as native and as mixture) skirted around representational claims of those Indian and Chinese migrants who, certainly in Jamaica, remained largely unincorporated as Indian and Chinese, though they were beginning to achieve a measure of prestige through the traditional alchemy of color in the Anglophone Caribbean: by their ability to lighten black skin.[18]

In the decade after Jamaican independence, then, certain radical lessons were being forgotten. Into this foray stepped Burning Spear, born Winston Rodney in 1948 and therefore a child of independence. Spear would have been a teenager when Chief Minister Alexander Bustamante bowed before Queen Elizabeth II on the signing of legislative documents making Jamaica independent. He would have experienced the incredulous excitement of his parents' generation at the changes afoot. He very likely would have watched news reports of the Independence ceremony at the National Stadium on August 1, 1962. But coming of age in newly independent Jamaica, Spear was also radicalized by accepting Rastafari. By the early 1970s, he smelled a rat.

When *Marcus Garvey* was released, several figures from Jamaica's revolutionary and political history had already been designated National Heroes under the auspices of the 1969 National Honours and Awards Act, all of them named-checked on *Marcus Garvey*. Garvey had been an inaugural National Hero, along with Paul Bogle, a Native Baptist preacher and leader of the 1865 Morant Bay Rebellion, and George William Gordon, a middle-class Jamaica assemblyman who was also a Baptist preacher sympathetic to the labor cause.[19] But Spear sings in the album's sixth song, "Old Marcus Garvey," that while "they been talking about" Bogle, Gordon, and Bustamante, no one was talking about Old Marcus Garvey:

> No one remember Old Marcus Garvey
> No one remember Old Marcus Garvey
> [Repeat]
> They been talking about Paul Bogle
> They been talking about William Gordon
> They been talking about Norman Washington Manley
> Including Bustamante
> No one remember Old Marcus Garvey
> No one remember Old Marcus Garvey

In what sense had post-Independence Jamaicans forgotten Garvey? How were they remembering his fellow National Heroes differently than they were him? There is no conventional temporal logic to Spear's claim, since if Manley and Bustamante would have been in contemporary memory and not Garvey, who had died decades previous, then what to make of our putatively better memory of Bogle and Gordon, who died a full century before? Indeed, why is Garvey's project implicitly kept separate from Bogle's here, when both were black radicals who critiqued British colonialism and envisioned justice for a black laboring class? I propose two reasons, one temporal and the other epistemological. Spear's act of recovery draws attention, first, to a different chronological system implicit in his music. Bogle and Gordon of 1865 coincide with Manley and Bustamante of 1962 with no conceptual dissonance, because for Burning Spear there is no necessary reason that time would proceed with any regularity. History's hastiness in these verses from the mid-nineteenth century to the mid-twentieth emphasizes both its repetitiveness and its recursivity. Cordoning Garvey off from the martyrs of 1865 also emphasizes the importance of Spear's Rastafari belief. Garvey is considered a prophet in Rastafari. He was considered prescient on the rise of a black emperor of Africa, whom Rastas would later identify as Ras Tafari Makonnen, crowned Haile Selassie I in 1930, emperor of Ethiopia. Emphasizing Garvey over and against Bogle and Gordon signals the priority of Spear's religious understanding in his music, which constitutes a belief in the spiritually elevated status of both Garvey and Selassie. This belief in turn has temporal implications.

queer

Rasta eschatology is fueled by an urgent belief in the impending end of current regimes of white colonialism, an urgency and ardency that has been experienced, so far at least, as deferral. Haile Selassie's future return is related, chiasmus-like, to Garvey's return from the past. "Jordan River" and "Resting Place" on *Marcus Garvey* as well as "Man in the Hills" on Spear's earlier album of the same name demonstrate this form of Rastafari eschatology that is in sympathy with Derrida's notion of the messianic: its content is perpetually deferred.[20] Selassie was the black emperor, but his death does not mean that the dream of his supremacy has ended. He may yet come back. Zion, the paradise of rest, does and does not refer to Ethiopia. This wavering between the material and the immaterial means that the symbolic is not abstract but is accompanied by a potent politics, materialized in bodily practices of the here and now and in pervasive and persistent political critique in Babylon.

Despite Garvey's embrace by Rastafari, a religion that was severely denigrated in Jamaica in early Independence, he was named a National Hero and enshrined in Jamaican national politics. But Garvey's project of black autonomy went in a different direction from that in which Jamaica's politicians were taking the new nation. Enshrining Garvey as they did was in fact the opposite of remembering him, and Spear's album is a rebuke to enshrinement over memory. Spear felt the need to conjure the spirit of Garvey to produce a national possession. Through a variety of turns, the album insists that Garvey is alive and well and that his presence will produce the love Jamaica needs, if only we can remember that he lives, that he is here. *Marcus Garvey* is a provocative example of history as possessive presence. When Spear asks, for instance, on "Old Marcus Garvey," "Who younger than Garvey?" It is an odd provocation, given that Garvey died at fifty two (prematurely, but not at an age usually considered young) and given that Garvey is, in fact, dead. But the spirit ceases to age. And if youth represents vitality, then Garvey's vivid presence in this album and, as Spear argues, in Jamaica itself, means that no one could be younger.

Marcus Garvey's aesthetics of possession are to be found not only conceptually but also in its most insistent formal feature: repetition. The album is full of echoes. Spear's vocals loop and drift around recurring refrains. The prevailing lyrical structure of the album, replicated on just about every song, is the echo. A refrain is established and repeated: "No one remember Old Marcus Garvey / No one remember Old Marcus Garvey." Or "Do you remember the days of slavery? / Do you remember the days of slavery?" The line is then repeated again in call-and-response fashion, providing the song with a verbal through-line that is like a backbone, supporting the lyrical and vocal digressions of Spear's solos, reminding him of what he can always depend on and come back to. For these songs are like bodies, made of backbones and pulsing blood, with vocals swelling out like muscles, the tightening sinews of Spear's upper register—a fit structure through which the spirit can pass. In "Old Marcus Garvey" the familiar reggae guitar thwack is like a heartbeat.[21] For the rest of the song, the drumbeat is like breath, regular and punctuated with startled intakes that are like stuttering accommodations to the consciousness of a spirit. The top guitar rhythm moves along in a regular rhythm, and the drumbeat is, as Fred Moten might say, in the break.[22] It is outside regular time, marking a different time, making a rupture that wedges open a space within the music for another realm of time. The drum's kit makes the break, and it exists in the break, in the space between heartbeat and breath, between the unconscious and the conscious.

The most unrelenting echoes occur on the song "Slavery Days." The opening refrain, "Do you remember the days of slavery?" is repeated continually throughout the song. It is an insistent question around which Spear offers his own memories. "The work was so hard," he says, "And they used us / Til they refused us." This is the most regular of the repetitions, almost unvarying, and with a two-part harmony that is a little off-pitch, a bit of a drone. *Do you remember the days of slavery* is echo, but it is also an insistent question, a nag.[23] The song's refrain enacts the tendency of the spirit to prompt to the point of distraction, to insist on itself until the subject is diminished and amplified in another sense—full of some other kind of knowledge, some other kind of person. The incantation of the refrain ("Mmmmmmm / Mmmmmmmm") is an invitation to remember something that has been forgotten. Incantations use the body, the vocal vibrations, to induce effects on the mind. The songs strip aesthetics down to the minimum, inducing spiritual memory not through overwhelming sensory effects but through the severe beauty of spare ritual. Spear's *mmmm*s vibrate like a body's shudder.

What can it mean, in 1975, to remember a labor system that ceased to exist 137 years earlier? Having been born in 1948 produces no barrier to Burning Spear's sense that he has an embodied memory of slavery, that he remembers it as if having lived through it himself. This living memory is an affront to the neocolonial state, a fugitive procedure by which, as Cheah writes, "a living past event [is] interiorized by memory so that it can be revivified."[24] Spear prompts listeners to remember those days, too. And how can contemporary listeners remember slavery rather than learn about it? Spear prompts us into memory by reminding us that "history" can recall. The line is: "History can recall, history can record / The days of slavery." At first glance, this line suggests the conventional charge that one should look to historical texts in order to correct ignorance. It seems to be a call for study. But the line's grammar positions history as the acting subject, recalling for itself the days of slavery. Personifying history, giving it the agency that is still conditional for Spear's listeners, suggests first that history is on the side of the listener, who, unremembering, lags behind history. If even *history* can recall, then surely we should, too. History seems to best the listener. Which consideration is the first glimmer that Spear's call to remember may not in fact be the same as his sense of recall. For history has bested black people before—historiography has often written black subjectivity out of its account. And given that the Burning Spear project implies a radical questioning of the very basis of materialism, and a keen understanding of the exploitations of modernity ("And they used us / Til they refused us"), it soon becomes apparent that history is not on the listener's side. This personification of history is also a categorical separation. History is not human, and its records are not sufficient. *Recall* connotes the rote and the practiced, not the learned or experienced.[25]

Spear's remembering is not, in fact, the same as whatever it is that history is recalling. His is a remembering from experience, from feeling; the call to listeners is to remember, too. "And they beat us," Spear prompts us. "And the work was so hard." The logic of the song argues that Spear remembers having experienced it himself. He suggests that "we"—the grammar of the song is first-person plural—were there, too. There are several assumptions about the addressee of the song, this "you" who may not be remembering. People who were slaves. People who should now remember that they were slaves. If the call is to a stimulation of the memories locked away in the subject, then there is an assumption that bodily presence in the era being remembered is not required for memory. Or, the opposite: the body *was* there, but in a very particular kind of way.

On *Marcus Garvey*, Burning Spear presents slavery as a living memory, something that happened to him personally, and at some temporality akin to yesterday. Layering the temporal complexity, Spear also channels the spirit of Marcus Garvey, becoming a conduit for the perspective of the famed Pan-Africanist. He is possessed by the spirit of Garvey; and to be possessed by a spirit is to be imbued with knowledge; to be, as Judy Rosenthal would argue, uniquely agentive rather than stripped of agency. Possession becomes the sign and the redress for historical dispossession. ("The dispossession accomplished by slavery became the model for possession in vodou: for making a man not into a thing but into a spirit," Joan Dayan writes.)[26] It is also a signal of a form of black temporality: that phenomenon Saidiya Hartman evokes, in her essay "The Time of Slavery," of the living being "coeval with the dead." More than the relation between the past and the present, the time of slavery is about "the horizon of loss, the extant legacy of slavery, the antinomies of redemption."[27] The existence of Burning Spear's ghostly album in 1975 was a sign that post-Independence Jamaican politics and economics were hospitable to ghosts, in Avery Gordon's sense. There is enough in that politics that is old to make ghosts comfortable. The dub version of *Marcus Garvey*, released a few months later, was appropriately called *Garvey's Ghost*. A dubside is also a flipside; the other side of a record, the underside of a track; a photo negative. On *Garvey's Ghost*, the instrumental tracks of *Marcus Garvey*, aesthetically distorted by various effects, including loops and extensions, appear with minimal words—except for ghostly traces of Spear's voice laid over in echoing, warbly effect. These are wholly new experiences of Spear's songs that make the meanings of the originals more vivid.[28]

We turn now from dub to Mackey, who's lengthier texts are also structured by invoked absences. The indeterminacy of N.'s epistolary interlocutor matches the ambiguous invocations of Burning Spear. Whoever Angel of Dust might be, her name registers an immaterial ontology, a combination of the mythologically celestial and evanescently material. For dust is that confounding substance whose presence is detectable only as trace. We see it but never know when or whence it arrives. It may disappear just as swiftly as it came, but for the moments it lingers, dust morphs those surfaces it touches, including air itself. The specter, always materially present as well as immaterial, may be metaphorized as dust, floating in a shaft of sunlight and warping it.

Where Spear registers possession by an attenuation of language (repetition), Mackey registers possession through the polysyllabic neologisms—

speaking in tongues. The paradox of this relationship between the two texts matches the paradox of historical haunt with which Mackey is concerned over the course of at least two decades: the effects of loss as surplus. This paradox is represented by a phantom limb, a sign on which Mackey ruminates over a series of essays which I will consider alongside the novel.

Legba's Missing Limb

The title of Nathaniel Mackey's four-volume work of fiction, *From a Broken Bottle Traces of Perfume Still Emanate*, gestures to the paradox that lies at the heart of his poetics. A fragrant spirit emanates from a container whose brokenness enables its release. These spirits linger, persisting despite time's passing. Mackey's theory of black art is encapsulated in this paradoxical mingling of sweetness and bitterness, brokenness and enabling. He refers to *Broken Bottle* as "a work that wavers with regard to genre."[29] We can pursue a line throughout his corpus in order to arrive at this idea of generic wavering, and part of the pleasure of this is observing Mackey develop his ideas iteratively, recursively. The work unfolds through a series of interlocking connections and conceptual associations. Images accrete. Like waves, they rush in, pull out again, and return with variations and with a different force. This style is all but impossible to resist. The writer on Mackey finds herself reproducing his rhetoric without at first realizing she is doing so. Not least because this is the very phenomenon with which my chapter is concerned—language as possessive force; aesthetics as metaphorized spiritual manifestation—I have chosen to see those moments in which Mackey arrives in my own language as exactly right. (This, after a remarkably fraught period in which the language refused to be revised.) For a few moments now, as I lay out the steps by which Mackey's aesthetics of diaspora came to be developed in relation to the Caribbean and to music, I will sound like him: multiply associative, accretive. Giving over my language in this way is in service to a larger idea, and is, in any event, inevitable. The Jamaican critic is overtaken by the African American artist; wounded kinship balmed by linguistic sympathy.

The recourse Mackey has to the Caribbean as a source of diasporic conceptualization functions like his relationship to music. In both sites, Mackey finds a form of loss that ultimately bestows aesthetic gifts. He is most compelled by theorizations in which music and the Caribbean are instantiated by a particular form of loss. It is the severing of a familial tie, and the insistent perception of that loss as a kind of phantom, that Mackey understands. His poetics is a suturing. We might think of his language as threading and looping, catching pieces of fabric at different points to create a seam. To suture the visible to the phantom, however, is no simple task. One strays, one misses, one tries again. The stitched crease might waver rather than describe a straight line. But it is only in this way that Mackey can bring us from Yoruban orisha to the Dogon, and to Federico Garcia Lorca and to the Caribbean—it is all the same to him: broken voice, haunted sibling. Mackey is fascinated by Burning Spear because Spear's vocals present that broken raspiness that is everything to Mackey as an embodiment of black diaspora. There is a whole world encompassed in the repetitions of Burning Spear's *Marcus Garvey*, in the sparseness of his most famous and arguably most accomplished record. And there is an answering expansion and elucidation in Mackey's poetics. It begins in 1980, five years after *Marcus Garvey*, with Mackey's essay on Caribbean history and poetics.

In "Limbo, Dislocation, Phantom Limb," Mackey writes about the ideas of Guyanese novelist Wilson Harris on the Caribbean history of forced migration, native decimation, forced labor, and other traumas of modernity as a crucible for American art. For Harris, the rupture of the Middle Passage need not be experienced as shameful loss, nor need it engender attempts at wholesale recovery.[30] Rather, as Mackey glosses Harris, the losses of transatlantic scattering are "that of an *opportune* deprivation or dispossession."[31] The limbo dance, created by slaves on the Middle Passage ship decks, becomes an embodied symbol of the first practice of diaspora art. The dance movement signals the cruelty of the cramped quarters below deck in the slave holds and signals as well slaves' survival: the mental, affective, and bodily practices by which unimaginable cruelty is survived through creative circumvention, dynamic invention, and subterfuge. As Harris says, limbo limns limb. The slave body's enactment of the liminal passage from Old to New World is also an enactment of dismemberment. Harris writes: "The limbo dance becomes the human gateway which dislocates (and therefore begins to free itself from) a uniform chain of miles across the Atlantic. . . . [It] therefore implies, I believe, a profound art of compensation which seeks to re-play a dismemberment of tribes . . . and at the same time a curious psychic re-assembly of the parts of the dead god or gods."[32]

Those dead gods—not dead really, but reborn (see, for instance, Wole Soyinka's erudite reading of the remaking of the orisha in the western hemisphere in his essay "The Fourth Stage")—inspire the creative imagination in which history's losses are transformed into "resourceful acts of bricolage."[33] Harris concludes: "The apparent void of history which haunts the black man may never be compensated until an act of imagination opens gateways between civilizations, between technological and spiritual apprehensions, between racial possession and dispossession. . . . Limbo and vodun are variables of an underworld imagination—variables of phantom limb and void and a nucleus of strategems in which limb is a legitimate pun on limbo, void on vodun."[34] Mackey's reckoning with this play between loss and gain in Harris's work was underwritten by an apparently discrepant figure in all of this: Federico Garcia Lorca. For Mackey's "Limbo, Dislocation, Phantom Limb" actually begins—at the very first sentence—with Lorca's "Play and Theory of the Duende" (1933).[35] For Mackey, the duende represents the mysterious presence of a spirit that inspires the flamenco singer, a spirit understood by idiom and memory to come from the north of Africa, from the Moors ("Eso es cante moro," *That's Moorish singing*, the saying goes). This is a spirit—i.e., a ghostly presence as well as an aesthetic attitude—that is connected in Lorca's mind and in Mackey's to New World spirituality and poetics. In a passage Mackey quotes at length from "Play and Function of the Duende," Lorca describes the moment he connected Old to New World, while listening to the inspired singing of an Andalusian singer, Pastora Pavon (known as La Niña de los Peines): "As though crazy, torn like a medieval weeper, La Niña de los Peines got to her feet, tossed off a big glass of firewater and began to sing with a scorched throat, without voice, without breath or color, but with duende. She was able to kill all the scaffolding of the song and leave way for a furious, enslaving duende, friend of sand winds, who made the listener rip their clothes with the same rhythm as do the blacks of the Antilles when, in the 'lucumi' rite, they huddled in heaps before the statue of Santa Barbara."[36] It is in relation to this passage that Mackey develops an idea of the torn voice as a doubled voice. There is in black music, he writes in "Cante Moro," "a forking of the voice, so that we hear the intersection of two lines of articulation—doubling the voice, splitting the voice, breaking the voice, tearing it."[37] This surplus articulation is also a disturbance of language such that conventional understanding mutates into something else, the articulation itself (poetry, experimental fiction in Mackey's case) takes on the nonrepresentational quality of music. "The [duende] voice becomes troubled," he writes. "Its eloquence becomes eloquence of another order, a broken, problematic, self-problematizing eloquence."[38] Spiritual inspiration occurs when seemingly absent, not strictly identifiable, though probably ancestral, force bends expression so that it is both less than communicative language (no one can say what this duende is) and, of course, more than communicative language (for no one can say whence this surplus).

The most important development from the question of the phantom limb, then, through the Lorcaian detour, is the move toward absent language—articulate noise. "The phantom limb bespeaks that reach, which continues beyond the grasping of something. It speaks of loss, it speaks of lack, but it also speaks of an insufficiency that's indigenous to the very act of reaching."[39] In "Sound and Sentiment, Sound and Symbol," perhaps Mackey's most famous essay, he rehearses the myth behind the song form of the Kaluli of Papua New Guinea—a song that is inspired by the loss of the sibling. Though Mackey does not say it outright, characteristically avoiding obviousness on this point, the clear implication is that Africans in the diaspora have lost siblings, too, and their songs are born of that loss. Something like an overarching poetics of black art in the West is attributed to this loss. A poetics of unconventional comprehensibility—like music, symbolic and lacking an easy transfer between sign and meaning—connects written to aural forms. And the theory of the lost sibling is how we get to Mackey's elegant encapsulation: "Music is wounded kinship's last resort."[40] This is an aesthetics of extremity, of exigency.

All of this explains Mackey's interest in music and musicians as well as his interest in a variety of forms of linguistic experimentation—most pertinently here reggae, Rasta speech, and the poetry of Kamau Brathwaite—language that thrives on neologisms and inversions to wring words out of joint, to make English strange to itself as a resistance to and a sign of the colonial oppression of language. To Calibanize it, in Mackey's appropriation of Kamau Brathwaite's famous trope. "I think of such things as scat," Mackey writes in *Bedouin Hornbook*,

> where the apparent mangling of articulate speech testifies to an "unspeakable" history such singers are both vanquishers and victims of.

This carries back, of course, to what I said about the moan and the south a few letters back, so I won't belabor it here. I will, however, add that one can hear the same sort of thing even in reggae, a scatlike gargling of "meaningless" sound in the singing of, among others, Burning Spear. Listen to "Jordan River" or, even better, the "live" version of "Man in the Hills," where you'll hear a kind of yodeling and even birdcalls about halfway thru.[41]

By the time of this, Mackey's first reference in *Bedouin Hornbook* to Burning Spear, the reader has been immersed in a series of letters from someone called only N. to someone referred to as Angel of Dust. The "sort of thing" that one can detect "even" here in reggae is of course of the same absent, inarticulable presence with which Mackey is fascinated and that I have been laboring to describe. And the "even" modifying the connection between the southern black moan and reggae suggests that there is something inapposite, or at the very least unexpected, about the relationship between Burning Spear's reggae and jazz. In part this is a question of geography—the US South can seem very far away from the Caribbean, in some senses, even though a mere two hundred years ago these regions were almost extensions of each other. But N. is arguing for a closeness between the "scatlike gargling of 'meaninglessness'" that we find in those moments of wordlessness in *Marcus Garvey* and "Man in the Hills" and the moan of southern bluesman. I am arguing, in apposition, for a closeness between the "mangling of articulate speech" of these musicians and the profusion of words we encounter in Mackey's fiction, novels that have sometimes been named jazz prose.[42] *Bedouin Hornbook* demonstrates the intensification of language to something approaching the unintelligible, if only at the level of the conventional plot. This intensification in turn recurs to music that inspired it.

The ur-text of *Bedouin Hornbook* is in Mackey's first series of "Andoumboulou" poems: "Songs" 5 and 7 contain the very first Angel of Dust letters.[43] In one interview, Mackey describes happening on the epistolary form in order to "unpack the poetry" for, at first, a certain friend, but soon enough for "a rather spectral audience."[44] In another interview, he suggests the connection between letter writing and absence as creating a kind of possession, noting that in the writing of a letter there is "the sense of being in conversation with the dead, the sense . . . that one is writing beyond one's self."[45] Letter writing is then—like photography, as Barthes explained in *Camera Lucida*—a way of dealing in death whose appearance is precisely death's opposite: the creation of a permanent record and forging a connection between the present and the future. The necessity of a letter is an absence, and to compose a letter is to attempt to bring into presence a kind of ghost.

This way of thinking about Mackey's turn to the epistolary brings to mind the very many connections between notions of diaspora and those of death, not least the structural paradox that diaspora represents. To conceive a connection among black people globally, for instance, is, at the very moment the thought is conceived, to bring to mind the fragmentation caused by the slave trade. Mackey's development of an aesthetic metaphor for diaspora in jazz communion and dispersion is another example of structural paradox, and this is also not an unfamiliar connection. However, Mackey makes it new by making it strange. The first set of images he finds for the black diaspora in *Bedouin Hornbook* are startling, and they fulfill multiple purposes. They establish the image of the leg, the hambone, that is riffed on throughout and that embodies the propulsion and sweep of the language of the novel, which is throughout characterized by a breathless erudition wed to poetic language games that are a part of the novel's aesthetics of haunt (words are constantly anagrammatically rearranged, as in conjuring). The images first occur when N. writes about a music composition he earlier sent to the Angel of Dust:

> The other composition you asked about I've since titled "Third Leg of the Sun." It actually grew out of a passage I'd read in Maya Deren's book on vodoun, a passage I might as well quote for you. "Legba," she writes, "who knows the divine language and through whom one might seek recourse from destiny, is himself the destined answer to the riddle of the Sphinx: he was once the new-born infant sun, lived through the fertile prime of his noon, and is now the old sun, walking with a cane—the 'third leg'—in the afternoon of life."
>
> This gave rise to the following questions, which I more or less tried to de-clench in that composition: Couldn't Ba have cut itself off from Legba and made the journey back to Egypt, have hidden out there like Stesichorus's Helen, a phantom limb calling itself "Ram" and at other times "Soul"? Couldn't Leg have followed suit, have introduced itself

as "Thigh," the Great Bear of the northern heavens, then almost immediately have left Egypt for Guatemala, calling itself "Huracan," and have come to be known there as "Heart of Heaven"? Couldn't the memory of Leg have merged with that of Set back in Egypt, Horus having wounded Set in the thing when he swallowed the moon? Why else would 1) Huracan, the Quiche Maya stormgod whose name sounds like "hurricane," be described as a huge thigh coming out of the clouds, 2) Set go by an alternate name Typhon, and 3) Typhon be what the Greeks called the hurricane buried in Tartaros?

More some other time.[46]

More, always more. N.'s letters flow as if fueled by inexhaustible resources. The metaphors for diaspora here are startling because their cultural conjunctions are so unfamiliar. Too, the enumerated hypotheses introduce quantification, which reminds us of spiritual possession as a kind of economy. N. is endowed with words that he spends. Afterward, he is spent. Reading, we are spent by their almost ceaselessness. This effect of possession as expenditure that we encounter in Mackey's novels is essential—recall Rosenthal on Gorovodu. Mackey, of course, does not discuss Gorovodu but rather Yoruba orisha practices among blacks in the New World. However, Ewe Gorovodu and Yoruba Ifa-Orisha have much in common, emerging in West African territories adjacent to each other and sharing overlapping histories, tenets, and practices, most fundamentally ritualized possession, ancestral veneration, and a belief in spiritual deities (orisha in Yoruba; vodus in Ewe) many of which are shared (including Legba). That Gorovodu venerates northern slave spirits as ancestral forces is a particularity that would be of special interest to Mackey, given his interest in and literary enactment of possession as expenditure and ravishment. Yoruba-based forms of possession function similarly to Ewe possession, both ecstatic moments of trance in which, as Rosenthal would put it, the overtaking of the subject is ravishment in all senses of the word—radical plunder, radical pleasure. This performance is an enactment of birth and death cycles and mirrors a historical epistemology in which things recur. History is brought back into the body through incantation. Mackey himself has written about the kind of possessive quality his writing sometimes takes, noting in the preface to his 2006 poetry collection *Splay Anthem* that "recursiveness, incantatory insistence, is liturgy and libation, repeated ritual sip, a form of sonic observance aiming to undo the obstruction it reports. . . . Recursion is conjunctive deprivation and possession, phantom limb, as if certain aroused and retained relations among consonants and vowels and progressions of accent were compensatory arms we reach with, compensatory legs we cross over on."[47]

Bedouin Hornbook's N. imagines a vision of the black diaspora in which the Yoruba orisha Legba encapsulates history's recursion and language's possessive brokenness. God of the crossroads, the intercessor, the deity imaged in Haitian vodou as an old man with a limp. Legba is enormously important in Yoruba-based religions, and it is not happenstance that Mackey holds on to him. It is Legba, of all the gods, whom we find at every turn in New World African spirituality.[48] In Mackey's narrative, Legba is the most portable—his name like a wishbone that can be cleanly split, easily cast in one direction and another. His philosophical embodiment as juncture means he can signify the site of both loss and potential connection. Robert Farris Thompson's description of the Yoruba god Eshu-Elegba, from which Legba derives, gives a sense of why he should come to figure so prominently in New World art and religion:

> According to a legend, at a crossroads in the history of the Yoruba gods, when each wished to find out who, under God, was supreme, all the deities made their way to heaven, each bearing a rich sacrificial offering on his or her head. All save one. Eshu-Elegbara wisely honoring beforehand the deity of divination with a sacrifice, had been told by him what to bring to heaven—a single crimson parrot feather (ekodide), positioned upright upon his forehead, to signify that he was not to carry burdens on his head. Responding to the fiery flashing of the parrot feather, the very seal of supernatural force and ashe, God granted Eshu the force to make all things happen and multiply (ashe). . . .
>
> Eshu consequently came to be regarded as the very embodiment of the crossroads. Eshu-Elegbara is also the messenger of the gods, not only carrying sacrifices, deposited at crucial points of intersection, to the goddesses and to the gods, but sometimes bearing the crossroads to us in verbal form, in messages that test our wisdom and compassion. . . .
>
> [Eshu is] the ultimate master of potentiality. Eshu becomes the imperative companion-messenger of each deity, the imperative messenger-companion of the devotee. The cult of Eshu-Elegbara thus transcends

the limits of ordinary affiliation and turns up wherever traditionally minded Yoruba may be.

So it was that Eshu-Elegbara became one of the most important images in the black Atlantic world.[49]

For Mackey, Legba grounds an idea of conjoined surplus and lack in diasporic aesthetics. Mackey thinks of Legba's limp as stemming from a lost limb, a consequence of the crossing from Old World to New. He writes:

> The master of polyrhythmicity and heterogeneity, [Legba] suffers not from deformity but multiformity, a "defective" capacity in a homogeneous order given over to uniform rule. Legba's limp is an emblem of heterogeneous wholeness, the image and outcome of a peculiar remediation. *Lame* or *limping*, that is, like *phantom*, cuts with a relativizing edge to unveil impairment's power, as though the syncopated accent were an unsuspected blessing offering anomalous, unpredictable support. Impairment taken to higher ground, remediated, translates damage and disarray into a dance. Legba's limp, compensating the difference in leg lengths, functions like a phantom limb. [His] deficit leg [transforms] into invisible supplement.[50]

The notion of a limping god, a god with a physical compromise, a liminal go-between from humanity to the divine, has a function in other West African cosmology that holds significance for Mackey—that of the Dogon. Mackey's interest in the religion of this Malian ethnic group is not dissimilar to his interest in the Yoruba, in that it emerges from an encounter with an artistic proffering around death and leads to a figure symbolizing lost kinship and the breach between the divine and the human, the material and the immaterial. Mackey's unreplicable yoking of the Dogon and the Yoruba is a kind of suturing—an intellectual and literary gesture that returns us to where we began. For reconnecting lost siblings is Mackey's instinct. His is an adventure that perceives broken connection and effects unlikely repair. In so doing, his poetics proposes a capacious black belonging and belonging-to, characterized by a forged and hard-worked likeness.

Mackey's engagement with the Dogon revolves around one particular aspect of Dogon creation myths that he encountered—we will not be surprised by this now—through a music recording. The *andoumboulou* are, according to certain recorded myths of the Dogon, a prehuman creature, the product of a god's coupling with the earth. The ur-text to *Bedouin Hornbook* is to be found in the very first series of poems entitled "Song of the Andoumboulou," published in the collection *Eroding Witness* in 1985. Heading up "Song of the Andoumboulou: 1" is an epigraph/quotation from Marcel Griaule's *Conversations with Ogotemmêli*, an ethnography of Dogon religion first published in French as *Dieu d'eau* in 1948.[51] In his interview with Peter O'Leary, Mackey described encounters with two texts about the Dogon that captured his imagination: a French recording of Dogon music entitled *Les Dogon* (1956) in which the liner notes identified the "Song of the Andoumboulou" as a funeral song; and *The Pale Fox*, a more elaborate text of Dogon mythology coauthored by Griaule and Germaine Deiterlen, first published in French as *Le renard pale* also in 1956.[52] Mackey first heard the record in the early 1970s, saying later: "It was aurally impressive in a way that I found ineradicable from my thinking." Later, when he read *The Pale Fox*, the music took on discursive significance, since Griaule and Dieterlen described who the *andoumboulou* were and how they fit into Dogon cosmology.[53]

Three conceptual constellations emerged for Mackey through his encounters with these texts. From *Conversations with Ogotemmêli* came the notion of "the creaking of the word" and language fabrication (explored in "Poseidon [Dub Version]" and summarized in the introduction to *Discrepant Engagement*.[54] Mackey mentions this idea in the introduction to *Paracritical Hinge*, this time bringing it all back to Burning Spear.[55]) From the music on *Les Dogon* came a preoccupation with death as muse, with the relationship between singing and the release of spirits—music as an archive of lost kin, letting go, and therefore transcending loss through creation. Mackey explains this in the O'Leary interview, saying that the recording of "Song of the Andoumboulou" suggested to him simultaneous lament and rebirth.[56] *Les Dogon* prompted Mackey's series of Andoumboulou poems. Finally, from *The Pale Fox* came the *andoumboulou* themselves—"a rough draft of human being," as Mackey came to think of them.[57] The song of these rough human drafts embodied a roughening of tonal quality that is the sign of musical mastery transcending to spiritual intensity.

Because scholarly work on the Dogon in English is relatively sparse and the history of its reception both in French and in English very complex, because Mackey's imaginative process is caught up with it in a way that is significant, and above all, because these receptions are a record of various hauntings, I would like to offer a brief word on the development of, and a controversy in, the field. Griaule's *Conversations with Ogotemmêli* is generally recognized as the introduction in the European scholarly imagination of the Dogon. When *The Pale Fox* appeared eight years later, shortly after Griaule's death, the two books together formed a dyad of Dogon myth in the West. Griaule himself came to have a mythical place in European Dogon studies. His research trips to Mali between 1931 and 1939 (referred to, significantly, as "missions"), his several students and collaborators who went on to publish on the Dogon (including his daughter, Geneviève Calame-Griaule) all meant that Griaule became a kind of guiding spirit in European anthropology of the Dogon.

In 1991 the Dutch anthropologist Walter van Beek published an article entitled "Dogon Restudied," which arrived as an intervention in the scholarly reception of Griaule's work.[58] Van Beek argued that Griaule's "cultural constructs" of the Dogon were unrecognizable both to the Dogon and to contemporary anthropologists of the field, that these constructions did not "offer productive insights into Dogon thinking," and that they were unfamiliar to the Dogon as "a meaningful part of their thinking and way of life."[59] In a later, companion piece to "Dogon Restudied," van Beek noted the positive use to which Griaule's representation of Dogon cosmology could be put—chiefly, as a refutation of racist notions of the supposedly simplistic religious cultures of "Africa."[60] But van Beek's concession as to the uses of "Griaule's Dogon" only reinforced his primary sense that the famous French anthropologist had, in a sense, invented the Dogon for the West. Writing of *Conversations with Ogotemmêli*, van Beek notes:

> At the time of first publication in 1948, the book was a revelation. Never before had such a coherent, mysterious, and deep set of ideas been found, seemingly governing all social life in an African community; never before had the secrets of an African society been exposed so clearly in order to show a native philosophy on par with what the Athenian and Indian civilizations offered to humanity. It was a victory over racist ideologies on Africa and Africans, a vindication of the negritude movement in swing at the same time. Africa really had something to offer to French intellectuals and to the rest of the world.[61]

Conversations with Ogotemmêli is based on Griaule's report of several weeks' conversation with an elder Dogon who, according to the book, explained to Griaule over a series of intense days their entire cosmology. *The Pale Fox* is rendered as a much more complicated, comprehensive research into this cosmology. Van Beek came to think of the works together as "ethnofiction, a fitting tribute to the joint creativity of anthropologist and informants."[62]

What Mackey encountered of the andoumboulou in *The Pale Fox* is, at least judging from my own encounter with the text, a quite convoluted narrative of the god Ogo's quest for premature knowledge, his subsequent banishment from the realm of the gods and separation from his twin-god, and his coupling with the earth (his mother) to create a new, imperfect life-form. It is the story of a god's fall, of incest, and of creation—elements that fit within archetypes of mythology. Here is the moment in *The Pale Fox* when the andoumboulou are explained:

> It is said: "His mother and the sky (it is) all one; it is as if he had stolen a piece of sky; Ogo . . . was (had as a symbol) 7; he entered into his mother, seeking to add (to himself) the word 8. (But) the word did not come very much to Ogo."
>
> The incest committed with his placenta, the earth, his "mother" was nevertheless productive. First to be born were the Yeban (yebeu), small creatures with big heads, discolored bodies, and fair limbs who, for shame of their condition, hide in the holes of the earth. They coupled and gave birth to the Andoumboulou (andummolo), who are even smaller than they are. All these beings were born single. All were incestuous because, like Ogo his progenitor, a Yeban male coupled with his daughter, an Andoumboulou woman. Thus, the Earth's interior became slowly populated with these beings who are the very first to attest to Ogo's failure and his lost twinness.[63]

The remarkable thing about what Mackey has done with Griaule's Dogon is that he has created another kind of lost kinship and then also created a suture. Between the Yoruba and this version of the Dogon (at least according to Van Beek and other recent anthropologists), there is very little in common. Part of Van Beek's contention about the problems with Griaule's Dogon is that they bear a surprising lack of resemblance to other West African cosmologies. But Mackey detects a lost connection. It is as if the Dogon and the Yoruba were separated (by Griaule?) and Mackey has put them back together. From the preface to *Splay Anthem*: "The song of the Andoumboulou is one of striving, strain, abrasion, an all but asthmatic song of aspiration. Lost ground, lost twinness, lost union and other losses variably inflect that aspiration, a wish, among others, to be we, that of the recurring two, the archetypal lovers who visit and revisit the poems, that of some larger collectivity an anthem would celebrate."[64] The scholarly controversy surrounding Griaule was still several years in the future when Mackey first heard *Les Dogon* and picked up *The Pale Fox*. Whether knowing all this would have changed his sense of the Dogon's relationship to his notion of the African diaspora is impossible to say—and it is, perhaps, no matter. What matters is that Mackey took the imaginative work of Griaule and Dieterlen and ran with it, creating his own Dogon imaginary. To this he added the Yoruba, essentially creating a new poetic, black diasporic imaginary, which, as I have been describing, draws on the inspiration of Burning Spear, too. By Griaule's account, Ogo will incessantly search for his lost twin, the partner he lost when he was cast out. In a sense Mackey's oeuvre is an incessant search for lost kin. In Burning Spear he found a far-flung brother. His suturing poetics is, emphatically, not a quest for origins or an attempt at recovery undergirded by shame at what has been lost. Rather, the strangely unfamiliar pairings that make up Mackey's idea of black diasporic art remind us precisely of what wholeness can never be recovered. And it is, in any event, a much weirder, more uncanny, and indeed more possessive vision of the diaspora than that conceived under the umbrella of "origins" and reclamation. It is as weird and as haunting as Burning Spear's voice.

Together, these two distinct artists conclude my book by offering unique takes on the possibilities for spirit possession. In Burning Spear's approach, embodiment of slave history and musical replication of a possession, he models a sense of black diasporic identity as unbounded, unfettered by mere considerations of historical time. And he provides a thesis for this approach to history in his urgent request that we "live good." For Mackey, the extravagant yoking of apparent unlikes, the making of twins out of figures apparently quite different, is another version of the metaphor of possession. For the doubling of the subject that the spirit produces when it enters her, the unity amid the strain of the body under possession, is like the poetics of diaspora—stretching far, stretching limbs, requiring imaginative openness and vulnerability. What these two artists offer as I conclude my book is a version of diasporic belonging that points to a rather contemporary experience of blackness waiting to be explored: it is the perception of diaspora as positioning the black subject always, somehow, "at large." Expansive, elusive, unbounded.

DANCEHALL'S URBAN POSSESSIONS

I would like to end this book by reflecting on a mythic Jamaican community, not a rural space with an aura of soulfulness (colloquially understood) but a rough urban one, a community known as Tivoli Gardens in the heart of Kingston. Like Erna Brodber's b l a c k s p a c e, with which I began this book, Tivoli Gardens represents a diasporic territory of soul. It is located within a nation and yet is extravagantly its own. Also, arguably through the contemporary musical form of dancehall, Tivoli is constituted, and I mean this more than metaphorically, by memories of the dead.

For a long time it has been easier for Jamaicans (and for others engaged in black cultural criticism) to consider the "roots" reggae culture with which Rastafari—and for that matter Brodber's reasonings and Emancipation reenactments—is aligned a more appropriate home for the enactment of diasporic spirituality and reclamation than rude, recalcitrant dancehall. And yet events that have occurred recently in Tivoli Gardens suggest that sometimes it is through the maddening, even criminally associated form of reggae's unruly spawn that a reckoning with the soul of black diaspora can occur.

The Tivoli Gardens community of Kingston has, like many inner-city communities globally, survived a series of incursions that mark into its landscape an archive of violations. Indeed, this community was created out of a fundamental dispossession: constructed in the 1960s after the razing of a set of improvised communities, including a long-standing Rastafari community known as Back-a-Wall, Tivoli emerged under the aegis of a newly independent postcolonial government in a gesture to "clean up" Jamaica's capital city.[1] In a familiar story of urban planning set against improvised use, the supposedly illicit presence of an indigenous, Creole religion,

Rastafari, was swept away with the trash dump alongside which it had existed—though the resulting community would never emerge as a beacon of government success. Indeed, what began as a bureaucratic urban project was, within a generation, a so-called political garrison: a neighborhood associated with armed political support—jettisoned by powerful MPs, including the former prime ministers Edward Seaga and Bruce Golding—and the site of violent eruptions around successive election seasons.

Tivoli has more recently been famous for two different phenomena, not unrelated: first, from around 2005 until 2010, a stretch of Spanish Town Road in the heart of Tivoli Gardens was home to the much-copied dancehall reggae event known as Passa Passa. At Passa Passa, the black body's intersection with the urban landscape was one of enormous wit and agency, if not supremacy: women danced on corner shop rafters; dandified men made a dance stage of the streets. After May 2010, however, Tivoli Gardens entered popular consciousness beyond Jamaica's borders for another reason. It was then that Jamaican armed forces fought a deadly battle with members of the community who refused to allow the government to detain and extradite to the United States Christopher "Dudus" Coke—the area don, or gang leader, whom the US government intended to try on multiple charges related to the international drug trade. And so in a remarkably compressed period of time, and sometimes all at once, this zone of western Kingston represented the urban landscape at the opposite extremes of its relationship to subaltern agency: on the one hand was the ecstasy and freedom of dance—the claiming of urban space by the body in extravagant movement through the appropriation of the built environment. On the other was the violent constraint of armed, state-sanctioned incursion; the death and trauma enacted on a community caught up in the crosshairs of legitimate and illegitimate political power.

The Passa Passa street dance was an extravagant instance of spatial reclamation, of subaltern subjects in the city transforming its infrastructure for their own purposes—a road becomes a stage, a sidewalk a parking lot. Its temporality—occurring in the middle of the week, beginning in the wee hours and ending when the sun was high and work commutes had begun—was a rebuke to capitalist time. And while Jamaican cultural studies scholar Carolyn Cooper has written about female dancing at dancehall events as an evocation of West African fertility rituals, Passa Passa was the height of the *male* dancing body in dancehall, enabling what I have referred to elsewhere as the rise of queer masculine embodiment at the very heart of an ostensibly homophobic culture.[2] It was said that at Passa Passa no crime could occur, because the event had been sanctioned—by Dudus, and therefore by the community more generally—as a space of pleasure and commerce, ritually suspended and carved out from the ordinary violence and drudgery of the everyday.

And yet Passa, by dint of its location in Tivoli, a space built on displacement and on a violent fiction of absence, would also gesture toward the difficulties, particularly the deaths, its rituals seemed to hold at bay. Here are two snippets from the Jamaican press about Tivoli, both written around the time of the Dudus extradition fracas, when Prime Minister Bruce Golding declared a state of emergency granting the police and the military extraordinary powers to enter a neighborhood that community members had blockaded. The first describes a system of justice set up and administered by Dudus in Tivoli: "Cohen said two youngsters, Greg and David, shot the son of 'Sexy Paul,' a well-respected Tivoli elder. The youngsters, whose job it was to watch the May Pen Cemetery, had reportedly told Dudus that men from Rema were responsible for the shooting, but were caught in a lie. They were shot and their bodies dumped on Darling Street. . . . According to Cohen, this system of punishing lieutenants was a new system that was started by Dudus when he took over the organisation after the death of his father, Lester Lloyd Coke, also known as 'Jim Brown.'"[3] The number of deaths just in these brief four sentences is perhaps the most immediately striking thing. The Tivoli elder is shot; then the boys who shot the elder are shot and their bodies dumped. We are reminded of Dudus's father's death—Lester Lloyd Coke, most readers of the article will have known, was killed in a prison riot while serving his long sentence on charges stemming from *his* reign as Tivoli's don. All of this leaves aside the numberless dead in the May Pen cemetery, which it was the duty of the so-called lieutenants to guard. Why this errand exists as a task for youth in Tivoli is less clear than the pointed irony that they were denied the honor of proper burial there. Though clearly, death is a matter of course in the realm of Tivoli and having familiarity with the arrangements for speedy and secretive burials could only be a boon to a gang-leader. The nameless dead interred beneath in the May Pen cemetery, who are referenced in the article, share with those Tivoli dwellers actually named a principle of aggregation that bespeaks the quantities of wasted/

spent lives in the community. Under the aegis of Dudus's highly organized, if illicit, means of administering justice, many numbers of people were killed, such that Tivoli itself could also be seen to house the dead.

And lest it be thought that only the gang-leaders and their minions were responsible for the extravagant waste of lives referred to in that first article, here is another, which describes how the Passa Passa street dance came to be in the first place. In June 2010, a reporter asked one of Passa Passa's organizers what would happen to the Tivoli street dance that was now imperiled by the extradition violence. The dance had not been held since April, when the first rumblings around Dudus's planned extradition presaged the explosion to come. Providing some history, the party promoter noted that "Passa Passa was started after security [police] forces led by Reneto Adams went into Tivoli in 2001 resulting in the death of 27 persons. After that episode, [the promoter Dylan Powe] said people were afraid to leave their community and so Passa Passa was started to cater to them. He also said the dance facilitated unity."[4] So Tivoli has been buffeted by state-sanctioned forces as well as informal ones, and its most famous event flouting the confinements imposed by violence itself emerged out of violence. Though that second article is called "Passa Passa Will Return," so far there are no signs that the street party will be able to revive its long-standing early morning traditions.

By thinking about the relationship between structures of possession and dispossession in African diasporic performance traditions, Passa Passa and Tivoli Gardens emerge with explanatory force for other spaces of black removal, incursion, and survival. And to the extent that they do, then, dancehall, too, can be seen to house soul, and to travel. Dancehall—with all its intense commodity culture and its violence, its apparent nihilism, its cultural recalcitrance. If the forces of capital continue to be unfairly stacked against the descendants of those who once were counted toward capitalist accumulation, then we should not be surprised that the performance traditions of these subjects comment in rigorous ways on consumption and expenditure. That these traditions have a framework for thinking about the relationship between capital's forces and spectacles of violence among them should also not surprise us at all. I would prefer to live in a world in which violence and loss did not puncture and circumscribe the lives of poor black subjects. But I want to suggest that these same subjects have principles and practices for structuring the losses around them, practices that powerfully evoke histories routinely ignored by dominant structures and that reframe questions of space, ownership, and memory in ways that allow them to claim space beneath their feet while claiming, unwittingly or not, a universe of traditions far beyond where they stand.

Ebony Mourning Tivoli, or Elegiac Bling

But how do people *outside* black spaces like Tivoli Gardens cope with and think through the losses these spaces have incurred? How does the critic or the artist approach a space of such enormous and painful signification? By way of conclusion, and through a form of artistic surrogation of my own, I turn to the Jamaican visual artist Ebony Patterson, whose recent work has found a way to grieve Tivoli's losses whilst celebrating its aesthetics of survival. How does Ebony mourn Tivoli? Well, first, she enumerates, numbering those who have died. These numbers literally frame her projects, providing their titles: *9 of 219*; *The Of 72 Project*. Patterson makes projects for the dead that are efforts in rigorous accounting, even as they are suffused with fanciful, baroque detail. *9:* the number of people who had been murdered during a week Patterson spent in Trinidad, making the piece she eventually exhibited at the Alice Yard arts complex. *219:* the number who had been killed in Trinidad all that year. *72:* one of the original estimates of the number of persons killed when soldiers, police, and gunmen clashed in Tivoli Gardens in May 2010. This eponymous numbering, tonally at odds, it might seem, with a project of mourning, gestures at the ethical impulse of Patterson's work: to render from statistical obscurity the disturbing particularity of the corpse.

The waste of spectacular violence, after all, is that even as it makes radically visible the loss of life, its very spectacle washes out the subjects who are its victims. Either the torments enacted on the dead are too macabre to look at—and so we look away. Or the numbers of the dead overwhelm us, and we cannot begin to grapple with each one, separable and specific. In *The Of 72 Project*, a set of mixed-media panels developed with the journal *Small Axe*, Patterson presents a highly articulated form of visual elegy, specific to the context of the contemporary Caribbean, with its landscape marked by increasingly unnerving numbers and displays of violence.

One name for the mode she develops in works reflecting on Jamaica's violence might be *elegiac bling*. There are a couple of elements that I think compose this mode, as it pertains to Patterson's work. For one thing, Patterson's engagement with dancehall employs a rich transfer between language and image, and not just because Patterson is a particularly articulate explicator of her work. Her pieces appear to narrate; and sometimes, as in *Of 72*, Patterson appends text that accompanies the project, not so much explaining as inviting story. This verbal capacity of her art means that it can hold many of the ideas of modern elegy, a literary form with the kind of social implications we hunger for in a time of crisis. Simultaneously, the aspects of Patterson's work that emphasize bling—that is to say, those striking and constitutive features of the art that signify on dancehall's relationship to its *things*—resist straightforward narration, if by that we mean realism or psychological explication. Rather, in Patterson's art, dancehall's possessions overwhelm narrative, a visual surfeit that, as I will show, is a match for the extraordinary qualities of violent grief. All this allows for a mode of mourning specific to dancehall's many tribes.

As Jahan Ramazani has observed, "we need elegies that, whilst imbued with grief, can hold up to the acid suspicions of our moment."[5] Ramazani's observation about modern elegy highlights our continued need for formal expressions of mourning amid a thoroughgoing failure of belief in the formal functions of state and community that elegies normally imply. The violent breakdown of the protective and communal function of the state represented by the Tivoli Gardens incursion, for instance, makes a mockery of the grand traditions of collective mourning contained by the traditional generic form of the elegy. In addition, the increasing attenuation of formal practices of grieving—at least in the bourgeois European and American contexts—has, as Ramazani points out, stripped away a felt need for the cathartic function of elegiac form. He writes: "Between 1880 and 1920, the period of mourning was shortened more and more in both America and Britain, until it extended little beyond a few days after the funeral. At the same time . . . mourning clothes were worn less and less; attention to mourning accouterments was diminishing in etiquette books, trade catalogues, and periodicals; flowers were supplanting black drapery in the parlor and somber badges on the front door, until these social symbols of grief virtually disappeared."[6] None of this, as it transpired, meant that elegy disappeared. Rather, modern forms of poetic elegy emerged that keyed to the skeptical and increasingly psychologized and interior forms of bourgeois mourning. Ramazani coins the phrase "melancholic mourning" to describe a tradition of twentieth-century elegy that captures the techniques of ambivalence, irony, and irresolution that mark the work of writers losing faith in the consolations of poetry. And he argues that modern poets "[assimilated] themselves to [the] reality" that grief was now accompanied by cynicism, even as they "reclaimed, redefined, and reinvigorated poetic mourning at the historical moment when social mourning was dwindling."[7]

Ramazani's ideas on elegy are instructive here, even as the situation in the contemporary Caribbean, and particularly among working-class people, evinces an entirely different set of implications. For one thing, elaborate funerary and ritualized grieving practices have continued to thrive in the Caribbean, reflecting more accustomed relationships to violent deaths, greater communal intimacy, and a striking investment in the commodity as a multifarious signifier of status, respect, and expression. As Annie Paul has described in an article on the lavish, elaborate, and very stylish cast of contemporary urban funerals in Jamaica, "the coffin or casket [in particular] acquires the expressiveness of a status symbol signifying the importance both of the deceased and the bereaved family or community. Often disproportionate amounts of money are invested by poor communities in custom-made designer caskets. In postcolonial Jamaica . . . painted and decorated caskets of various kinds seem to be the latest art objects to have surfaced, registering with fetishistic fervor the ever escalating death rate in the country."[8] Mourners' pride in spending on beautiful funeral clothing, and funerals that themselves emphasize beauty and expense, are a keen reminder that, as Joseph Roach would have it, spectacles of violence and spectacles of masquerade are cognate, each ritualizing lavish expenditure (on the one hand of life; on the other of money).[9] And make no mistake that contemporary Kingston funerals for community "dons" or dancehall heroes such as the dancer Bogle become sartorial processions that achieve the status of masking. Of the funeral of a well-known Spanish Town don in 2005, Paul notes the following news report: "Some women wore heels with pants; others were clad in short skirts with matching jackets. One woman, who gave her name only as Sherine, said her outfit 'cost over 10 grand' ($10,000) [about $100 US dollars]. She said that if it were anyone else that had died, she would not have bothered to buy anything new. 'But a di big man, so mi haffi show up big time,' she said."[10] Jahan Ramazani's analysis of modern Euro-American poets' adaptation to the new tonal requirements of elegy noted the incorporation of ambivalence, the rejection of tropes of ascension, overcoming, or majesty in poems of modern loss. Yet as these descriptions of certain forms of Jamaican funerals suggest, splendor remains an expectation of rituals of grieving in that Caribbean space. The adaptations that contemporary mourners make to the new, or perhaps not-so-new, situation of extravagant death among them is that the commodity forms of capitalism—objects such as guns, money, and jewels—that are often implicated with violent deaths in urban communities in Jamaica themselves become the signifiers of ritualistic mourning.

The Of 72 Project attends to a moment of violent eruption in Jamaica that threatens, by the very nature of its reporting and the nature of state involvement, to efface the particulars of the human beings affected. To reintroduce those losses as particular and nameable, Patterson created seventy-two collaged fabric remembrances for each of the reportedly seventy-two people (many reported more) slain during those days in May. What makes this project remarkable as a mode of elegy is Patterson's use of dancehall aesthetics, themselves tied to forms of consumerism and spectacle not fully separable either from state practice, or from the accouterments of don-ship. Each mixed-media panel (fabric, embroidery, rhinestones, digital photography) depicts a face that is partly obscured and evinces Patterson's characteristically filigreed style, in which faces and fabric are embroidered with highly ornate and detailed gestures.

She began with studies—paintings and collage on paper—that, at least when first I discovered them at her website, appeared to me more beautiful, more fully achieved, than the final mixed-media project published in *Small Axe*. On consideration, that is precisely the point, of course. If we take, for instance, the study *1 of 72*, there is something striking about the simultaneous vibrancy and delicacy of the colors—that gold doily, the rosy pinks and cheerful violets and sunny oranges. The clean lines of the carefully rendered head, centered and gazing directly at the viewer, as well as the balanced placement of the objects on the page—each butterfly perfectly weighs itself across from its mate—all this *proportion* appeals to the eye and, finally, relaxes. Though these studies are collage, just as the final project is collage, the crucial difference is that in the finished pieces Patterson chooses to emphasize the "foundness" of the found objects—to accentuate the sense of having retrieved, or salvaged from waste, items that when grouped together she makes into art, against all odds. Comparing the two phases of the project, one is reminded of the art critic Petrine Archer's idea that in the long tradition of Jamaican masquerade—the very long tradition dating back to the seventeenth century—the use of found objects as spectacular embellishment can signify *difficulty*, struggle, not just creative reuse. "Performances," Archer writes, "that collage together costumes of ribbon, feathers, tinsel, raffia, and found objects represent the remnants of displaced rituals recycled and salvaged with the economic imperative of survival."[11]

In the study *4 of 72*, that dangling red flower gestures at the slightly more disturbing effect of the completed project—what we see in, say, *43 of 72* in the final series. There, the red flower is upturned but off-center. Its mate is diagonally positioned but slightly smaller—the proportions are askew. A photograph has been interpolated where the painting used to be in the study, and while the gaze is direct, as in the studies, it is far more challenging. That gold doily embellishment is *manifestly* a doily, and it has become lurid; tonal delicacy is abandoned. The leaved backdrop behind the head is evenly placed but cruder than the swirled backdrops of the studies, and the appended mask on the face appears deliberately off-scale. Perhaps most striking of all, the colors and patterns of the various cloths Patterson has used clash. Their undertones conflict, they do not please. And so though each bandana-ed panel in *The Of 72 Project* is in fact an object of glitzy honor, when put in dialogue with the studies that precede them, something other than beauty emerges as their object. Patterson has drawn attention to waste, to loss, to salvage, and she seeks to discomfit, not merely to please, to prompt the viewer into some experience, however minor, of pain.

The *Of 72* panels are composed of bandana material, itself a recycled style for dancehall men, ubiquitous in the 1970s and again a few years back. Patterson is reflecting on dancehall style, on ambiguous masculinity—indeed, masculinity itself, its imperatives, its injunctions, are a source of grief for Patterson. And the faces of each subject in the series are shielded by an improvised bandana, so that a repetitious effect functions on each individual piece as well as in the project as a whole. This repetition suggests the recurrence of violence in Jamaica, the brutality of its patterns—what Deborah Thomas has referred to recently as the "repertoire of violence" from the very inception of Jamaica as colonial space to the present, with each iteration appearing exceptional when it is in fact part of a series.[12]

FIGURE E.1. Ebony G. Patterson, *Untitled Study I* from the series *Of 72*, 2011. Mixed media on paper, 16 x 10 ¼ in. IMAGE COURTESY OF THE ARTIST AND MONIQUE MELOCHE GALLERY, CHICAGO.

FIGURE E.2. Ebony G. Patterson, *Untitled Study VI* from the series *Of 72*, 2011. Mixed media on paper, 16 x 10 ¼ in. IMAGE COURTESY OF THE ARTIST AND MONIQUE MELOCHE GALLERY, CHICAGO.

The repetitiousness and the shifts function as well to tweak the viewer's potentially anaesthetized response so that a sensation of numberless losses shifts into an apprehension of particular and exquisite subjectivity. Throughout the body of her work, the delicacy of Patterson's technique and the warmth of her representation of black faces and bodies rebukes conventional wisdom that dancehall is all brutal hard edges. Yet the sparkle of the rhinestones and sequins is flinty, and gestures to the long, hard history of bling. Indeed the brilliance of elegiac bling is that its glints startle. Look at that gold medallion anchoring "43 of 72" for long enough and its dangling embellishments start to take on the menacing aspect of spikes or prickles. Bling startles. It shoots out sharp-edged rays that can slice through bullshit.

The art historian Krista Thompson's essay on contemporary African American visual artists and hip hop "shine" was inspiring for me in defining Patterson's elegiac bling. Thompson points out that in the work of the artist Kehinde Wiley, like the album art of 1990s hip hop, surface sheen accentuates an engagement with art history in which sparkle marked prestige. This is a visual history where, indeed, the "shine" of black skin, oiled down to appeal to buyers, was often itself incorporated into canvases as one of a number of bling objects marking a subject's saturation with luxury commodities. To narrow in on a particularly resonant moment in Thompson's argument: "Bodily shine helped to increase slaves' worth, to heighten their assimilation and visual verisimilitude to the world of objects. In this way, the reflective surface of the black body—what might be characterized as the visual production of the slave sublime—serves to blind buyers, if you will, to the slave's humanity. It sealed them, as Fanon so succinctly described it, 'in crushing objecthood.'" Bling's sublime, used also in hip hop's cognate form of dancehall, pushes toward the recuperation of subjecthood in the post-slavery era while retaining every ounce of its ambivalence. We see this in Kehinde Wiley's manipulation and resignification of the history of this shiny visual trope, say in his 2005 painting *Portrait of Andries Stilte*, a versioning on a painting completed in 1640 by Johannes Verspronck called *Andries Stilte as Standard-Bearer*. Krista Thompson notes that

> Wiley's canvases attempt to capture ... [the] corporeal experience of vision [which] recalls the physiological and even painful experience of light that is so intrinsic to bling. Inspired by ways of seeing in hip-hop,

FIGURE E.3. Ebony G. Patterson, #48 from *Of 72 Project*, 2012. Digital photo on fabric bandana with embroidery and hand-embellished elements, 20 x 16 inches. IMAGE COURTESY OF THE ARTIST AND MONIQUE MELOCHE GALLERY, CHICAGO.

Wiley glances at how the early portrait painters used light to convey the prestige of their subjects to the beholder. Thus, what is new in Wiley's bling-informed new-Baroque aesthetic is not another era of flamboyant fashions but a new way of foregrounding literally how painters constructed opulence and power through surfacism and light.[13]

Furthermore, Wiley, like Ebony Patterson, foregrounds the aesthetic and political implications of framing—the way in which the presentation of subjects within an art setting draws attention to the ambivalence of subject and object, particularly when the subject/object is racialized. In Wiley's painting *St. Sebastian II*, where the ornate black frame becomes an almost oppressive feature of the painting itself, Thompson argues that the artist critiques "what might be described as 'enframing,' the process by which certain subjects and practices are reified as powerful through art."[14] Patterson's work in *Of 72* also imposes framing techniques, though interestingly, the repetition and apparent reproducibility of her images, spread across the pages of *Small Axe* in even, four-part reproductions, offers a different mode of critique by implicitly arguing *against* certain constructions of value. The elegiac function of the self-conscious "enframed" presentation in *Of 72*, wed to the almost exhausting repetition, suggests something like Achille Mbembe's idea of subaltern superfluity.[15] The lives lost are constructed, through their wastage, as infinitely replaceable, even as they are necessary to the functioning power of capital and the state. Furthermore, Patterson's emphasis on framing undercuts representational prestige, even as it draws attention to its history in portrait art. Her subjects represent the missing, the wasted, the lost. Thus Patterson offers a way of engaging with our "acid suspicions" about the losses of these lives: that in the dialectic between objecthood and subjecthood referenced by bling, there are many quarters in which the seventy-two, poor and black, remain frozen as objects.

Finally—and this is the brilliance of elegiac bling—Patterson's use of objects and aesthetics from dancehall renders the pieces somehow familiar in their extravagance. Bling mourning takes the materials at hand and transforms those objects into something more than their vestigial parts, gesturing to the power of the ordinary, to Jamaican subjects' ability to continue functioning in the wake of violence. "The re-creation of ordinariness," Deborah Thomas writes in *Exceptional Violence*, "the development of new though unspectacular ways of moving through everyday life—is in this context something extraordinary." For Thomas, as for Patterson in *Of 72*, the work of memory and mourning in the aftermath of catastrophe is often approached by those directly impacted by it through rituals of the everyday. Furthermore, the extravagance and detail of the material and method of her work makes reference to the superfluity of beauty, the work it accomplishes within the space of death by not in any transactional sense being useful. Like the aesthetic work of slaves in their apportioned plots of land, Patterson's bling "transform[s] the landscape of death and suffering into a space of pleasure, of aesthetic value."[16] Indeed, the rigorous time commitment of the bead work, the fabric manipulation, even the repeated digital processing on the photographs, compares to what Simon Gikandi refers to as "surplus time"—the adducing of time as itself an aesthetic material, in defiance of the rigid organization of time on plantations, the now prevalent waste of time in the extravagantly under-employed Kingston ghetto. The daily work of Patterson's method is a part of the quotidian putting together of life after catastrophe that she memorializes.

What does an elegy do? Of the raw, hazardous materials of loss, arts of mourning strain, striate, and attempt to produce something potable, something even pure. The reason for doing this is mysterious, of course, as mysterious as those motivations guiding any act of creation. For the transformation of the waste of loss into the shine of elegy does not, in fact, provide comfort. Clean elegiac lines of poetry may organize our disordered thoughts. Perhaps they offer language when we can find none of our own, for horror mutes. But many poetic elegies thematize their own ineptness. Remember Kamau Brathwaite elegizing Mikey Smith in the poem "Stone":

> When the stone fall that morning out of the johncrow sky
> it was not dark at first . . . that opening on to the red sea humming
> but something in my mouth like feathers.[17]

The particular menace of Jamaican violence: the bad tidings of the johncrow, the sea now red, not blue, carrying the blood that always sits just below the Atlantic surface. This opening marks a kind of intelligibility, the sort of intelligibility offered by that which is recognizable. But then, later in the poem, is this: "& there was a loud booodoooooooooooooooooogs." And then

this: "**murdererrrrrrrrrrrrrrrrrrrrrrrrrrrrrrrrrrrrrrrrrrrrrrrrrrrrrrrrrrrrrrrrrrrrr**";
infinite *r*'s, bold typeface. And then this:

> *bom si. cai si. ca boom ship bell. bom si. cai si. ca boom ship bell*
> & a laughin more blood & spittin out
> **lawwwwwwwwwwwwwwwwwwwwwwwwwwwwwwwwwwwwwwwwwwd**[18]

Brathwaite demonstrates the break of language that is also a surfeit, that excess lettering, like elegiac blinging, pointing to a kind of insufficiency in the art of mourning, especially in moments of violent crisis or when the waste of life is spectacular. Ebony Patterson's work achieves a new mode of Jamaican memorial by not shying away from the simultaneous boon and emptiness of commodity spectacle in the life of its most potent and popular forms. The act of the elegy is not comfort, but recognition contorted to produce something like alertness. Something happened. It happened, and this offering marks the place where we try to grieve it.

Territories of the Soul has offered a set of models in which the grief of loss and displacement, part and parcel of black diaspora, is managed and molded into extraordinary practices of identity and space. C. L. R. James's loves; Baldwin and Lamming's jousting; Salkey's queer elusiveness; and the possessive embrace and suturing of Burning Spear and Nathaniel Mackey—these artists create in strange and unique ways versions of what Erna Brodber has literally set up in the mountains of Woodside, St. Mary: black space. They have shown us some of the ways to belong in the black diaspora. When I watch the shining people of Tivoli, of Johannesburg, of New Orleans, of Oakland, I am continually reminded that there are thousands and thousands of ways more.

NOTES

INTRODUCTION: *The Queer Elsewhere of Black Diaspora*

1 Stuart Hall, unpublished Interview with Bill Schwartz, 2004, 4–5, 7–8; manuscript supplied to the author by Bill Schwartz.

2 Ibid., 10.

3 Ibid., 10–11.

4 Ibid., 16–17.

5 Ibid.

6 Writing of the hard-won claims to London spaces by black migrants in the nineteen-seventies, Phillips writes: "So in Britain the spaces we inhabited also became territories of the soul." *London Crossings: A Biography of Black Britain* (London: Continuum Press, 2001) 203.

7 Jose Muñoz, "Introduction: Feeling Utopia," in *Cruising Utopia: The Then and There of Queer Futurity* (New York: New York University Press, 2009), 1.

8 Ibid., 17.

9 Recent queer studies allows me to think through questions of time and affinity in a way that makes sexuality deeply integral rather than epiphenomenal to my readings. However, it is often the case that scholars focused on queer time fail to take into account raced or diasporic test cases—as well as the different formulations of history registered by the temporal ruptures that mark black diaspora. I seek to bring, therefore, the critical endowment of such queer theorists as Lee Edelman, Chris Nealon, Elizabeth Freeman, and Heather Love into conversation with global black cultures and textual practices. Reading, for instance, Freeman's notion of chrononormativity alongside Muñoz's formulation of queer utopia (in which queerness is that which is yet to be accomplished) establishes a temporal horizon of queerness that accommodates itself to Jamaican Rastafari's ever-deferred messianic eschatology. Chris Nealon argues that pre-Stonewall queer texts display "an overwhelming desire to *feel historical*" that impel narratives of the foundling picked up and grafted onto a family unit. Nealon, *Foundlings: Lesbian and Gay Historical Emotion*

before Stonewall (Durham, NC: Duke University Press, 2001), 8. The versions of familial affinity I track here, while related to Nealon's description of queer scatter and unconventional historicity, emphasize the affirmative possibilities of paired unlikes within a racial category—blackness—of putative sameness. And Heather Love's writing on failed genealogies and David Eng's on the "poststructural family" both involve a reckoning with the intimacy of alterity that I explore, particularly in chapter 4, through black diasporic practices and aesthetics of spirit possession—a form of intimacy not often brought into dialogue with queer theory. Eng, *The Feeling of Kinship: Queer Liberalism and the Racialization of Intimacy* (Durham, NC: Duke University Press, 2010), 84; Love, *Feeling Backward: Loss and the Politics of Queer History* (Cambridge, MA: Harvard University Press, 2009).

10 By way of swift and necessarily partial citation in the realm of black queer of color studies I would point to Cathy Cohen's challenge to queer activism "Punks, Bulldaggers, and Welfare Queens: The Radical Potential of Queer Politics," *GLQ: A Journal of Lesbian and Gay Studies* 3, 4 (1997): 437–465, as a touchstone of critical intervention in queer studies that informs my reading of black diasporic forms as both resistant and queer. Roderick Ferguson's analysis of the exclusion of black subjects from archival and disciplinary formations as a form of sexualized abjection assists my reading of archives, particularly those in London, where the absence of black figures in records does not necessarily signify their discursive or material absence in the city. Ferguson, *Aberrations in Black: Toward a Queer of Color Critique* (Minneapolis: University of Minnesota Press, 2004). Gloria Wekker's study of the female Surinamese tradition of *mati* is revelatory in its analysis of a particular form of queer of color expression, as well as in the implications to which it points for the study of other queer expressions that do not line up neatly with Western ideas of same-sex eros. Wekker, *The Politics of Passion: Women's Sexual Culture in the Afro-Surinamese Diaspora* (New York: Columbia University Press, 2006). Her rigorous study of Winti, the spiritual tradition that infuses *mati*, makes clear the connections between Afro-diasporic spirituality and queer sexuality, a connection that until recently has not been examined. Her analysis of Winti rituals and their profound ties to black Surinamese identity also informs my analysis of spirit possession as a mode of diasporic belonging. M. Jacqui Alexander's work explores this connection profoundly as well. Alexander, *Pedagogies of the Crossing: Meditations on Feminism, Sexual Politics, Memory, and the Sacred* (Durham, NC: Duke University Press, 2006). Like any critic of black diasporic queer sexuality, I am a child of Audre Lorde. Her essay "The Uses of the Erotic as Power," is paradigmatic in any understanding of sexuality as touching all aspects of how one daily exists in the world. Lorde, *Sister Outsider: Essays and Speeches* (Freedom, CA: The Crossing Press, 1984), 53–59.

11 Not surprisingly, since he is a fountainhead of critical thought around diaspora, Hall comes closest to reconciling these dialectical formulations and

critical drifts. In his influential essay "Cultural Identity and Diaspora," *Framework* 36 (1989): 222–237, for instance, he argued that what is known as "the African Diaspora" is composed of narratives of identity in which constitutive difference is narrated into contingent, strategic likeness.

12 I use performative surrogation in the context of diaspora and transatlantic circulation as it is classically described in Joseph Roach's *Cities of the Dead: Circum-Atlantic Performance* (New York: Columbia University Press, 1996). Surrogation is marked by a symbolic figure filling a vacant space, performing a function of communal binding that is always at once necessary and insufficient.

13 The pairing of poet-critic with musician is also compelled by Mackey's intense interest in music (he once had his own radio show) and his incorporation of musical ideas into his poetics as well as his creative writing. He is often referred to as a jazz writer. See for example Fritz Gysin, "From 'Liberating Voices' to 'Metathetic Ventriloquism': Boundaries in Recent African-American Jazz Fiction," in *Jazz Poetics: A Special Issue, Callaloo* 25, 1 (winter 2002): 274–287; Norman Finkelstein, "Nathaniel Mackey and the Unity of All Rites," *Contemporary Literature* 49, 1 (2008): 24–55; Paul Hoover, "Pair of Figures for Eshu: Doubling of Consciousness in the Work of Kerry James Marshall and Nathaniel Mackey," *Callaloo* 23, 2 (spring 2000): 728–748;

14 Lisa Lowe, "The Intimacies of Four Continents," in *Haunted by Empire: Geographies of Intimacy in North American History*, ed. Ann Laura Stoler (Durham, NC: Duke University Press, 2006), 191–212.

15 Erna Brodber, e-mail to the author, August 25, 2011.

16 Ian Baucom, *Specters of the Atlantic: Finance Capital, Slavery, and the Philosophy of History* (Durham, NC: Duke University Press, 2005).

17 A Jamaica Information Service document dates the stoppage of national Emancipation Day celebrations to the first Independence Day celebration, August 6, 1962. According to the brochure, the holiday was restored in 1997. "The observance of Emancipation Day as a public holiday began in 1893, at which time it was observed on the first Monday in August. Between 1895 and 1962, it was celebrated on August 1, unless the date fell on a Saturday or Sunday. When Jamaica became an independent nation in 1962, the official observance of Emancipation Day was discontinued in favour of Independence Day, which is observed on August 6. However, since 1997, Emancipation Day as a public holiday was re-introduced and observed on August 1, except when the day falls on a Sunday; in which case it is celebrated on Monday August 2." "The Observance of Emancipation Day in Jamaica," Jamaica Information Service, online brochure, http://www.jis.gov.jm/special_sections/festiva12k10/pdf/Observance.pdf.

18 Barry Higman's thorough article on the history of Emancipation Day celebrations points out that 1838 festivals included church services with sermons on the necessity of former slaves continuing to work with industry. Higman,

"Slavery Remembered: The Celebration of Emancipation in Jamaica," *Journal of Caribbean History* 12 (1979): 55–74. My own essay on Jamaican performance traditions explores the relationship between these celebrations and expressions of freedom after abolition. See Nadia Ellis, "Jamaican Performance in the Age of Emancipation," in *Victorian Jamaica*, ed. Tim Barringer and Wayne Modest (Durham, NC: Duke University Press, forthcoming).

19 Higman, "Slavery Remembered," 57, 59.

20 Deborah Thomas, *Modern Blackness: Nationalism, Globalization and the Politics of Culture in Jamaica* (Durham, NC: Duke University Press, 2004), 30. I describe this process in more detail in chapter 4, where I also briefly adumbrate the West Indian–specific notion of "brownness."

21 Erna Brodber, *The Second Generation of Freemen in Jamaica* (Gainesville: University of Florida Press, 2004).

22 Erna Brodber, "Programme Audit, Jamaica Cultural Development Commission," December 1989, 22. Facsimile copy provided to the author by Erna Brodber.

23 Brodber, "Programme Audit," 22–23.

24 The results of Brodber's extraordinary undertaking to document the fate of the "grandchildren" of Emancipation first appeared as her doctoral thesis. It was later published in *The Second Generation of Freemen in Jamaica, 1907–1944* (Gainesville: University Press of Florida, 2004).

25 "If national holidays are to serve their celebratory functions within the culture, it must be clear to the nation why the occasions they celebrate are so important that it can take a whole day and sometimes more, from productive activity to note it." Brodber, "Programme Audit," 22.

26 "The committee which ordered me to do this audit, said that it was a best seller among and eagerly read by the members of parliament and my own representative had told me so. Also an old school mate who happened to work in the prime minister's office had told me that my audit was what had caused emancipation day to be back on the agenda of holidays." Brodber, e-mail to author, August 25, 2011.

27 Earl Witter, Q. C., Office of the Defender, *Interim Report To Parliament Concerning Investigations Into The Conduct Of The Security Forces During The State Of Emergency Declared May, 2010 — West Kingston/Tivoli Gardens 'Incursion'—The Killing Of Mr. Keith Oxford Clarke And Related Matters*, April 29, 2013 (1).

CHAPTER 1: *The Attachments of C. L. R. James*

1 C. L. R. James, "La Divina Pastora," in *Spheres of Existence: Selected Writings* (London: Allison and Busby, 1980), 5–8.

2 "I knew at a relatively young age what the word *diaspora* meant—though to this day that word makes me visualize a diaspore, the white Afro-puff of a dan-

delion being blown by my lips into a series of wishes across our old backyard: to be known, to be loved, to belong." Emily Raboteau, *Searching for Zion: The Quest for Home in the African Diaspora* (New York: Atlantic Monthly, 2013), 8.

3 C. L. R. James to Arthur Schlesinger, Jr., Arthur Schlesinger Papers, John F. Kennedy Presidential Library Archives, Boston. I offer immense thanks to Simon Gikandi for drawing my attention to this letter, as well as sharing with me his own copy of it. The same is true for James's missive to Willard Thorp.

4 C. L. R. James to Willard Thorp, Arthur Schlesinger Papers, John F. Kennedy Presidential Library Archives, Boston,

5 C. L. R. James, *Mariners, Renegades, and Castaways: The Story of Herman Melville and the World We Live In* (New York: privately published, 1953).

6 C. L. R. James, *Mariners, Renegades, and Castaways: The Story of Herman Melville and the World We Live In*, 2nd rev. ed. (Detroit: Bewick, 1978). Simon Gikandi again receives my gratitude, this time for drawing my attention to this telling discrepancy in the editions.

7 James, *Mariners, Renegades, and Castaways: The Story of Herman Melville and the World We Live In* (Lebanon, N.H.: University Press of New England, 2001).

8 Paul Gilroy, *Postcolonial Melancholia* (New York: Columbia University Press, 2005).

9 Selwyn Cudjoe, "C. L. R. James Misbound," *Transition* 58 (1992): 126.

10 See, for example, Natasha Barnes's exegesis of cultural nationalism in the Jamaican context. Barnes, *Cultural Conundrums: Gender, Race, Nation, and the Making of Caribbean Cultural Politics* (Ann Arbor: University of Michigan Press, 2006).

11 Norman Girvan, foreword to *Tribute to a Scholar: Appreciating C. L. R. James*, ed. Bishnu Ragoonath (Kingston: Consortium Graduate School of Social Sciences, 1990), vii.

12 Paul Buhle, introduction to *C. L. R. James: His Life and Works*, ed. Buhle (London: Allison and Busby, 1986), 22.

13 Selwyn Cudjoe's introduction to *C. L. R. James: His Intellectual Legacies* bears marks of similar anxieties and impossibilities: "We regret that the essays gathered in this volume do not emphasize enough the collaborative nature of James's intellectual production. But history would treat us unkindly if we did not at least acknowledge and pay tribute to the nature of that collective enterprise as it manifested itself in the Johnson-Forest Tendency." See Cudjoe, introduction to *C. L. R. James: His Intellectual Legacies*, ed. Selwyn R. Cudjoe and William E. Cain (Amherst: University of Massachusetts Press, 1995), 1–2.

14 Walter Rodney, "The African Revolution," in Buhle, *C. L. R. James: His Life and Work*, 30.

15 Richard Small, "The Training of an Intellectual, the Making of a Marxist," in Buhle, *C. L. R. James: His Life and Work*, 58.

16 Paul Buhle, *C. L. R. James: The Artist as Revolutionary* (London: Verso, 1988), 1.

17 George Lamming, *The Pleasures of Exile* (London: Alison and Busby, 1984), 47.

18 Ibid., 36.

19 Quoted in Cudjoe, introduction, 1–2.

20 C. L. R. James, *The Future in the Present: Selected Writings* (London: Allison and Busby, 1977); C. L. R. James, *Spheres of Existence: Selected Writings* (London: Allison and Busby, 1980); C. L. R. James, *At the Rendezvous of Victory: Selected Writings* (London: Allison and Busby, 1984); Scott McLemee and Paul Le Blanc, *C. L. R. James and Revolutionary Marxism: Selected Writings of C. L. R. James 1939–1949*, Revolutionary Studies (Atlantic Highlands, NJ: Humanities Press, 1994).

21 Grant Farred, Introduction to *Rethinking C. L. R. James*, ed. Grant Farred (Oxford: Blackwell, 1996), 1.

22 In a letter to Constance Webb from Pyramid Lake Ranch in Sutcliff, Nevada, where he had gone to earn some money whilst while awaiting the divorce papers, James writes: "I have seem some of the handsomest men I have seen in my life, face and figure. How well they look! I saw a cowboy to-day, about 35, about 6 ft exactly, so straight, so slim, his shoulders square, but almost as narrow as his hips, and his whole body as flat as a pancake, and his eyes blue; and they were slow, easy-going." C. L. R. James, *Special Delivery: The Letters of C. L. R. James to Constance Webb, 1939–1948* (Oxford: Blackwell, 1996), 334.

23 C. L. R. James, *Minty Alley* (London: New Beacon, 1971).

24 Stuart Hall, "C. L. R. James: A Portrait," in *C. L. R. James's Caribbean*, ed. Paget Henry and Paul Buhle (Durham, NC: Duke University Press, 1992), 3.

25 C. L. R. James, *Beyond a Boundary* (London: Hutchinson Press, 1963; reprint, Durham, NC: Duke University Press, 1993), 3.

26 Ibid.

27 Ibid., 4.

28 Ibid.

29 Ibid., 90.

30 Ibid.

31 The phrase, which Kaufman and Patterson quote in their article, is J. A. Mangan's. It is a good summation one of their article's main arguments. See Jason Kaufman and Orlando Patterson, "Cross-national Cultural Diffusion: The Global Spread of Cricket," *American Sociological Review* 70 (February 2005): 82–110.

32 Kaufman and Patterson, "Cross-national Cultural Diffusion," 91.

33 James, *Beyond a Boundary*, 40–41.

34 James, *Beyond a Boundary*, 40.

35 Homi Bhabha, "Of Mimicry and Man: The Ambivalence of Colonial Discourse," *October* 28 (spring 1984): 125–133.

36 Ibid., 127.

37 Ibid., 130–131.

38 Anne Cheng, *The Melancholy of Race: Psychoanalysis, Assimilation, and Hidden Grief* (Oxford: Oxford University Press, 2001).

39 Ibid., 12.

40 Ibid., 18.

41 James, *Beyond a Boundary*, 39.

42 Ibid., 29.

43 Ibid., 39.

44 Ibid., 40.

45 Cecil Headlam, *Ten Thousand Miles through India and Burma: An Account of the Oxford University Authentics' Cricket Tour with Mr. KL Key in the Year of the Durbar* (London: Dent, 1903), quoted in Kaufman and Patterson, "Cross-national Cultural Diffusion," 92.

46 Denise Riley, *Impersonal Passion: Language as Affect* (Durham, NC: Duke University Press, 2005), 2.

47 Unreferenced text quoted in James, *Beyond a Boundary*, 5.

48 Ibid., 5–6.

49 Ibid., 20.

50 Ibid., 7.

51 Ibid., 5.

52 Ibid., 17, 18.

53 Ibid., 6.

54 Ibid., 30.

55 Ibid., 41.

56 Sylvia Wynter, "Beyond the Categories of the Master Conception: The Counterdoctrine of the Jamesian Poiesis," in *C. L. R. James's Caribbean*, ed. Paget Henry and Paul Buhle (Durham, NC: Duke University Press, 1992), 69.

57 Ibid.

58 Joseph Roach, *Cities of the Dead: Circum-Atlantic Performance* (New York: Columbia University Press, 1996).

59 Joseph Roach, *It* (Ann Arbor: University of Michigan Press, 2007), 17.

60 James, *Special Delivery*, 73.

61 Ibid., 89.

62 Ibid., 74.

63 Ibid., 76.

64 Ibid., 76–77.

65 C. L. R. James, *C. L. R. James on the "Negro Question,"* ed. Scott McLemee (Jackson: University of Mississippi Press, 1996).

66 Anna Grimshaw and Keith Hart, introduction to C. L. R. James, *American Civilization*, ed. Grimshaw and Hart (Oxford: Blackwell, 1993), 23.

67 The letter is dated September 1, 1943; *Special Delivery*, 72.

68 Lauren Berlant, *The Female Complaint: The Unfinished Work of Sentiment in American Culture* (Durham, NC: Duke University Press, 2008), 140.

69 Ibid., 121–122.

70 Ibid., 170.

71 James, *Special Delivery*, 72.

72 Quoted in James, *American Civilization*, 142.

73 Ibid., 143.

74 Ibid., 73.

75 James, *Special Delivery*, 72.

76 Ibid.

77 James, *American Civilization*, 122.

78 James, *Special Delivery*, 72.

79 Peter Linebaugh and Marcus Rediker, *The Many-Headed Hydra: Sailors, Slaves, Commoners, and the Hidden History of the Revolutionary Atlantic* (Boston: Beacon Press, 2000).

80 Yogita Goyal, *Romance, Diaspora, and Black Atlantic Literature* (Cambridge: Cambridge University Press, 2010), 2, 3.

81 Roach, *It*, 3.

82 Roach, *It*, 3.

83 *Now, Voyager*, dir. Irving Rapper (1942; Burbank, CA: Warner Home Video, 2001), DVD.

84 James, *Special Delivery*, 42.

85 Ibid., 46.

86 Ibid., 89. In a particularly evocative moment on the same page he writes: "But tonight I'll have my own party—Webb in red, sleepy and therefore giving herself away, all instinct and feeling and unawakened passion and power—and me, an intellectual to my fingertips, but arriving through observation and study at what you know instinctively. It would be a wonderful party—a voyage of discovery and understanding, constantly to discover and understand, the eternal instinct of life with the understanding of civilization. You see why I love you?"

87 Ibid., 208.

88 Ibid., 253.

89 Ibid., 298 (italics in the original).

90 Ibid., 298 (italics in the original).

91 Ibid., 74–75.

92 Ibid., 99.

93 Ibid., 77.

94 Ibid., 78.

95 Ibid., 83 (emphasis in the original).

96 And indeed, when James later gave a talk on black women writers in 1981 (published in the magazine *Cultural Correspondence*), he did not make the connection to this earlier moment in his cultural and political interests. "I find it astonishing and revealing," he writes of *Sula* (a book he admired), "that Toni Morrison should insist that this tremendous insight come from a poor Black woman, on the lowest level of American human society." In other words James is only just catching up to the reality that poor black women can em-

body important cultural critique. It is as if Ethel Waters's majesty—to name only the one prominent black woman James gave notice—never happened. C. L. R. James, "Three Black Women Writers: Toni Morrison, Alice Walker, Ntozake Shange," in *The C. L. R. James Reader*, ed. Anna Grimshaw (Oxford: Blackwell, 1992), 413.

CHAPTER 2: *The Fraternal Agonies of Baldwin and Lamming*

1 For more context surrounding Diop, his founding of *Presence Africaine*, and the various meetings he sponsored under its auspices, see Eileen Julien, "Terrains de Rencontre: Cesaire, Fanon, and Wright on Culture and Decolonization," *Yale French Studies* 98 (2000): 149–166, and Benetta Jules-Rosette, "Antithetical Africa: The Conferences and Festivals of Presence Africaine, 1956–1973," in Jules-Rosette, *Black Paris: The African Writers' Landscape* (Urbana: University of Illinois Press, 1998), 49–78.

2 "Le 1er Congres International des Ecrivains et Artistes Noirs (Paris—Sorbonne— 19–22 Septembre 1956), Compte Rendu Complet," special issue, *Presence Africaine: Revue Culturelle du Monde Noir*, nos. 8–9–10 (June–November 1956).

3 George Lamming, "The Negro Writer and His World," *Presence Africaine* 8–9–10 (1956), 318–325.

4 James Baldwin, "Princes and Powers," in *Nobody Knows My Name*, in *Collected Essays* (New York: Dial Press, 1961; reprint, New York: Library of America, 1998), 143–169.

5 Lamming, *The Pleasures of Exile* (London: Murray Joseph, 1960, reprint, Ann Arbor: University of Michigan, 1993). Baldwin, *Notes of a Native Son* (Boston: Beacon Press, 1955).

6 Baldwin, *Go Tell It on the Mountain* (New York: Dial Press, 1953); Lamming, *In the Castle of My Skin* (London: Michael Joseph, 1953).

7 Heather Love, *Feeling Backward: Loss and the Politics of Queer History* (Cambridge, MA: Harvard University Press, 2009), 98.

8 Ibid., 93.

9 Lamming, "Negro Writer," 320 (emphasis in the original).

10 Ibid.

11 Ibid.

12 George Lamming, introduction to *In the Castle of My Skin* (Ann Arbor: University of Michigan, 1991), xxxviii.

13 Joseph Roach, *Cities of the Dead: Circum-Atlantic Performance* (New York: Columbia University Press, 1996), 6.

14 Kingsley Amis, "Fresh Winds from the West," *Spectator*, May 2, 1958, 565–566.

15 Caribbean Artists Movement Collection, George Padmore Institute, London (hereafter the CAM Collection). Anne Walmsley did herculean work to interview and document the history of the movement, and she generously deposited her materials, along with others that have been gathered, at the Padmore Institute.

16 Anne Walmsley, *The Caribbean Artists Movement, 1966–1972: A Literary and Cultural History* (London: New Beacon Books, 1992).

17 Kamau Brathwaite remembers Salkey dissuading him from asking Lamming, Selvon, and Harris to join. Lamming did, however, do a reading at the first CAM conference. Brathwaite also notes that, unsurprisingly, "Naipaul was approached and he dismissed the idea of CAM rather cavalierly." Transcript of Anne Walmsley interview with Edward [Kamau] Brathwaite, March 15, 1986, CAM Collection, GB 2904 CAM/6/9. Page 33.

18 Transcript of Anne Walmsley interview with Andrew Salkey, March 20, 1986. CAM Collection, GB 2904 CAM/6/64. Page 4.

19 Edward [Kamau] Brathwaite to Bryan King, November 30, 1966, CAM Collection, GB 2904 CAM/3/1. Brathwaite to Edward Lucie-Smith, December 12, 1966, CAM Collection, GB 2904 CAM/3/3.

20 Brathwaite to Edward Lucie-Smith, December 12, 1966, CAM Collection, GB 2904 CAM/3/3.

21 Roland Penrose to Edward [Kamau] Brathwaite, May 4, 1967, CAM Collection, GB 2904 CAM/3/69.

22 Ibid.

23 Louis James, interview by Anne Walmsley, CAM Collection, May 27, 1986, GB 2904 CAM/6/34. Page 22.

24 Gordon Rohlehr to Edward [Kamau] Brathwaite, January 12, 1967, CAM Collection, GB 2904 CAM/3/11.

25 Kenneth Ramchand to Edward [Kamau] Brathwaite, January 4, 1967, CAM Collection, GB 2904 CAM/3/7.

26 She continues: "It could so easily become cosily incestuous. One can sort of see why Selvon and Naipaul hold themselves aloof." Veronica Jenkin to Edward [Kamau] Brathwaite, February 5, 1967, CAM Collection, GB 2904 CAM/3/18.

27 Andrew Salkey, interview by Anne Walmsley, CAM Collection, GB 2904 CAM/6/64. Page 21.

28 Lamming, *Pleasures*, 29.

29 Ibid., 30.

30 James Baldwin, *Notes of a Native Son* (Boston: Beacon Press, 1955) 6, quoted in Lamming, *Pleasures*, 31.

31 Ibid.

32 Lamming, *Pleasures*, 31.

33 Ibid.

34 Ibid, 33.

35 Baldwin, "Princes and Powers," 143.

36 Ibid.

37 Ibid., 147.

38 Ibid.

39 Ibid., 148.

40 Ibid., 146.

41 Ibid., 147.

42 Ibid., 159.

43 Ibid., 146.

44 James Baldwin, "My Dungeon Shook," *The Fire Next Time*, in *Collected Essays* (New York: Library of America, 1998), 295.

45 Ibid., 293.

46 Baldwin, "Princes and Powers," 157.

47 Ibid.

48 Ibid.

49 Ibid.

50 Julien, "Terrains de Rencontre," 165.

51 Baldwin, "Princes and Powers," 160.

52 Ibid.

53 Ibid., 161 (italics in the original).

54 Akin Adesokan, "Baldwin, Paris, and the 'Conundrum of Africa,'" *Textual Practice* 23, 1 (2009): 73–97.

55 Ibid., 91.

56 Ibid., 78.

57 Ibid.

58 In chapter 4, I linger on the difference between *black* and *brown* in the Caribbean. Suffice it to say for the moment that *brown* denotes light-skinned and connects with certain social privileges and assumptions about economic privileges.

59 Hortense Spillers, "Mama's Baby, Papa's Maybe: An American Grammar Book," *Diacritics* 17, 2 (1987): 64–81.

60 Ibid., 80 (emphasis in the original).

61 Ibid. (italics in the original).

62 Ibid.

63 Lamming, *Pleasures*, 116.

64 Ibid., 9.

65 Ibid.

66 George Lamming, "The West Indian People," *New World Quarterly* 2, 2 (1966–1967), 64.

67 Ibid.

68 Foundational ethnographies of Haitian vodou ritual that I have consulted describe cults of the *lwa*, or dieties, beliefs in the power of spirits, and various careful rituals of burial, mourning, and celebration. But they do not include a "ceremony of the souls." See Alfred Metreaux, *Voodoo in Haiti* (New York: Schocken Books, 1959), 243–264 and Melville Herskovits, *Life in a Haitian Valley* (New York: Anchor Books, 1971), 200–221. Immense gratitude to Kate Ramsay for pointing me to these references, as well as for her recent book on Haitian religious culture, colonialism, and the law, which is a revelation. See Ramsay, *The Spirits and the Law: Vodou and Power in Haiti* (Chicago: University of Chicago Press, 2011).

69 Lamming, *Pleasures*, 96.

70 Ibid., 10.

71 Ibid., 11.

72 Ibid., 12.

73 Gordon Rohlehr, "The Problem of the Problem of Form: The Idea of an Aesthetic Continuum and Aesthetic Code-Switching in West Indian Literature," *Caribbean Quarterly* 31, 1 (March 1985): 15, 5.

74 Ibid., 2.

CHAPTER 3: *Andrew Salkey and the Queer Diaspora*

1 Alexander Baron, *The Lowlife* (London: Harvill Press, 2001), 19.

2 The arrival of the *Empire Windrush* in 1948 with 490 Caribbean migrants has become a symbol for the sea change in modern British racial identity, its landing seen as inaugurating a wave of colonial immigration to British cities that forever altered the racial landscape, and racial language, of the nation. The founding of the Institute of Race Relations in 1958 registered the government's relationship to these changing demographics and discourses. See Ambalavaner Sivanandan, *Race and Resistance: The I.R.R. Story* (London: Race Today, 1974). For a brief history of the development of the field of Race Relations as well as a critique of some of its limitations, see Chris Waters, "'Dark Strangers in Our Midst': Discourses of Race and Nation in Britain, 1947–1963," *Journal of British Studies* 36 (April 1997): 207–238. Mike Phillips and Trevor Phillips, *Windrush: The Irresistible Rise of Multi-racial Britain* (London: HarperCollins, 1998) marked the fiftieth anniversary of the ship's landing and helped to initiate a contemporary discourse of the "*Windrush* generation"—a term that became inextricably connected with discourses of modern multicultural Britain and whose representation was solidified by the immense popularity of such novels as Zadie Smith's *White Teeth* (2000) and Andrea Levy's *Small Island* (2004).

3 Baron, *The Lowlife*, 20–21.

4 Monica Miller, *Slaves to Fashion: Black Dandyism and the Styling of Black Diasporic Identity* (Durham, NC: Duke University Press, 2009), 144.

5 Cally Blackman, *One Hundred Years of Menswear* (London: Laurence King Publishing, 2012).

6 "Fuck the social order and the Child in whose name we're collectively terrorized; fuck Annie; fuck the waif from *Les Mis*; fuck the poor, innocent kid on the Net; fuck Laws both with capital *l*s and small; fuck the whole network of Symbolic relations and the future that serves as its prop." Lee Edelman, *No Future: Queer Theory and the Death Drive* (Durham, NC: Duke University Press, 2004), 29.

7 Heather Love, *Feeling Backward: Loss and the Politics of Queer History* (Cambridge, MA: Harvard University Press, 2009), 98.

8 Salkey, *Escape to an Autumn Pavement* (London: Hutchinson, 1960), 136.

9 Ibid., 38.

10 Jose Esteban Muñoz, *Cruising Utopia: The Then and There of Queer Futurity* (New York: New York University Press, 2009), 26.

11 Ibid., 75, 80.

12 I use that charged term "sheebeen" purposely to invoke the Race Relations sociologist Sheila Patterson's telling of the festive goings-on occurring in some London clubs in the new post-*Windrush* scenario because it captures the exoticism and colonial intrigue that tinged much of bourgeois white society's attitude toward it. Patterson describes "unattached men and, in later years, teenagers, who were regulars at the various local coloured clubs and shebeens" in south London; or again the "lively and anti-social café society elements" to be found in northwest London. See Patterson, *Dark Strangers: A Sociological Study of the Absorption of a Recent West Indian Migrant Group in Brixton, South London* (London: Tavistock Press, 1963), 279, 294. For his part, unattached men in various colored clubs were precisely MacInnes's métier and his trio of London novels, *City of Spades* (1957), *Absolute Beginners* (1959), and *Mr. Love and Justice* (1960) were among the first to chronicle the new lives being made by black migrants in Notting Hill and Soho. Not unrelated to my topic here, but somewhat exceeding its scope MacInnes also wrote a book called *Loving Them Both* that claimed West Indian men were "unusually bisexual. . . . [Though] if any Caribbean is going to have it off with you at all, the conditions are that he must really like you (indispensable), that you are discreet, and that the time and place are very right." MacInnes, *Loving Them Both: A Study of Bisexuality and Bisexuals* (London: Martin, Brian and O'Keeffe, 1973), 42–43.

13 Muñoz, *Cruising Utopia*, 103.

14 Samuel Selvon, *The Lonely Londoners* (1956).

15 George Lamming, *The Emigrants* (1954).

16 For important readings of McKay's vision of diasporic community as masculine vagabondage, see Brent Hayes Edwards, *The Practice of Diaspora: Literature, Translation, and the Rise of Black Internationalism* (Cambridge, MA: Harvard University Press, 2003), chap. 4; and Michelle Stephens, *Black Empire: The Masculine Global Imaginary of Caribbean Intellectuals in the United States, 1914–1962* (Durham, NC: Duke University Press, 2005), chap. 6.

17 Salkey, *Escape*, 164.

18 Ibid., 176.

19 Ibid., 180.

20 Ibid., 48–49.

21 Ibid., 195.

22 Ibid., 25.

23 Omi'seke Natasha Tinsley, *Tiefing Sugar: Eroticism between Women in Caribbean Literature* (Durham, NC: Duke University Press, 2010), 3.

24 The *mati* tradition in the Suriname is certainly one of the most structured and historically archived homosocial/queer practices in the Caribbean and

Gloria Wekker's study of women in Suriname is a revelation. Wekker, *The Politics of Passion: Women's Sexual Culture in the Afro-Surinamese Diaspora* (New York: Columbia University Press, 2006). Evelyn Blackwood notes the existence of homosocial and homoerotic ties between women in the Anglophone Caribbean — ties that are, ironically, usually elided in discussions preoccupied with the familial "missing man" and the failure of the patriarchal ideal. See Blackwood, "Wedding Bell Blues: Marriage, Missing Men, and Matrifocal Follies," *American Ethnologist* 32, 1 (February 2005): 3–19.

25 George Lamming, *The Pleasures of Exile* (London: Alison and Busby, 1984), 39.

26 Andrew Salkey, *Quality of Violence* (London, Hutchinson, 1959).

27 Arthur Drayton, "Awkward Questions for Jamaicans," *Journal of Commonwealth Literature* 7 (1969): 125–127.

28 Andrew Salkey, *The Late Emancipation of Jerry Stover* (London: Hutchinson, 1968); Salkey, *The Adventures of Catullus Kelly* (London: Hutchinson, 1969). One notable exception is the marriage of Erasmus and Bridget in that novel, which is portrayed with warmth and humor. Needless to say, they are not the main focus of *The Adventures of Catullus Kelly*.

29 Between 1959, when Salkey published his first novel *A Quality of Violence*, and 1979 when his biography was included in Daryl Cumber Dance's *Caribbean Writers*, I can find two newspaper reviews and six academic responses (including book reviews) to the whole of Salkey's work. Anonymous, "Review of Andrew Salkey's *Escape to an Autumn Pavement*," *Times Literary Supplement* 7 (July 1960): 15; L. E. Brathwaite, "*A Quality of Violence*: Andrew Salkey," *Bim* 8, 31 (1960): 219–220; Bill Carr, "A Complex Fate," in *The Islands in Between*, ed. Louis James (London: Oxford University Press, 1968); Arthur Drayton, "Awkward Questions for Jamaicans," *Journal of Commonwealth Literature* 7 (1969): 125–127; Gerald Moore, "*The Late Emancipation of Jerry Stover*: Andrew Salkey," *Bim* 12, 48 (1969): 268–269; David Arnason, "Review of *the Late Emancipation of Jerry Stover*," *World Literature Written in English (WLWE)* 10 (1971): 90–92; Barrie Davies, "The Sense of Abroad: Aspects of the West Indian Novel in England," *World Literature Written in English (WLWE)* 1, 2 (1972): 67–80; and Donald Herdeck, "Andrew Salkey," in *Caribbean Writers: A Bio-Bibliographical-Critical Encyclopedia*, ed. Daryl Cumber Dance, 186–188 (Washington, DC: Three Continents Press, 1979). Peter Nazareth gives Salkey's work sustained attention in his monograph, following on his earlier essay on *The Adventures of Catullus Kelly*. See Nazareth, "Sexual Fantasies and Neo-colonial Repression in Andrew Salkey's *The Adventures of Catullus Kelly*," *WLWE* 28, 2 (1988): 341–356, and Nazareth, *In the Trickster Tradition: The Novels of Andrew Salkey, Francis Ebejar and Ishmael Reed* (London: Bogle Louverture Press, 1994). Despite a conference in London celebrating Salkey's life and work and Salkey's continued prolific output, it is not until 1998 that we get another major academic essay, Michelle Derose's piece on the long poem *Jamaica*: Derose, "'Is the Lan' I Want': Reconfiguring

Metaphors and Redefining History in Andrew Salkey's Epic 'Jamaica,'" *Contemporary Literature* 39, 2 (1998): 212–237.

30　Andrew Salkey, "Johnnie, London, 1960," in *Our Caribbean: A Gathering of Gay and Lesbian Writing from the Antilles*, ed. Thomas Glave (Durham, NC: Duke University Press, 2008), 325–335. Salkey, *Escape to an Autumn Pavement* (London: Peepal Tree Press, 2009).

31　Salkey, *Escape*, 102, 105.

32　Matt Houlbrook, *Queer London: Perils and Pleasures in the Sexual Metropolis, 1918–1957* (Chicago: University of Chicago Press, 2005).

33　Dick: "'I want you to return my love for you, Johnnie. And before you can do that, you've got to come to terms with what I spoke about earlier on. There's no mystery attached to it; no depravity either.'" Salkey, *Escape*, 188.

34　Ibid., 158.

35　Ibid., 179.

36　Ibid., 19.

37　Ibid., 20.

38　Ibid.

39　Baron, *Lowlife*, 60–61.

40　Richard Hoggart, *The Uses of Literacy* (London: Chatto and Windus, 1957), 260.

41　Ibid., 239.

42　Ibid., 241–242.

43　Ibid., 244.

44　Ibid., 246.

45　Ibid., 252–253.

46　Salkey, *Escape*, 21.

47　Ibid., 22.

48　Eve Kosofsky Sedgwick, *Between Men* (New York: Columbia University Press, 1985), 102.

49　Salkey, *Escape*, 135.

50　Ibid., 186.

51　Contrasting his relationship with Dick to that of Fiona, Johnnie thinks, "We're as near happiness together as Fiona and I are cut off from it right now." Ibid., 110.

52　*Pool of London*, dir. Basil Dearden (London: Ealing Studios, 1951); *Sapphire* (London: Artna Films, 1959). *Flame in the Streets*, dir. Roy Baker (Rank Organization Film Productions Limited and Somerset Productions, 1961).

53　Anne McClintock, *Imperial Leather: Race, Gender, and Sexuality in the Colonial Contest* (London: Routledge, 1995).

54　I have described this type with reference to C. L. R. James in chapter 1.

55　Quoted in Stephen Bourne, *Black in the British Frame: The Black Experience in Film and Television* (London: Continuum Press, 2001), 145.

56　This idea is set up very early on in Dearden's film, when the police detectives look through Sapphire's clothes. They inspect her modest brown skirt and say "Nice, plain things," before rummaging beneath to find a lacy red slip that gives them pause. Later, the policemen investigate a club where Sapphire used to go dancing, a place where, inexplicably, "Lily" girls—black girls passing for white—gather. A black man starts playing the drums, and suddenly the nice looking blonde girls reveal their "true selves" to the flabbergasted policemen by dancing to the beat.

57 The father of the household, Ted Harris, bristles at his economic circumstances ("We can't afford to eat in cafes") and sees Sapphire as the barrier between his son David and an architecture scholarship in Rome. If David married Sapphire, he would not be able to afford to take the scholarship, and the family's chance at economic improvement would slip away.

58 "Boys are finding it hard to make the payments on the car and the telly," Mitch argues, suggesting that the new standards of living in many working-class homes are coming at a stretch.

59 There are implications of the labor union in Jacko's more financially solid home life as well. When Jacko receives a long-awaited letter from the London branch of the union saying that they support his promotion to national president, Jacko's wife Nell becomes excited about the prospect of moving to a better house. When Jacko balks at the idea and is confused by Nell's bitter disappointment, it is his father who explains, "Maybe having a bathroom is just as important to her as having a union is to you."

60 John Hill, *Sex, Class, and Realism: British Cinema 1956–1963* (London: BFI Books, 1986), 103.

61 Ian Baucom, *Out of Place: Englishness, Empire, and the Locations of Identity* (Princeton: Princeton University Press, 1999), chap. 6.

62 Ivar Oxaal, *Black Intellectuals Come to Power: The Rise of Creole Nationalism in Trinidad and Tobago* (Cambridge, MA: Schenkman, 1968), 59.

63 Marcus Collins, "Pride and Prejudice: West Indian Men in Mid-Twentieth-Century Britain," *Journal of British Studies* 40, 3 (2001): 391–418.

64 Quoted in Collins, "Pride and Prejudice," 396–397.

65 Martin Francis, "The Domestication of the Male? Recent Research on Nineteenth- and Twentieth-Century British Masculinity," *Historical Journal* 45, 3 (2002): 644.

66 Stephen Brooke, "Gender and Working Class Identity in Britain during the 1950s," *Journal of Social History* 34, 4 (2001): 773–795.

67 Ibid., 784.

68 Though it is true that Young and Wilmott also recognized that traditional gender roles were retained in other ways and that mothers remained the foundation and ground of home life. Brooke, "Gender and Working Class Identity," 784–785.

69 Collins, "Pride and Prejudice," 403.

70 Baron, *Lowlife*, 114.

71 Ibid.

72 Ibid., 157.

73 Salkey, *Escape*, 122.

74 Ibid., 199

75 Ibid., 201.

76 Ibid., 195.

77 Ibid., 212.

78 Jose Muñoz, *Cruising Utopia*, 32.

79 I thank Kathleen Frederickson for the felicitous phrase "excess of civility." For accounts of the Montague, Pitt-Rivers, Croft-Cooke, and Wildeblood cases, see H. Montgomery Hyde, *The Love That Dared Not Speak Its Name: A Candid History of Homosexuality in Britain* (Boston: Little Brown, 1970), 216–228.

80 The Sexual Offences Act, which came as a result of the Wolfenden Report, was passed in 1967 and overturned existing "sexual indecency" laws, thereby decriminalizing sexual acts between adult men. The Commonwealth Immigrants Act was passed in 1962. Instead of the automatic right of entry that West Indians had as United Kingdom and Colonies citizens, the 1962 Act placed prospective migrants in voucher categories based on whether they had already set up employment in Britain. The Immigration Act of 1971 would make the racial basis of these restrictions much clearer: "patrial" tenets meant that Commonwealth citizens and subjects were now required to have genealogical history in Britain. Overwhelmingly, colonials with British-born descendants were white. See Kathleen Paul, *Whitewashing Britain: Race and Citizenship in the Postwar Era* (Ithaca, NY: Cornell University Press, 1997), especially chaps. 5 and 6; and Ian Baucom, introduction to *Out of Place*.

81 This zero-sum contest between (black) race and (queer) sexuality is another important reason to trace the variations in the archive of difference during the postwar era. The competing abjections we view here—the spectacle of identical language used to describe problems that were seen as categorically different—help to explain the problem of identity politics we observe decades later.

82 See Waters, "Dark Strangers"; and Sivanandan, *Race and Resistance*.

83 Houlbrook, *Queer London*, 239.

84 Quoted in Paul, *Whitewashing Britain*, 127.

85 The journal's name change in 1974 to *Race and Class* and the assumption of leadership by Ambalavener Sivanandan might be seen as one useful benchmark of another phase in the history of the discourse.

86 Michael Banton, *The Coloured Quarter: Negro Immigrants in an English City* (London: Jonathan Cape, 1955); Ruth Glass, *London's Newcomers: The West Indians in London* (London: Centre for Urban Studies and George Allen and Unwin, 1960); Patterson, *Dark Strangers*; Anthony Richmond, *Colour Prejudice in Britain: A Study of West Indian Workers in Liverpool, 1941–1951* (London: Routledge and Paul, 1954).

87 The historian Laura Tabili tells the story of this law, which required "coloured" sailors to give up their passports in exchange for restrictive alien cards. She argues this was a signal moment in the construction of racial difference in twentieth-century Britain not just by disgruntled and racist British seamen or local authorities but (more importantly) by the central government. Her vivid and rigorously documented account of Stepney's part in the widespread labor disturbances of 1919 also describes why the area gained a reputation for class and race warfare. Despite these disturbances, Michael Banton suggests that there had been relatively peaceful relations among the various communities in Stepney throughout the 1920s and 1930s. See Tabili, "The Construction of Racial Difference in Twentieth-Century Britain: The Special Restriction (Coloured Alien Seamen) Order, 1925," *Journal of British Studies* 33, 1 (1994): 54–98.

88 Banton, *Coloured Quarter*, 153.

89 Ibid., 228. Of east and docklands London's queer bona fides, Matt Houlbrook notes working-class venues in "east and south London-dockside pubs" where "dock laborers, sailors from across the world, and families mingled freely with flamboyant local queans and slumming gentlemen in a protean milieu where queer men and casual homosexual encounters were an accepted part of everyday life." Houlbrook, *Queer London*, 88.

90 Banton, *Coloured Quarter*, 110.

91 To take just one example, the films of Isaac Julien are central in generating debate along these lines. In *Looking for Langston*, a meditation on the Harlem Renaissance becomes a celebration of (and mourning for) the suppressed gay culture of the black poets associated with the movement. In Julien's later film *Frantz Fanon, Black Skin White Mask*, a piquant moment involving Fanon's notorious assertion that homosexuality was not very often found in Martinique is illustrated with the Fanon character staring at the naked torso of a black man. Julien's only feature film, *Young Soul Rebels*, presents the intersection of race, class, nationhood, and sexuality as a charged site of identity in 1970s Britain.

92 Apart from providing documentation suggesting what was known about homosexuality and concerns around migrant labor in Stepney, Edith Ramsay's papers are an important record of the neighborhood's postwar social history. Ramsay herself emerges as a fascinating figure, at turns compassionate, imperious, egotistic, and selfless. Her papers suggest she poured significant amounts of her time and energy into improving Stepney for some of its least represented inhabitants. She had a particular interest in eliminating "vice" (especially prostitution) from the area, though she demonstrated sensitivity to the complexity surrounding these issues.

93 Edith Ramsay, "Inadequate Housing Stock for Migrants in Stepney," October 7, 1961, Edith Ramsay Collection, P/RAM/3/2/1, Tower Hamlets Local History Archive, London, p. 4.

94 Ramsay, notes on Colonial House, Leman Street E1, n.d., Edith Ramsay Collection, P/RAM/3/2/2, p. 1.

95 Kenneth Leech to Edith Ramsay, 8 February 1963, Edith Ramsay Collection, P/RAM/1/3/2. Leech's keen language of surveillance, intense eagerness to gain access to the community, and curious moments of anxiety about how all this might appear—he notes emphatically at one point in this letter that any mingling with the disreputables of Stepney would be "*not* for any reason or with any ulterior motive but simply in order to make friends"—all of this reads as queer desire too. But that is analysis for another occasion.

96 Ibid.

97 A resident named Wilfred Reeve wrote to her in 1961 to say that "there have been acts of indecency in that area for which persons have been arrested and charged." July 4, 1961, p. 3, Edith Ramsay Collection, P/RAM/2/1/5. She has a news clipping about a Maltese night-club owner who in 1957 was asked to deny that his café was "a well-known haunt of prostitutes and homosexuals." And in one of her memos, Ramsay writes about a place in Stepney called the Creole Club that "has a shocking reputation": "[Godfrey] Hodgson visited the Creole late one evening, and was met by a white man, drunk, who apologised. . . . The man introduced Hodgson to an African who was obviously his 'boyfriend' and charged the African to look after Hodgson. The African offered him: Men, boys, women, drink after hours, minor and major drugs." Ramsay, untitled memo about registered clubs in Stepney, May 1, 1960; Edith Ramsay Collection, P/RAM/2/1/5.

98 Ramsay, "Memorandum on the Welfare of Colonials in East London," n.d., Edith Ramsay Collection, P/RAM/3/2/2.

99 Quoted in Glass, *London's Newcomers*, 71.

100 Ibid.

101 For a detailed history of the relationship between male homosexuality and the YMCA movement in the U.S. context, see John Donald Gustav-Wrathall, *Take the Young Stranger by the Hand: Same-Sex Relations and the Y.M.C.A.* (Chicago: University of Chicago Press, 1998). He argues that as the Y became more anxious about the obviously homosocial tenor of its hostels and gyms and began to focus more on the physical and spiritual sculpting of "proper" Christian masculinity, the YMCAs became even *more* known for gay cruising. As the space for legitimated male-male love shrank, the arena for subversive male desire grew. To my knowledge, a similar history of the British YMCA movement has not yet been written, though the homosocial structure of the YMCA's hostels and gyms would parallel those in the United States.

102 T. Fitzgerald, Letter from the Home Office to the Commissioner of the Metropolitan Police, October 26, 1959. National Archives, Kew, London, MEPO 2/10011 26A. Offences by Coloured Immigrants. The record of Mason's struggles to conduct even a limited study of black settlement and crime

is fascinating. The deputy superintendent of the Metropolitan Police, a Mr. C. Robertson, repeatedly denied Mason's request to ask local authorities questions about crime and race. He relented finally, only after repeated requests by Mason, possible backdoor dealings, and the permission of the Home Office. Fitzgerald's letter shows that the Home Office requested that the terms of the study be changed from race to "territories of origin." (In the end this was not done.) The hypocrisy here is revealing, and adds another sliver of evidence to Kathleen Paul's monumental archival work on the role of the central government in fostering and covering up race prejudice during the era of Caribbean migration. The new migrant laws successively reduced the ability of black colonials and subjects to enter Britain, even as the language became more and more benign, to do with "country of origin" and "patrial lineage" rather than color. The IRR exchanges can be found in the files MEPO 2/10011, Metropolitan Police: Offences by Coloured Immigrants: Police Statistics for Institute of Race Relations and MEPO 2/9563— Metropolitan Police: Prime Minister Requests Information Regarding Attitudes Towards the Increasing Number of Coloured People Arriving in London, both in National Archives, Kew, London. These two files include letters from Mason to C. Robertson at the Metropolitan Police, Robertson's responses to those letters, and Robertson's letter to the Home Office informing them of Mason's requests.

103   Patterson, *Dark Strangers*, 223.

104   Ibid., 294.

105   Ibid., 288.

106   Ibid., 279–280.

107   It is a curious fact that any researcher of postwar black, gay life in London is indebted to MacInnes—cranky and politically suspect, he was nonetheless unique among English writers during this period in his attentiveness to black migration. Critics justifiably suspect that MacInnes's privileged cynicism did a disservice to the black migrants he apparently admired, in part because his novels are so much about his own struggles with his attraction to black men. In a black-authored book on Notting Hill in the 1960s, two separate Caribbean sources refer to Colin MacInnes arriving to "pick up he guys and all of that" (Phillips and Phillips, *Windrush*, 73). For more on MacInnes's complicated relationship to black London and black men, see Tony Gould, *Inside Outsider: The Life and Times of Colin MacInnes* (London: Chatto and Windus, 1983; and Daniel Farson, *Soho in the Fifties* (London: Michael Joseph, 1987).

108   Quoted in Houlbrook, *Queer London*, 88.

109   See Glass, *London's Newcomers*, 51, 53–54; Banton, *Coloured Quarter*, 93.

110   See Farson, *Soho in the Fifties*; Oliver Bennett, "Licor-Ish Allsorts," *Guardian*, January 16, 1999; and "Karl Weschke" (obituary), *Telegraph.co.uk*, February 23, 2005.

111　William Feaver's gloss of the painting describes the "known characters . . ." as "Jeff Bernard on the left elbow cocked against the mantle piece; John Deakin facing an indignant Henrietta Moraes . . . Bruce Bernard listening respectfully to Francis Bacon; and Muriel turning her sallow face to Ian the barman and ordering another round on someone's behalf. Lucian Freud, looking levelly out of the pictures, serves as the one who knows what's going on." Michael Andrews, William Feaver, Paul Moorhouse, and Tate Britain, *Michael Andrews* (London: Tate, 2001), 51.

112　Military and Metropolitan Police sources I pursued in the National Archives at Kew are found in the following files: AIR 2/10673—RAF Personnel and Women's Auxiliary Air Force Personnel: Homosexual Offences and Abnormal Sexual Tendencies; HO 213/1592—Home Office: Applications for Naturalisation: Effect of Homosexual Offences; WO 93/58—Army and RAF: Homosexual Offences; MEPO 2/1779—Metropolitan Police: Coloured Men Stranded in London; MEPO 2/9715—Metropolitan Police: Vice in Stepney.

113　Generally the exemption applied for number 40—preserving the privacy of a "third party" if he or she were not the enquirer. However, exemption 32 was also applied: it guards against "risk to law-enforcement."

114　"Charges of Indecency: Army [1952–1954]," Homosexual Offences in the Army and RAF, WO 93/58, National Archives, Kew, London.

115　I quote from a personal transcription of the audio recording housed in the Sound Archives of the British Library in the collection of the Hall-Carpenter Oral History Project (456/124). I have deleted repeated words and holding phrases for the sake of clarity. The 1980s saw the publication of several autobiographical texts of gay life in Britain including two published with Routledge by the Hall Carpenter Oral History project: Gay Men's Oral History Group, *Walking after Midnight: Gay Men's Life Stories* (London: Routledge, 1989), and Lesbian Oral History Group, *Inventing Ourselves: Lesbian Life Stories* (London: Routledge, 1989). The gay male volume does not include narratives by Caribbean-born men. The women's collection features a woman of Caribbean descent and women from Africa and Asia who became involved in Afro-Caribbean- and Asian-identified women's liberation groups, though after the period under consideration here.

116　Les Ballets Nègres deserves its own history. Berto Pasuka (who had changed his name from Wilbert Passley) left Jamaica for England in 1939 and performed in cabaret and revue acts in London until 1946, when Richie Riley joined him from Jamaica and the two formed Les Ballets Nègres. The company had several successful seasons in London and Europe between 1946 and 1953, at which point its business manager convinced some of the dancers to perform in Holland with him as leader. Angry and disillusioned, Pasuka disbanded the company and moved to Paris. He died in 1963. See Leon Robinson, "A Celebration of Les Ballets Negres: 1946–1953," *Dance*

Theatre Journal 15, 3 (1999): 26–29. There are very few scholarly references to Les Ballets Nègres. In 1950, Fernau Hall mentions Les Ballets Nègres in his book on English dance—though he includes the company under a section on the choreographer Ernest Berk and gives Berk credit for transforming Pasuka's "raw material" into sophisticated art. Hall is untroubled in this assertion by his own analysis of Ballets Nègres' debut. He noted that "it was impossible to distinguish in the final production the contributions of the various participants." Hall, *Modern English Ballet: An Interpretation* (London: Andrew Melrose, 1950), 146. Larraine Nicholas's tantalizingly titled essay only footnotes Les Ballets Nègres, though the note does gently undermine Hall's take on Berk, writing that "recent research suggests that Fernau Hall (1950) may have overemphasized the modern dance contribution made by Ernest Berk to their first productions." See Nicholas, "Dancing in the Margins? British Modern Dance in the 1940s and 1950s," in *Rethinking Dance History: A Reader*, ed. Alexandra Carter (London: Routledge, 2004), 119–131.

Katherine Dunham's company had already changed its name from Ballet Nègre by the time her group first toured London in 1948, though the homonym is notable. For more on her company and its tour in London see Ramsay Burt, "Katherine Dunham's Floating Island of Negritude: The Katherine Dunham Dance Company in London and Paris in the Late 1940s and Early 1950s," in Carter, *Rethinking Dance History*, 94–106.

117 Again, one is put in mind of Monica Miller's black dandy in *Slaves to Fashion*—in particular the black swell, the erstwhile colonial figure who makes a splash in the metropolis through his sartorial flair and a racial and gendered statement simultaneously.

118 Would that I could confirm this. No materials were deposited with the taped interview in the British Library Sound Archive and despite repeated attempts, I was not able to look at photographs in the personal collection where they are currently held.

119 One of the directors of the Hall Carpenter Oral History Project, Margot Farnham, has confirmed that respondents would have been told what the project was about: "Respondents [were] aware this was a lesbian and gay social history, so looking at history including lesbian and gay identity in the context of the rest of their life and the significant developments of the age they live in" (e-mail to the author, February 22, 2006). Farnham did not know Riley and is not in contact with the person who interviewed him, Juliet Margets, whom I was unable to locate.

CHAPTER 4: *Burning Spear and Nathaniel Lackey at Large*

1 His poetry, on the other hand, and especially in the wake of his 2006 National Book Award win for *Splay Anthem*, has been given some significant attention.

2 Nathaniel Mackey, "Sound and Sentiment, Sound and Symbol," *Callaloo* 30 (1993): 29–54. Republished in Mackey, *Discrepant Engagement: Dissonance, Cross-culturality, and Experimental Writing* (Cambridge: Cambridge University Press, 1993), 162–179.

3 Burning Spear [Winston Rodney], *Marcus Garvey* (Island Records, 1975). The dub version, *Garvey's Ghost*, appeared one year later (Island Records, 1976). References in this text will be to the rerelease double album containing both recordings, *Marcus Garvey/Garvey's Ghost* (Mango Records, 1990).

4 Henry Louis Gates, Jr., *The Signifying Monkey: A Theory of Afro-American Literary Criticism* (New York: Oxford University Press, 1989).

5 Robert Farris Thompson, *Flash of the Spirit: African and Afro-American Art and Philosophy* (New York: Vintage, 1984).

6 Nathaniel Mackey, *Eroding Witness: Poems* (Urbana: University of Illinois Press, 1985); Mackey, "Sound and Sentiment, Sound and Symbol," 32.

7 *Bedouin Hornbook* first appeared as a stand-alone text, though it is noted in the title page as volume 1 of *From a Broken Bottle Traces of Perfume Still Emanate* (Lexington: University of Kentucky, 1986). The first three volumes of the novel have been collected together as *From a Broken Bottle Traces of Perfume Still Emanate*, vols. 1–3 (New York: New Directions, 2010). All references in this text to *Bedouin Hornbook* will be to this latter publication.

8 "There is something disappeared, departed in the apparition itself as reapparition of the departed"; Jacques Derrida, *Specters of Marx: The State of the Debt, the Work of Mourning, and the New International* (New York: Routledge, 1994), 6.

9 Avery Gordon, *Ghostly Matters: Haunting and the Sociological Imagination* (Minneapolis: University of Minnesota Press, 1997), 19.

10 Pheng Cheah, *Spectral Nationality: Passages of Freedom from Kant to Postcolonial Literatures of Liberation* (New York: Columbia University Press, 2003).

11 Ibid., 317.

12 Ibid., 320.

13 Ibid., 391.

14 "For, paradoxically, it is exactly such a haunting gap or discrepancy that allows the African diaspora to 'step' and 'move' in various articulations." Brent Hayes Edwards, Prologue, *The Practice of Diaspora* (Cambridge, MA: Harvard University Press, 2003), 15.

15 Alexander, "Pedagogies of the Sacred: Making the Invisible Tangible," in *Pedagogies of Crossing: Meditations on Feminism, Sexual Politics, Memory, and the Sacred* (Durham, NC: Duke University Press, 2005), 294, 329. "Propelled to seek a different source, I began to undertake linguistic spiritual work with a Bakongo teacher so that I could follow Thisbe from a plantation located about seven miles from the Mojuba crossroads of my childhood back to the Mayombe region of Central Africa to discover Kitsimba, who refused to be cluttered beneath an array of documents of any kind, whether generated by

the state, by plantation owners, or by me. . . . The idea, then, of knowing self through Spirit, to become open to the movement of Spirit in order to wrestle with the movement of history . . . are instances of bringing the self into intimate proximity with the domain of Spirit" (ibid., 294–295).

16 Deborah Thomas, *Modern Blackness: Nationalism, Globalization, and the Politics of Culture in Jamaica* (Durham, NC: Duke University Press, 2004).

17 Rex Nettleford is one of the earliest and most astute explicators of the relationship between color and class in Jamaica, and especially in relation to the categories *black* and *brown*. See his *Caribbean Cultural Identity: The Case of Jamaica*, rev. ed. (Kingston: Ian Randle Press, 2003), and *Mirror, Mirror: Identity, Race, and Protest in Jamaica*, rev. ed. (Kingston: LMH, 2000). Deborah Thomas's description of the nexus of brownness and discourses of "creole" and folk nationalism in Jamaica is one of astonishing lucidity. See her *Modern Blackness*, pt. 1, "The Global-National," in particular. Note as well Shalini Puri's consideration of discourses of hybridity (and the limits of postcolonial theory's discourses of hybridity) in the Caribbean, especially in Trinidad and Tobago. Puri, *The Caribbean Postcolonial* (Houndsmill, Basingstoke: Palgrave Macmillan, 2004).

18 The story around Chinese and Indian political incorporation in Trinidad and in Guyana is different than in Jamaica. In these other two countries with larger Asian populations, political movements organized specifically around ethnicity could be formed. In Jamaica, however, discourses of multiethnic democracy actually foreclosed the full inclusion of Asian subjects *as* Asian.

19 Both Bogle and Gordon were executed on orders of Governor Eyre in the aftermath of 1865, as were dozens of Jamaican workers. The event came to be one of the death throes of British colonialism in the Caribbean, evidence of its brutality. Tim Watson's study emphasizes how integral Morant Bay was in British political and social consciousness, undoing any easy notion of separation between metropole and colony. See Watson, *Caribbean Culture and British Fiction in the Atlantic World, 1780–1870* (Cambridge: Cambridge University Press, 2008).

20 The Rasta eschatology that Burning Spear espouses is a clarifying example of Derrida's idea of "the messianic without messianism"—that is, a hoped-for return that confounds teleology because it is infinitely deferred and yet produces an urgent political critique of the here and now. Derrida, *Specters of Marx*, 89.

21 The drumroll, martial in its delivery, introduces "Old Marcus Garvey," a rhythm that is never repeated; it is reminiscent of Garvey's martial metaphors, his military garb, but this album does not take up Garvey's politics of military display. Rather, it is a meditation on the soul. Garvey's spirit lives now and infuses the album with soul.

22 I am thinking too of the other break that DJ Kool Herc was about to create: the punctuation in electronic music, that pulsing irregular heartbeat, that

would become hip-hop, the genesis of a whole new kind of performed subjectivity: the b-boy, the b-girl. The movement of Herc from Kingston to the Bronx in 1967 is the start of another track of performed black history and culture of which Burning Spear is the beginning. See Jeff Chang, *Can't Stop, Won't Stop: A History of the Hip-Hop Generation* (New York: Picador, 2005), and Norman Stolzoff, *Wake the Town and Tell the People: Dancehall Culture in Jamaica* (Durham, NC: Duke University Press, 2000).

23 "Cajoling is in the nature of the ghost." Avery Gordon, *Ghostly Matters*, 6.

24 Cheah, *Spectral Nationality*, 320.

25 These considerations owe much to Diana Taylor's elegant formulations surrounding the archive and the repertoire. Taylor delineates a distinction between the prestige of written colonial documents, which both supplant and are in aggravated contest with the embodied practices, the repertoire, of native people and their descendants in Mexico. This distinction seems to bear on Burning Spear's dichotomy between history's recall and the listener's implicitly embodied remembering. Note, however, that Taylor's account is underwritten by a deconstruction of archive and repertoire in which each is defined by reference to the other. History's animation, its recall, makes it a little like a dancer, no? Or maybe a musician. Taylor, *The Archive and the Repertoire* (Durham, NC: Duke University Press, 2003).

26 Joan Dayan, *Haiti, History, and the Gods* (Berkeley: University of California Press, 1995), 36.

27 Saidiya Hartman, "The Time of Slavery," *South Atlantic Quarterly* 101, 4 (2002): 759.

28 Carter Mathes's fascinating essay on Martin Luther King Jr. and Peter Tosh in 1970s Jamaica, "Circuits of Political Prophecy: Martin Luther King Jr., Peter Tosh, and the Black Radical Imaginary," *Small Axe* 14, 2 (June 2010): 17–41, resonates here for several reasons. One particularly resonant moment is his reference to Tosh's use of dub effects: "For Tosh, technologies of amplification and modulation are vital tools, allowing his voice to be heard during the One Love Peace Concert through his use of echo and reverb effects, emphasizing a haunting quality to his spoken words, and granting them a level of authority through lingering, resonating cuts of sound that persist beyond their utterance. This utilization of a dub aesthetic (not as a reflection of dub musical style per se but as a phenomenological orientation toward time and sound) becomes an equalizer of sorts that increases his stature as political commentator beyond the pale of the Jamaican political arena" (36–37).

29 Nathaniel Mackey, introduction to "Door Peep (Shall Not Enter)," in *Paracritical Hinge: Essays, Talks, Notes, Interviews* (Madison: University of Wisconsin Press, 2005), 15.

30 Nathaniel Mackey, "Limbo, Dislocation, Phantom Limb: Wilson Harris and the Caribbean Occasion," in *Discrepant Engagement*, 162–179. Previously

published as "Limbo, Dislocation, Phantom Limb: Wilson Harris and the Caribbean Occasion," *Criticism* 22 (winter 1980): 57–86.

31 Ibid., 165 (italics in the original).

32 Quoted in Mackey, "Limbo, Dislocation, Phantom Limb," 169–170.

33 Wole Soyinka, "The Fourth Stage," in *Art, Dialogue, and Outrage: Essays on Literature and Culture* (New York: Pantheon, 1994); Mackey, "Limbo, Dislocation, Phantom Limb," 170.

34 Quoted in Mackey, "Limbo, Dislocation, Phantom Limb," 170.

35 Frederico Garcia Lorca, "Play and Theory of the Duende," in *In Search of Duende* (New York: New Directions, 1998), 48–62; originally published in Spanish, the essay's title is sometimes rendered "Theory and Function of the Duende."

36 Lorca, "Duende," 53.

37 Nathaniel Mackey, "Cante Moro," in *Paracritical Hinge*, 193.

38 Ibid., 182.

39 Nathaniel Mackey, interview by Peter O'Leary, in *Paracritical Hinge*, 292.

40 Mackey, "Sound and Sentiment," 29.

41 Mackey, *Bedouin Hornbook*, 68.

42 See, for instance, Fritz Gysin, "From 'Liberating Voices' to 'Metathetic Ventriloquism': Boundaries in Recent African-American Jazz Fiction," *Jazz Poetics: Callaloo* 25, 1 (winter 2002): 274–287.

43 Mackey, *Eroding Witness*, 50, 54.

44 Mackey, interview by Peter O'Leary, 298.

45 Nathaniel Mackey, interview by Edward Foster, in *Paracritical Hinge*, 276.

46 Mackey, *Bedouin Hornbook*, 7.

47 Nathaniel Mackey, preface to *Splay Anthem* (New York: New Directions Books, 2006), xiv, xv.

48 He is known in vodou as Papa Legba. In Cuban Santeria and other Hispanophone orisha traditions, he is Ellegua. In Brazil, Exu.

49 Thompson, *Flash of the Spirit*, 18–19.

50 Mackey, "Sound and Sentiment," 40 (italics in the original).

51 Marcel Griaule, *Conversations with Ogotemmêli: An Introduction to Dogon Religious Ideas* (Oxford: Oxford University Press, 1965).

52 Marcel Griaule and Germaine Dieterlen, *The Pale Fox*, trans. Stephen C. Infantino (Baltimore: Afrikan World Books, 1986); first published as *Le renard pale* (Paris: l'Institut d'Ethnologie, 1965).

53 Mackey, interview by Peter O'Leary, 294.

54 "[The title of this book] is an expression coined in reference to practices that, in the interest of opening presumably closed orders of identity and signification, accent fissure, fracture, incongruity, the rickety, imperfect fit between word and world. . . . Recalling the derivation of the word discrepant from a root meaning 'to rattle, creak,' I relate discrepant engagement to the name the Dogon of West Africa give their weaving block, the base on which the loom

they weave upon sits. They call it the 'creaking of the word.' It is the noise upon which the word is based, the discrepant foundation of all coherence and articulation, of the purchase upon the world fabrication affords." Mackey, introduction to *Discrepant Engagement*, 19.

Six years later in "Paracritical Hinge," a talk delivered at the Guelph Jazz Festival Colloquium, Mackey quoted the same passage, adding that fiction writing—that is, the writing of *From a Broken Bottle*, his only novel so far—is "the practice of mine out of which, more than any single other, the critical formulation I call discrepant engagement emerged. That practice is the writing of fiction, specifically that of a work called *From a Broken Bottle Traces of Perfume Still Emanate*, running through which are installments of a scribal-performative undertaking known as "The Creaking of the Word," a name borrowed from the Dogon of Mali that I see as related to—a parent or an ancestor to—discrepant engagement." Mackey, "Paracritical Hinge," in *Paracritical Hinge*, 207–208.

55 "The book wants to say, by way of recourse to that figure [Burning Spear] something about the rickety fit of its parts." Mackey, introduction to "Door Peep," 18.

56 Mackey, interview by Peter O'Leary, 293.

57 Nathaniel Mackey, "Palimpsestic Stagger," in *Paracritical Hinge*, 60. Mackey, preface to *Splay Anthem*, x–xi.

58 Walter E. A. van Beek, "Dogon Re-studied: A Field Evaluation of the Work of Marcel Griaule," *Current Anthropology* 32, 2 (April 1991): 139–167. In a sign of the stir the article made in the field, van Beek's research was precirculated to several prominent anthropologists in the field, and their responses were published alongside his article.

59 Ibid., 139.

60 Walter E. A. van Beek, "Haunting Griaule: Experiences from the Restudy of the Dogon," *History in Africa* 31 (2004): 43–68.

61 Ibid., 79.

62 Ibid., 65.

63 Griaule and Dieterlen, *Pale Fox*, 209–210.

64 Mackey, preface to *Splay Anthem*, xi.

EPILOGUE: *Dancehall's Urban Possessions*

1 Many scholars have written about the creation of Tivoli Gardens as it has become an exemplar of modern day political patronage and violence in Jamaica. See for example, Obika Grey, *Radicalism and Social Change in Jamaica, 1960–1972* (Knoxville: University of Tennesee Press, 1991) and Amanda Sives, "Changing Patrons, from Politician to Drug Don: Clientelism in Downtown Kingston, Jamaica," *Latin American Perspectives* 29.5 (September 2002) 66–89. Writing about the particular Rasta character of Back-a-Wall, Clinton Hutton quotes Rasta elder Mortimo Planno: "Back-o-Wall, Ackee Walk, Dungle, was

Rastafari community. Dem call it squatta land. We buil' up shacks an' live in dem an' tings." Hutton, "Oh Rudie: Jamaican Popular Music and the Narrative of Urban Badness in the Making of Postcolonial Society," *Caribbean Quarterly* 56.4 (December 2010) 33.

2 Ellis, "Out and Bad: Towards a Queer Performance Hermeneutic of Jamaican Dancehall," *Small Axe* 15, 2 (2011): 7–23.

3 Fern White, "Deadly Dudus Tales," *Daily Gleaner*, May 23, 2010.

4 Curtis Campbell, "Passa Passa Will Return," *Daily Gleaner*, June 16, 2010.

5 Jahan Ramazani, *Poetry of Mourning: The Modern Elegy from Hardy to Heaney* (Chicago: University of Chicago Press, 1994), x.

6 Ibid., 11.

7 Ibid.

8 Annie Paul, "'No Grave Cannot Hold My Body Down': Rituals of Death and Burial in Postcolonial Jamaica," *Small Axe* 23 (June 2007): 143.

9 Joseph Roach, *Cities of the Dead: Circum-Atlantic Performance* (New York: Columbia University Press, 1996).

10 Quoted in Paul, "No Grave," 146.

11 Petrine Archer, "Accessories/Accessaries; or, What's in Your Closet?," *Small Axe* 32 (July 2010): 101.

12 Deborah Thomas, *Exceptional Violence* (Durham, NC: Duke University Press, 2011).

13 Krista Thompson, "The Sound of Light: Reflections on Art History in the Visual Culture of Hip-Hop," *Art Bulletin* 41, 4 (December 2009), 492.

14 Ibid., 493.

15 Achille Mbembe, "The Aesthetics of Superfluity," *Public Cultures* 16, 1 (2004): 373–405.

16 Gikandi, *Slavery and the Culture of Taste* (Princeton: Princeton University Press, 2011), 242.

17 Kamau Brathwaite, "Stone," in *Middle Passages* (New York: New Directions, 1993), 59–65.

18 Ibid.

BIBLIOGRAPHY

Adesokan, Akin. "Baldwin, Paris, and the 'Conundrum of Africa.'" *Textual Practice* 23, 1 (2009): 73–97.

Alexander, M. Jacqui. "Danger and Desire: Crossings Are Never Undertaken All at Once or Once and for All." *Small Axe* 12, 2 (2007): 154–166.

Alexander, M. Jacqui. *Pedagogies of Crossing: Meditations on Feminism, Sexual Politics, Memory, and the Sacred*. Durham, NC: Duke University Press, 2006.

Alexander, M. Jacqui. "Pedagogies of the Sacred: Making the Invisible Tangible." In *Pedagogies of Crossing: Meditations on Feminism, Sexual Politics, Memory, and the Sacred*, 287–332. Durham, NC: Duke University Press, 2005.

Amis, Kingsley. "Fresh Winds from the West." *Spectator*, May 2, 1958, 565–566.

Andrews, Michael, William Feaver, Paul Moorhouse, and Tate Britain (Gallery). *Michael Andrews*. London: Tate, 2001.

Anonymous. "Review of Andrew Salkey's *Escape to an Autumn Pavement*." *Times Literary Supplement* 7 (July 1960): 15.

Anonymous. "It's Official: Pride Gets New Home." *Pink Paper*, January 13, 1994, 1.

Anonymous, "Black and Proud in Brixton." *Capital Gay*, July 15, 1994, 2.

Arnason, David. "Review of *The Late Emancipation of Jerry Stover*." *World Literature Written in English* 10 (1971): 90–92.

Baldwin, James. *Collected Essays*. New York: Library of America, 1998.

Baldwin, James. *Go Tell It on the Mountain*. New York: Dial Press, 1953.

Baldwin, James. "My Dungeon Shook." In *The Fire Next Time*, in *Collected Essays*. New York: Library of America, 1998.

Baldwin, James. *Notes of a Native Son*. Boston: Beacon Press, 1955.

Baldwin, James. "Princes and Powers." In *Nobody Knows My Name*. In *Collected Essays*, 143–169. New York: Library of America, 1988.

Banton, Michael. *The Coloured Quarter: Negro Immigrants in an English City*. London: Cape, 1955.

Barnes, Natasha. *Cultural Conundrums: Gender, Race, Nation, and the Making of Caribbean Cultural Politics*. Ann Arbor: University of Michigan Press, 2006.

Baron, Alexander. *The Lowlife*. London: Harvill Press, 2001.

Barthes, Roland. *Camera Lucida: Reflections on Photography*. New York: Hill and Wang, 1981.

Baucom, Ian. *Out of Place: Englishness, Empire, and the Locations of Identity*. Princeton: Princeton University Press, 1999.

Baucom, Ian. *Specters of the Atlantic: Finance Capital, Slavery, and the Philosophy of History*. Durham, NC: Duke University Press, 2005.

Bennett, Louise. "Colonization in Reverse." In *Selected Poems*, edited by Mervyn Morris. Kingston: Sangsters, 1982. 106–7.

Bennett, Oliver. "Licor-Ish Allsorts." *The Guardian*, January 16, 1999. http://www .theguardian.com/lifeandstyle/1999/jan/16/weekend.oliverbennett; accessed April 22, 2015.

Berman, Paul, Paul Buhle, and Sojourner Truth Organization. *C. L. R. James: His Life and Work*. Chicago: Sojourner Truth Organization, 1981.

Best, Stephen. "Neither Lost nor Found: Slavery and the Visual Archive." *Representations* 113, 1 (winter 2011): 150–163.

Bhabha, Homi. "Of Mimicry and Man: The Ambivalence of Colonial Discourse." *October* 28 (spring 1984): 125–133.

Blackman, Cally. *One Hundred Years of Menswear*. London: Laurence King, 2012.

Blackwood, Evelyn. "Wedding Bell Blues: Marriage, Missing Men, and Matrifocal Follies." *American Ethnologist* 32, 1 (2005): 3–19.

Bourne, Stephen. *Black in the British Frame: The Black Experience in Film and Television*. London: Continuum Press, 2001.

Brathwaite, Kamau. "Stone." In *Middle Passages*. New York: New Directions, 1993, 59–65.

Brathwaite, L. E. "*A Quality of Violence*: Andrew Salkey." *Bim* 8, 31 (1960): 219–220.

Brodber, Erna. *The Second Generation of Freemen in Jamaica*. Gainesville: University of Florida Press, 2004.

Brooke, Stephen. "Gender and Working Class Identity in Britain during the 1950s." *Journal of Social History* 34, 4 (2001): 773–795.

Buhle, Paul. *C. L. R. James: The Artist as Revolutionary*. London: Verso, 1988.

Buhle, Paul, ed. *C. L. R. James: His Life and Work*. London: Allison and Busby, 1986.

Burning Spear [Winston Rodney]. *Marcus Garvey*. Kingston: Island Records, 1975.

Burt, Ramsay. "Katherine Dunham's Floating Island of Negritude: The Katherine Dunham Dance Company in London and Paris in the Late 1940s and Early 1950s." In *Rethinking Dance History: A Reader*, edited by Alexandra Carter, 94–106. London: Routledge, 2004.

Carpio, Glenda. "Conjuring the Mysteries of Slavery: Voodoo, Fetishism, and Stereotype in Ishmael Reed's *Flight to Canada*." *American Literature* 77, 3 (2005): 563–589.

Carr, Bill. "A Complex Fate." In *The Islands in Between*, edited by Louis James. London: Oxford University Press, 1968.

Chang, Jeff. *Can't Stop, Won't Stop: A History of the Hip-Hop Generation*. New York: Picador, 2005.

Cheah, Pheng. *Spectral Nationality: Passages of Freedom from Kant to Postcolonial Literatures of Liberation.* New York: Columbia University Press, 2003.

Cheng, Anne Anlin. *The Melancholy of Race.* Oxford: Oxford University Press, 2001.

Clarke, Richard. "Lamming, Marx and Hegel." *Journal of West Indian Literature,* November 2008, 42–53.

Collins, Marcus. "Pride and Prejudice: West Indian Men in Mid-twentieth-century Britain." *Journal of British Studies* 40, 3 (2001): 391–418.

Cudjoe, Selwyn. "C. L. R. James Misbound." *Transition* 58 (1992): 124–136.

Cudjoe, Selwyn. Introduction to *C. L. R. James: His Intellectual Legacies,* edited by Selwyn R. Cudjoe and William E. Cain, 1–19. Amherst: University of Massachusetts Press, 1995.

David, Hugh. *On Queer Street: A Social History of British Homosexuality, 1895–1995.* London: HarperCollins, 1997.

Davies, Barrie. "The Sense of Abroad: Aspects of the West Indian Novel in England." *World Literature Written in English* 1, 2 (1972): 67–80.

Dayan, Joan. *Haiti, History, and the Gods.* Berkeley: University of California Press, 1995.

D'Emilio, John. "Homophobia and the Trajectory of Postwar American Radicalism: The Career of Bayard Rustin." *Radical History Review* 62 (1995): 80–103.

Derose, Michelle. "'Is the Lan' I Want': Reconfiguring Metaphors and Redefining History in Andrew Salkey's Epic 'Jamaica.'" *Contemporary Literature* 39, 2 (1998): 212–237.

Derrida, Jacques. *Specters of Marx: The State of the Debt, the Work of Mourning, and the New International.* New York: Routledge, 1994.

Dhondy, Farrukh. *C. L. R. James.* London: Weidenfeld and Nicolson, 2001.

Drayton, Arthur. "Awkward Questions for Jamaicans." *Journal of Commonwealth Literature* 7 (1969): 125–127.

Du Bois, W. E. B. "Of Our Spiritual Strivings." In *The Souls of Black Folk.* Chicago: A. C. McClurg, 1909, 1–12.

Edwards, Brent Hayes. Prologue to *The Practice of Diaspora: Literature, Translation, and the Rise of Black Internationalism.* Cambridge, MA: Harvard University Press, 2003.

Edwards, Brent Hayes. "The Uses of Diaspora." *Social Text* 19, 1 (2001): 45–73.

Ellis, David. "The Produce of More Than One Country: Race, Identity, and Discourse in Post-Windrush Britain." *Journal of Narrative Theory* 31, 2 (2001): 214–232.

Ellis, Nadia. "Out and Bad: Towards a Queer Performance Hermeneutic of Jamaican Dancehall," *Small Axe* 15, 2 (2011): 7–23.

Eng, David. *The Feeling of Kinship: Queer Liberalism and the Racialization of Intimacy.* Durham, NC: Duke University Press, 2010.

Farred, Grant. Introduction to *Rethinking C. L. R. James,* edited by Grant Farred, 1–14. Oxford: Blackwell, 1996.

Farson, Daniel. *Soho in the Fifties.* London: Michael Joseph, 1987.

Francis, Martin. "The Domestication of the Male? Recent Research on Nineteenth- and Twentieth-Century British Masculinity." *Historical Journal* 45, 3 (2002): 637–652.

Gates, Henry Louis. *The Signifying Monkey: A Theory of Afro-American Literary Criticism*. New York: Oxford University Press, 1989.

Gikandi, Simon. *Slavery and the Culture of Taste*. Princeton: Princeton University Press, 2011.

Gikandi, Simon. *Writing in Limbo*. Ithaca, NY: Cornell University Press, 1992.

Gilbert, Helen, and Joanne Tompkins. *Post-colonial Drama: Theory, Politics, Practice*. London: Routledge, 1996.

Gilman, Sander. *Difference and Pathology: Stereotypes of Sexuality, Race, and Madness*. Ithaca, NY: Cornell University Press, 1985.

Gilroy, Paul. *The Black Atlantic: Modernity and the Double Conscious*. Cambridge, MA: Harvard University Press, 1993.

Gilroy, Paul. *Postcolonial Melancholia*. New York: Columbia University Press, 2005.

Girvan, Norman. Foreword to *Tribute to a Scholar: Appreciating C. L. R. James*, edited by Bishnu Ragoonath, vii–x. Kingston: Consortium Graduate School of Social Sciences, 1990.

Glass, Ruth. *London's Newcomers: The West Indians in London*. London: Centre for Urban Studies and George Allen and Unwin, 1960.

Gordon, Avery. *Ghostly Matters: Haunting and the Sociological Imagination*. Minneapolis: University of Minnesota Press, 1997.

Gould, Tony. *Inside Outsider: The Life and Times of Colin Macinnes*. London: Chatto and Windus, 1983.

Goyal, Yogita. *Romance, Diaspora, and Black Atlantic Literature*. Cambridge: Cambridge University Press, 2010.

Grey, Obika. *Radicalism and Social Change in Jamaica, 1960–1972*. Knoxville: University of Tennessee Press, 1991.

Griaule, Marcel. *Conversations with Ogotemmêli: An Introduction to Dogon Religious Ideas*. Oxford: Oxford University Press, 1965.

Griaule, Marcel, and Germaine Dieterlen. *The Pale Fox*. Translated by Stephen C. Infantino. Baltimore: Afrikan World Books, 1986.

Gustav-Wrathall, John Donald. *Take the Young Stranger by the Hand: Same-Sex Relations and the Y.M.C.A.* Chicago: University of Chicago Press, 1998.

Gysin, Fritz. "From 'Liberating Voices' to 'Metathetic Ventriloquism': Boundaries in Recent African-American Jazz Fiction." In *Jazz Poetics: A Special Issue, Callaloo* 25, 1 (winter 2002): 274–287.

Hall Carpenter Archives Gay Men's Oral History Group. *Walking after Midnight: Gay Men's Life Stories*. London: Routledge, 1989.

Hall Carpenter Archives Lesbian Oral History Group. *Inventing Ourselves: Lesbian Life Stories*. London: Routledge, 1989.

Hall, Fernau. *Modern English Ballet: An Interpretation*. London: Andrew Melrose, 1950.

Hall, Stuart. "C. L. R. James: A Portrait." In *C. L. R. James's Caribbean*, edited by Paget Henry and Paul Buhle, 3–16. Durham, NC: Duke University Press, 1992.

Hall, Stuart. "Cultural Identity and Diaspora." *Framework* 36 (1989): 222–237.

Harper, Phillip Brian. "Eloquence and Epitaph: Black Nationalism and the Homophobic Impulse in Responses to the Death of Max Robinson." *Social Text* 28 (1991): 68–86.

Harper, Phillip Brian. "The Evidence of Felt Intuition: Minority Experience, Everyday Life, and Critical Speculative Knowledge." *GLQ: A Journal of Lesbian and Gay Studies* 6, 4 (2000): 641–657.

Hartman, Saidiya V. *Lose Your Mother: A Journey along the Atlantic Slave Route*. New York: Farrar, Straus and Giroux, 2007.

Hartman, Saidiya V. "The Time of Slavery." *South Atlantic Quarterly* 101 (2004): 757–777.

Hartman, Saidiya V. "Venus in Two Acts," *Small Axe* 26 (2008): 1–14.

Herdeck, Donald. "Andrew Salkey." In *Caribbean Writers: A Bio-Bibliographical-Critical Encyclopedia*, edited by Daryl Cumber Dance, 186–188. Washington, DC: Three Continents Press, 1979.

Herskovits, Melville. *Life in a Haitian Valley*. New York: Anchor Books, 1971.

Higman, Barry. "Slavery Remembered: The Celebration of Emancipation in Jamaica." *Journal of Caribbean History* 12 (1979): 55–74.

Hill, John. *Sex, Class and Realism*. London: BFI Books, 1986.

Hoggart, Richard. *The Uses of Literacy*. London: Chatto and Windus, 1957.

Hooper, Richard, ed. *Colour in Britain*. London: British Broadcasting Corporation, 1965.

Hoover, Paul. "Pair of Figures for Eshu: Doubling of Consciousness in the Work of Kerry James Marshall and Nathaniel Mackey." *Callaloo* 23, 2 (spring 2000): 728–748.

Houlbrook, Matt. *Queer London: Perils and Pleasures in the Sexual Metropolis, 1918–1957*. Chicago: University of Chicago Press, 2005.

Hutton, Clinton. "Oh Rudie: Jamaican Popular Music and the Narrative of Urban Badness in the Making of Postcolonial Society." *Caribbean Quarterly* 56.4 (December 2010)

Hyde, H. Montgomery. *The Love That Dared Not Speak Its Name: A Candid History of Homosexuality in Britain*. Boston: Little Brown, 1970.

Jamaica Information Service. "The Observance of Emancipation Day in Jamaica." Originally posted at http://www.jis.gov.jm/special_sections/festiva12k10/pdf/Observance.pdf. That page is now defunct; however in a sign of the archival times, the original article is preserved on in a post from July 31, 2013 on Facebook, at the official page of the Jamaica Olympics. https://www.facebook.com/JamaicaOlympics/posts/394985340602597. Accessed April 22, 2015.

James, C. L. R. *American Civilization*. Oxford: Blackwell, 1993.

James, C. L. R. *At the Rendezvous of Victory: Selected Writings*. London: Allison and Busby, 1984.

James, C. L. R. *Beyond a Boundary*. London: Hutchinson, 1963.

James, C. L. R. *C. L. R. James on the "Negro Question."* Edited by Scott McLemee. Jackson: University of Mississippi Press, 1996.

James, C. L. R. *The Future in the Present: Selected Writings*. London: Allison and Busby, 1977.

James, C. L. R. "La Divina Pastora." In *Spheres of Existence: Selected Writings*. London: Allison and Busby, 1980, 5–8.

James, C. L. R. *Letters from London: Seven Essays by C. L. R. James*. Edited by Nicholas Laughlin. Oxford: Signal Books, 2003.

James, C. L. R. *Mariners, Renegades, and Castaways: The Story of Herman Melville and the World We Live In*. 2nd rev. ed. Detroit: Bewick, 1978.

James, C. L. R. *Mariners, Renegades, and Castaways: The Story of Herman Melville and the World We Live In*. Lebanon, NH: University Press of New England Press, 2001.

James, C. L. R. *Minty Alley*. London: New Beacon, 1971.

James, C. L. R. *Special Delivery: The Letters of C. L. R. James to Constance Webb, 1939–1948*. Cambridge, MA: Blackwell, 1995.

James, C. L. R. *Spheres of Existence: Selected Writings*. London: Allison and Busby, 1980.

James, C. L. R. "Three Black Women Writers: Toni Morrison, Alice Walker, Ntozake Shange." In *The C. L. R. James Reader*, edited by Anna Grimshaw. Oxford: Blackwell, 1992.

Jameson, Frederic. "Marx's Purloined Letter." *New Left Review* 209 (1995): 75–109.

Jeffery-Poulter, Stephen. *Peers, Queers, and Commons: The Struggle for Gay Law Reform from 1950 to the Present*. London: Routledge, 1991.

Jules-Rosette, Benetta. "Antithetical Paris: Conferences and Festivals of Presence Africaine, 1956–1973." In Jules-Rosette, *Black Paris: The African Writers' Landscape*. Urbana: University of Illinois Press, 1998, 49–78.

Julien, Eileen. "Terrains de Rencontre: Cesaire, Fanon, and Wright on Culture and Decolonization." *Yale French Studies* 98 (2000): 149–166.

Julien, Isaac, dir. *Frantz Fanon, Black Skin White Mask*. California Newsreel, 1995. DVD.

Julien, Isaac, dir. *Looking for Langston*. Sankofa, 1989. DVD.

Julien, Isaac, dir. *Young Soul Rebels*. ILC Prime, 1991. DVD.

"Karl Weschke." Obituary. *The Telegraph*, February 23, 2005. http://www.telegraph.co.uk/news/obituaries/1484141/Karl-Weschke.html. Accessed April 22, 2015.

Kaufman, Jason, and Orlando Patterson. "Cross-national Cultural Diffusion: The Global Spread of Cricket." *American Sociological Review* 70 (February 2005): 82–110.

Kennedy, Elizabeth Lapovsky. "'But We Could Never Talk about It': The Structures of Lesbian Discretion in South Dakota, 1928–1933." In *Inventing Lesbian Cultures in America*, edited by Ellen Lewin, 15–39. Boston: Beacon Press, 1996.

Lamming, George. *In the Castle of My Skin*. London, Michael Joseph, 1953.

Lamming, George. Introduction to *In the Castle of My Skin*, Ann Arbor: University of Michigan, 1991, xxxv–xlvi.

Lamming, George. "The Negro Writer and His World." *Presence Africaine* 8–9–10 (1956): 318–125.

Lamming, George. *The Pleasures of Exile*. London: Alison and Busby, 1984.

Lamming, George. "The West Indian People." *New World Quarterly* 2, 2 (1966–67): 63–74.

"Le 1er Congres International des Ecrivains et Artistes Noirs (Paris—Sorbonne—19–22 Septembre 1956), Compte Rendu Complet." Special issue, *Presence Africaine: Revue Culturelle du Monde Noir*, nos. 8–9–10 (June-November 1956).

Linebaugh Peter, and Marcus Rediker. *The Many-Headed Hydra: Sailors, Slaves, Commoners, and the Hidden History of the Revolutionary Atlantic*. Boston: Beacon Press, 2000.

"London Councils Battle for Pride." *Capital Gay*, November 11, 1994, 3.

Lorca, Frederico Garcia. "Play and Theory of the Duende." *In Search of Duende*, 48–62. New York: New Directions, 1998.

Love, Heather. *Feeling Backward: Loss and the Politics of Queer History*. Cambridge, MA: Harvard University Press, 2009.

Lowe, Lisa. "The Intimacies of Four Continents." In *Haunted by Empire: Geographies of Intimacy in North American History*, edited by Ann Laura Stoler. Durham, NC: Duke University Press, 2006, 191–212.

MacInnes, Colin. *Loving Them Both: A Study of Bisexuals and Bisexuality*. London: Martin, Brian and O'Keeffe, 1973.

Mackey, Nathaniel. *Bedouin Hornbook*. Los Angeles: Sun and Moon Press, 1999.

Mackey, Nathaniel. "Cante Moro." In *Paracritical Hinge: Essays, Talks, Notes, Interviews*. Madison: University of Wisconsin Press, 2005, 181–198.

Mackey, Nathaniel. *Discrepant Engagement: Dissonance, Cross-culturality, and Experimental Writing*. Cambridge: Cambridge University Press, 1993.

Mackey, Nathaniel. *Eroding Witness: Poems*. Urbana: University of Illinois Press, 1985.

Mackey, Nathaniel. *From a Broken Bottle Traces of Perfume Still Emanate*. Vols. 1–3. New York: New Directions, 2010.

Mackey, Nathaniel. Interview by Edward Foster. In *Paracritical Hinge: Essays, Talks, Notes, Interviews*. Madison: University of Wisconsin Press, 2005, 268–285.

Mackey, Nathaniel. Interview by Peter O'Leary. In *Paracritical Hinge: Essays, Talks, Notes, Interviews*. Madison: University of Wisconsin Press, 2005, 286–300.

Mackey, Nathaniel. "Introduction: Door Peep (Shall Not Enter)." In *Paracritical Hinge: Essays, Talks, Notes, Interviews*. Madison: University of Wisconsin Press, 2005, 3–20

Mackey, Nathaniel. "Limbo, Dislocation, Phantom Limb: Wilson Harris and the Caribbean Occasion." In *Discrepant Engagement: Dissonance, Cross-Culturality, and Experimental Writing*. Cambridge: Cambridge University Press, 1993, 162–179.

Mackey, Nathaniel. "Palimpsestic Stagger." In *Paracritical Hinge: Essays, Talks, Notes, Interviews*. Madison: University of Wisconsin Press, 2005. 59–68.

Mackey, Nathaniel. "Paracritical Hinge." In *Paracritical Hinge: Essays, Talks, Notes, Interviews*. Madison: University of Wisconsin Press, 2005, 207–227.

Mackey, Nathaniel. *Paracritical Hinge: Essays, Talks, Notes, Interviews*. Madison: University of Wisconsin Press, 2005.

Mackey, Nathaniel. "Sound and Sentiment, Sound and Symbol." *Callaloo* 30 (1987): 29–54.

Mackey, Nathaniel. *Splay Anthem*. New York: New Directions Books, 2006.

Mathes, Carter. "Circuits of Political Prophecy: Martin Luther King Jr., Peter Tosh, and the Black Radical Imaginary." *Small Axe* 14, 2 (June 2010): 17–41.

McLemee, Scott, and Paul Le Blanc. *C. L. R. James and Revolutionary Marxism: Selected Writings of C. L. R. James 1939–1949*. Revolutionary Studies. Atlantic Highlands, NJ: Humanities Press, 1994.

Metraux, Alfred. *Voodoo in Haiti*. New York: Schocken Books, 1959.

Moore, Gerald. "*The Late Emancipation of Jerry Stover*: Andrew Salkey." *Bim* 12, 48 (1969): 268–269.

Morris, Rosalind. "Giving Up Ghosts: Notes on Trauma and the Possibility of the Political from Southeast Asia." *positions* 16, 1 (2008): 229–258.

Morrison, Toni. *Beloved: A Novel*. New York: Knopf, 1987.

Mort, Frank. "Mapping Sexual London: The Wolfenden Report on Homosexual Offences and Prostitution 1954–1957." *New Formations* 37 (1999): 92–113.

Moten, Fred. *In the Break: The Aesthetics of the Black Radical Tradition*. Minneapolis: University of Minnesota Press, 2003.

Muñoz, Jose. *Cruising Utopia: The Then and There of Queer Futurity*. New York: New York University Press, 2009.

Nazareth, Peter. *In the Trickster Tradition: The Novels of Andrew Salkey, Francis Ebejar and Ishmael Reed*. London: Bogle Louverture Press, 1994.

Nazareth, Peter. "Sexual Fantasies and Neo-colonial Repression in Andrew Salkey's *The Adventures of Catullus Kelly*." *World Literature Written in English (WLWE)* 28, 2 (1988): 341–356.

Nealon, Chris. *Foundlings*. Durham, NC: Duke University Press, 2001.

Nettleford, Rex. *Caribbean Cultural Identity: The Case of Jamaica*. Rev. ed. Kingston: Ian Randle Press, 2003.

Nettleford, Rex. *Mirror, Mirror: Identity, Race, and Protest in Jamaica*. Rev. ed. Kingston: LMH, 2000.

Niaah, Sonjah Stanley. *DanceHall: From Slaveship to Ghetto*. Ottawa: University of Ottawa Press, 2010.

Nicholas, Larraine. "Dancing in the Margins? British Modern Dance in the 1940s and 1950s." In *Rethinking Dance History: A Reader*, edited by Alexandra Carter, 119–131. London: Routledge, 2004.

Nixon, Rob. "Caribbean and African Appropriations of *The Tempest*." *Critical Inquiry* 13, 3 (1987): 557–578.

Nyong'o, Tavia. *The Amalgamation Waltz*. Minneapolis: University of Minnesota Press, 2009.

Ové, Horace, dir. *Baldwin's Nigger*. London: British Film Institute, 2004.

Oxaal, Ivar. *Black Intellectuals Come to Power: The Rise of Creole Nationalism in Trinidad and Tobago.* Cambridge, MA: Schenkman, 1968.

Palmié, Stefan. *Wizards and Scientists: Explorations in Afro-Cuban Modernity and Tradition.* Durham, NC: Duke University Press, 2002.

Parés, Luis Nicolau, and Roger Sansi, eds. *Sorcery in the Black Atlantic.* Chicago: University of Chicago Press, 2011.

Patterson, Sheila. *Dark Strangers: A Sociological Study of the Absorption of a Recent West Indian Migrant Group in Brixton, South London.* London: Tavistock, 1963.

Paul, Annie. "'No Grave Cannot Hold My Body Down': Rituals of Death and Burial in Postcolonial Jamaica." *Small Axe* 23 (June 2007): 142–162.

Paul, Kathleen. *Whitewashing Britain: Race and Citizenship in the Postwar Era.* Ithaca, NY: Cornell University Press, 1997.

Phelan, Peggy. *Mourning Sex: Performing Public Memories.* London; New York: Routledge, 1997.

Phillips, Charlie, and Mike Phillips. *Notting Hill in the Sixties.* London: Lawrence and Wishart, 1991.

Phillips, Mike. *London Crossings: A Biography of Black Britain.* London: Continuum, 2001.

Phillips, Mike, and Trevor Phillips. *Windrush: The Irresistible Rise of Multi-racial Britain.* London: HarperCollins, 1998.

Pouchet Paquet, Sandra. Foreword to *The Pleasures of Exile*, edited by George Lamming, vii–xxvii. Ann Arbor: University of Michigan Press, 1992.

Puar, Jasbir. *Terrorist Assemblages: Homonationalism in Queer Times.* Durham, NC: Duke University Press, 2007.

Puri, Shalini. *The Caribbean Postcolonial.* Houndsmill, Basingstoke: Palgrave Macmillan, 2004.

Ramazani, Jahan. *Poetry of Mourning: The Modern Elegy from Hardy to Heaney.* Chicago: University of Chicago Press, 1994.

Ramazani, Jahan. "The Wound of History: Walcott's *Omeros* and the Postcolonial Poetics of Affliction." *PMLA* 112, 3 (1997): 405–417.

Ramsay, Kate. *The Spirits and the Law: Vodou and Power in Haiti.* Chicago: University of Chicago Press, 2011.

Riley, Denise. *Impersonal Passion: Language as Affect.* Durham, NC: Duke University Press, 2005.

Roach, Joseph. *Cities of the Dead: Circum-Atlantic Performance.* New York: Columbia University Press, 1996.

Roach, Joseph. *It.* Ann Arbor: University of Michigan Press, 2007.

Robinson, Leon. "A Celebration of Les Ballets Negres: 1946–1953." *Dance Theatre Journal* 15, 3 (1999): 26–29.

Rodney, Walter. "The African Revolution." In *C. L. R. James: His Life and Work*, edited by Paul Buhle, 30–48. London: Allison and Busby, 1986.

Rohlehr, Gordon. "The Problem of the Problem of Form: The Idea of an Aesthetic Continuum and Aesthetic Code-Switching in West Indian Literature." *Caribbean Quarterly* 31, 1 (March 1985): 1–52.

Rosenthal, Judy. *Possession, Ecstasy, and Law in Ewe Voodoo*. Charlottesville: University of Virginia Press, 1998.

Salkey, Andrew. *The Adventures of Catullus Kelly*. London: Hutchinson, 1969.

Salkey, Andrew. *Escape to an Autumn Pavement*. London: Hutchinson, 1960.

Salkey, Andrew. "Johnnie, London, 1960." In *Our Caribbean: A Gathering of Gay and Lesbian Writing from the Antilles*, edited by Thomas Glave. Durham, NC: Duke University Press, 2008, 325–335.

Salkey, Andrew. *The Late Emancipation of Jerry Stover*. London: Hutchinson, 1968.

Salkey, Andrew. *Quality of Violence*. London: Hutchinson, 1959.

Sandhu, Sukhdev. *London Calling: How Black and Asian Writers Imagined a City*. London: HarperCollins, 2003.

Schwarz, Bill. "C. L. R. James and George Lamming: The Measure of Historical Time." *Small Axe* 14 (2003): 39–70.

Schwarz, Bill. "Not Even Past Yet." *History Workshop Journal* 57 (spring 2004): 101–115.

Scott, David. *Refashioning Futures: Criticism after Postcoloniality*. Princeton: Princeton University Press, 1999.

Scott, David, and George Lamming. "The Sovereignty of the Imagination: An Interview with George Lamming." *Small Axe* 12 (2002): 72–200.

Selvon, Samuel. *The Lonely Londoners*. New York: Longman, 1956.

Silberman, Seth Clark. "'Youse Awful Queer, Chappie': Reading Black Queer Vernacular in Black Literatures of the Americas, 1903–1967." PhD diss., University of Maryland, College Park, 2005.

Sivanandan, Ambalavaner. *Race and Resistance: The I.R.R. Story*. London: Race Today, 1974.

Sives, Amanda. "Changing Patrons, from Politician to Drug Don: Clientelism in Downtown Kingston, Jamaica." *Latin American Perspectives* 29.5 (Sep. 2002) 66–89.

Small, Richard. "The Training of an Intellectual, the Making of a Marxist." In *C. L. R. James: His Life and Work*, edited by Paul Buhle, 49–60. London: Allison and Busby, 1986.

Spillers, Hortense. "Mama's Baby, Papa's Maybe: An American Grammar Book." *Diacritics* 17, 2 (1987): 64–81.

Stephens, Michelle. *Black Empire: The Masculine Global Imaginary of Caribbean Intellectuals in the United States, 1914–1962*. Durham, NC: Duke University Press, 2005.

Stolzoff, Norman. *Wake the Town and Tell the People: Dancehall Culture in Jamaica*. Durham, NC: Duke University Press, 2000.

Sylvester, Mark. "Gay Hate Gang Beat Up Marchers." *South London Press*, June 21, 1994.

Tabili, Laura. "The Construction of Racial Difference in Twentieth-Century Britain: The Special Restriction (Coloured Alien Seamen) Order, 1925." *Journal of British Studies* 33, 1 (1994): 54–98.

Taussig, Michael T. *The Devil and Commodity Fetishism in South America*. Chapel Hill: University of North Carolina Press, 1980.

Taussig, Michael T. "History as Sorcery." *Representations* 7 (1984): 87–109.

Taylor, Diana. *The Archive and the Repertoire*. Durham, NC: Duke University Press, 2003.

Thomas, Deborah. *Exceptional Violence*. Durham, NC: Duke University Press, 2011.

Thomas, Deborah. *Modern Blackness: Nationalism, Globalization, and the Politics of Culture in Jamaica*. Durham, NC: Duke University Press, 2004.

Thompson, Krista. "The Sound of Light: Reflections on Art History in the Visual Culture of Hip-Hop." *Art Bulletin* 41, 4 (December 2009): 481–505.

Thompson, Robert Farris. *Flash of the Spirit: African and Afro-American Art and Philosophy*. New York: Vintage, 1984.

Tinsley, Omi'seke Natasha. *Tiefing Sugar: Eroticism between Women in Caribbean Literature*. Durham, NC: Duke University Press, 2010.

Tomkins, Silvan. "What Are Affects?" In *Shame and Its Sisters: A Silvan Tomkins Reader*, edited by Eve Kosofsky Sedgwick and Adam Frank, 33–74. Durham, NC: Duke University Press, 1995.

van Beek, Walter E. A. 1991. "Dogon Restudied: A Field Evaluation of the Work of Marcel Griaule." *Current Anthropology* 32, 2 (1991): 139–167.

van Beek, Walter E. A. "Haunting Griaule: Experiences from the Restudy of the Dogon." *History in Africa* 31 (2004): 43–68.

Walcott, Derek. "A Tribute to C. L. R. James." In *C. L. R. James: His Intellectual Legacies*, edited by Selwyn R. Cudjoe and William E. Cain, 34–48. Amherst: University of Massachusetts Press, 1995.

Walmsley, Anne. *The Caribbean Artists Movement, 1966–1972: A Literary and Cultural History*. London: New Beacon Books, 1992.

Waters, Chris. "'Dark Strangers' in Our Midst: Discourses of Race and Nation in Britain, 1947–1963." *Journal of British Studies* 36 (1997): 207–238.

Watson, Tim. *Caribbean Culture and British Fiction in the Atlantic World, 1780–1870*. Cambridge: Cambridge University Press, 2008.

Weeks, Jeffrey. *Coming Out: Homosexual Politics in Britain from the Nineteenth Century to the Present*. London: Quartet, 1990.

Wekker, Gloria. *The Politics of Passion: Women's Sexual Culture in the Afro-Surinamese Diaspora*. New York: Columbia University Press, 2006.

Witter, Earl. Q. C., Office of the Defender, *Interim Report To Parliament Concerning Investigations Into The Conduct Of The Security Forces During The State Of Emergency Declared May, 2010 — West Kingston/Tivoli Gardens 'Incursion'—The Killing Of Mr. Keith Oxford Clarke And Related Matters*, April 29, 2013.

Wynter, Sylvia. Afterword to "Beyond Miranda's Meanings: Un/silencing the 'Demonic Ground' of Caliban's 'Woman.'" In *Out of the Kumbla: Caribbean Women and Literature*, edited by Carole Boyce Davies and Elaine Savory Fido. Trenton, NJ: African World Press, 1990, 355–372.

Wynter, Sylvia. "Beyond the Categories of the Master Conception: The Counter-doctrine of the Jamesian Poiesis." In *C. L. R. James's Caribbean*, edited by Paget Henry and Paul Buhle, 63–91. Durham, NC: Duke University Press, 1992.

Wynter, Sylvia. "The Ceremony Must Be Found: After Humanism." *boundary 2*, 12–13 (spring-autumn 1984): 19–70.

INDEX

Adams, Reneto, 180
Adesokan, Akin, 82–83
aesthetics: black, 164–65, 176; dance-
    hall and, 190; diaspora and, 5; haunt
    and, 169; of possession, 148–49,
    160–61, 163, 176; of Rastafari, 149
affinity, 6; black global, 7–8, 69;
    diasporic, 5, 8; disavowal of, 8; for
    England, 67–68; nationalism and,
    13; queer, 193n9; queer diasporic,
    9–10
African Diaspora studies, 5, 10
Alexander, M. Jacqui, 156–57, 194n10,
    215n15
Amis, Kingsley, 69
Anderson, Lindsay, 84
andoumboulou: Mackey on, 175–76; in
    The Pale Fox, 175. See also *Bedouin
    Hornbook* (Mackey)
Andrews, Michael, 141
Archer, Petrine, 185
Arts Festival (Jamaica), 13–15
Aviance, Kevin, 99

Back-a-Wall (Kingston), 177, 219n1
Baldwin, James, 2, 7–8, 62–66, 192;
    on Africans, 77–78; Americanness
    in, 76–77; on Black American
    subjectivity, 82; blackness and, 77;
    on Cesaire, 82; civil rights move-
ment, support for, 79; on colonial
    blacks, 78; on colonialism, 77; at
    Congress of Negro Writers and
    Artists, 75–78; *The Fire Next
    Time*, 79; *Go Tell It on the Moun-
    tain*, 63–64; on Lamming, 63, 73,
    80–82, 90; on Lasebikan, 82–83;
    on "Negro," 89–90; "Princes and
    Powers," 62, 75–83; on Tutuola, 81;
    US politics, investment in, 64–65;
    West, relation to, 65; at West Indian
    Students Association, 83–90. *See
    also* Lamming, George
Baldwin's Nigger, 83–90
Banton, Michael, 132, 134–35, 210n87;
    black masculinity in, 135; on homo-
    sexuality, 135; interracial relation-
    ships in, 135
Baron, Alexander, 95. *See also Lowlife,
    The* (Baron)
Barthes, Roland, 169
Baucom, Ian, 11, 114
Bedouin Hornbook (Mackey), 150, 167,
    215n7; "Andoumboulou" poems,
    168–69; Burning Spear in, 168;
    haunt aesthetics of, 169; "Song of
    the Andoumboulou," 173. *See also*
    Mackey, Nathaniel
Bergman, Ingrid, 51
Berk, Ernest, 214n116

James, C. L. R. (*continued*)
performance in, 7, 35–36, 43–44, 52; restraint in, 25–26, 36, 39, 44; screens stars and, 7, 26, 44–51, 54; *Special Delivery*, 26; subjectivity in, 36–39; surrogation in, 50; Trotskyism and, 22, 43, 47, 52; on US race relations, 27; visibility in, 26; vitality in, 51, 59–60; Webb, correspondence with, 41, 47, 49, 52, 56–61, 198n22, 200n86; white femininity in, 48–49, 59; whiteness in, 7; on women, 20, 58–59. See also *Beyond a Boundary*; Webb, Constance
James, Louis, 71
Jameson, Frederic, 150
Jane and Louisa Will Soon Come Home (Brodber), 16–17
jazz, 140, 168; bebop, 1; in Mackey, 169; modernism and, 1–2; Stuart Hall and, 1–4
Jenkin, Veronica, 72
Jewett, Sarah Orne, 65–66
Johnson, Linton Kwesi, 72
Johnson-Forest Tendency, 30, 47
Jones, Arthur, 40–41, 42
Julien, Eileen, 79–80
Julien, Isaac, 210n91

Kaufman, Jason, 34–35
King, Bryan, 70
King, Martin Luther, Jr., 217n28
kinship: difference and, 82, 88
Kumina, 151

Lamming, George, 2, 7–8, 30, 62–75, 101, 192, 202n171; on Baldwin, 73–75, 90; on CAM, 72; as "Caribbean Artist," 70; England, affinity for, 67–68; *In the Castle of My Skin*, 64; misrecognition in, 7, 65, 75; "The Negro Writer and His World," 62–63, 80, 86, 87; *The Pleasures of*

Exile, 64, 68–69, 91–93; Rohlehr on, 93–94; subjectivity in, 68–69; on vodou, 91–93; West, relation to, 65; "The West Indian People," 92; on West Indian writers, 67, 71, 80, 104–5. See also Baldwin, James
land: b l a c k s p a c e and, 16; ownership of, 12–13; ritual and, 16
LaRose, John, 69
Lasebikan, E. L., 82–83
Leech, Kenneth, 136–37, 211n95
Legba, 148, 150, 169–72, 218n48
Les Ballets Nègres, 143, 213n116
Les Dogon, 173, 176
limbo, 165–66
Linebaugh, Peter, 53
literature, West Indian, 72–73; British cultural studies and, 113; class and, 104–5; queerness in, 108
Little, Kenneth, 134
Lorca, Federico García, 165, 166
Lorde, Audre, 194n10
Lord Montague, 131
loss, 181, 184–85, 188–92; diaspora and, 5, 152–55, 192; in Mackey, 164–67, 171–76; Middle Passage as, 5–6, 165; in Patterson, 185, 188–90; as queer, 4; in Salkey, 98–99; spirit possession and, 149; subjectivity and, 37, 88
L'Ouverture, Toussaint, 60
Love, Heather, 65, 193n9; *Feeling Backwards*, 98
Lowe, Lisa, 10
Lowlife, The (Baron), 95, 127–29; class in, 110–11, 120, 128; labor in, 128–29; queer diasporic in, 98
Lucie-Smith, Edward, 70

MacInnes, Colin, 100, 140, 205n13; on black migration, 212n107
Mackey, Nathaniel, 2, 9–10, 148–54, 192; absence in, 152–53, 163; black

aesthetics of, 152, 164–65, 167, 172; blackness and, 149; bodies in, 9; on Burning Spear, 151, 165, 173, 176; "creaking of the word" in, 148, 173, 218n54; diasporic aesthetics of, 164–65, 176; diasporic belonging, model of, 149; diasporic cultural practice of, 148; diasporic subjectivity and, 155; *Discrepant Engagement*, 150, 151; double voice in, 166–67; *From a Broken Bottle*, 164, 219n54; haunt in, 152, 164, 173–74; jazz in, 169; "Limbo, Dislocation, Phantom Limb," 165; on Lorca, 166–67; loss in, 164–67, 171–76; on music, 148, 167, 173, 195n13; *Paracritical Hinge*, 150; phantom limb in, 152–53, 154, 164, 167, 169–70, 172; on reggae, 167–68; recursion in, 152, 170–71; seriality of, 151; "Sound and Sentiment," 152–53; spirit possession in, 163–64, 168–71; *Splay Anthem*, 175, 214n1; wavering in, 164–65

Mais, Roger, 66, 67

Manley, Michael, 1, 29

Manley, Norman, 158

Marcus Garvey (Burning Spear album), 9–10, 150, 151, 155–63; aesthetics of possession of, 160–61; the body in, 162; dub version of, 163; history in, 160, 162; "Old Marcus Garvey," 159–61, 216n21; repetition in, 152, 160; slavery in, 161–63; "Slavery Days," 161; spirit possession in, 156, 161, 163; wordlessness in, 168. *See also* Burning Spear

Margets, Juliet, 144–46, 214n119

Marley, Bob, 149

Marson, Una, 20

masculinity: black, 118–19, 125, 135; blackness and, 132; civilization and, 114; class and, 125, 131; dancehall and, 185; diaspora and, 205n16;

in film, 118–19; intimacy and, 90; nationalism and, 104; nationality and, 129; in Salkey, 108, 114

Mason, Philip, 139–40, 141

Mathes, Carter, 217n28

Mbembe, Achille, 190

McCarty, Kevin, 100

McClintock, Anne, 117

McKay, Claude, 20, 73; homosocial vagabondage of, 101, 205n16

McLean, Donald, 132

McLemee, Scott, 47

melancholia, 37–38, 65

Melville, Herman, 73

Middle Passage, 88; as loss, 5–6, 165

migration, Caribbean: class and, 1, 96, 100–107, 110–15, 118, 123–30, 140–41; to Britain, 95–96, 101, 115, 133–34, 97 fig. 3.1, 204n2; Commonwealth Immigrants Act (1962), 209n80; domesticity and, 101, 102–3; homosexuality and, 101; Immigration Act (1971), 132, 209n80; immigration laws, 212n102; sexuality and, 141–42. *See also* immigrants, Caribbean

Miller, Monica, 96, 214n117

mimicry, 36

misrecognition: of Baldwin and Lamming, 7–8, 65, 75; in literature, 7

modernity: diaspora and, 2

Momma Don't Allow, 84–85

Morant Bay Rebellion, 158, 216n19

Moten, Fred, 148

mourning: consumerism and, 183–84; elegy and, 182–83; in Jamaica, 183

Muñoz, Jose Esteban, 1, 99–100; on queer futurity, 103; queer utopianism of, 3, 4–5, 99, 100, 193n9

Naipaul, V. S., 69, 202n17, 202n26

nationalism, 11; affinity and, 13; Caribbean, 12, 25, 31, 157; creole, 12, 158;